IMAGES
of America

SPRINGVILLE

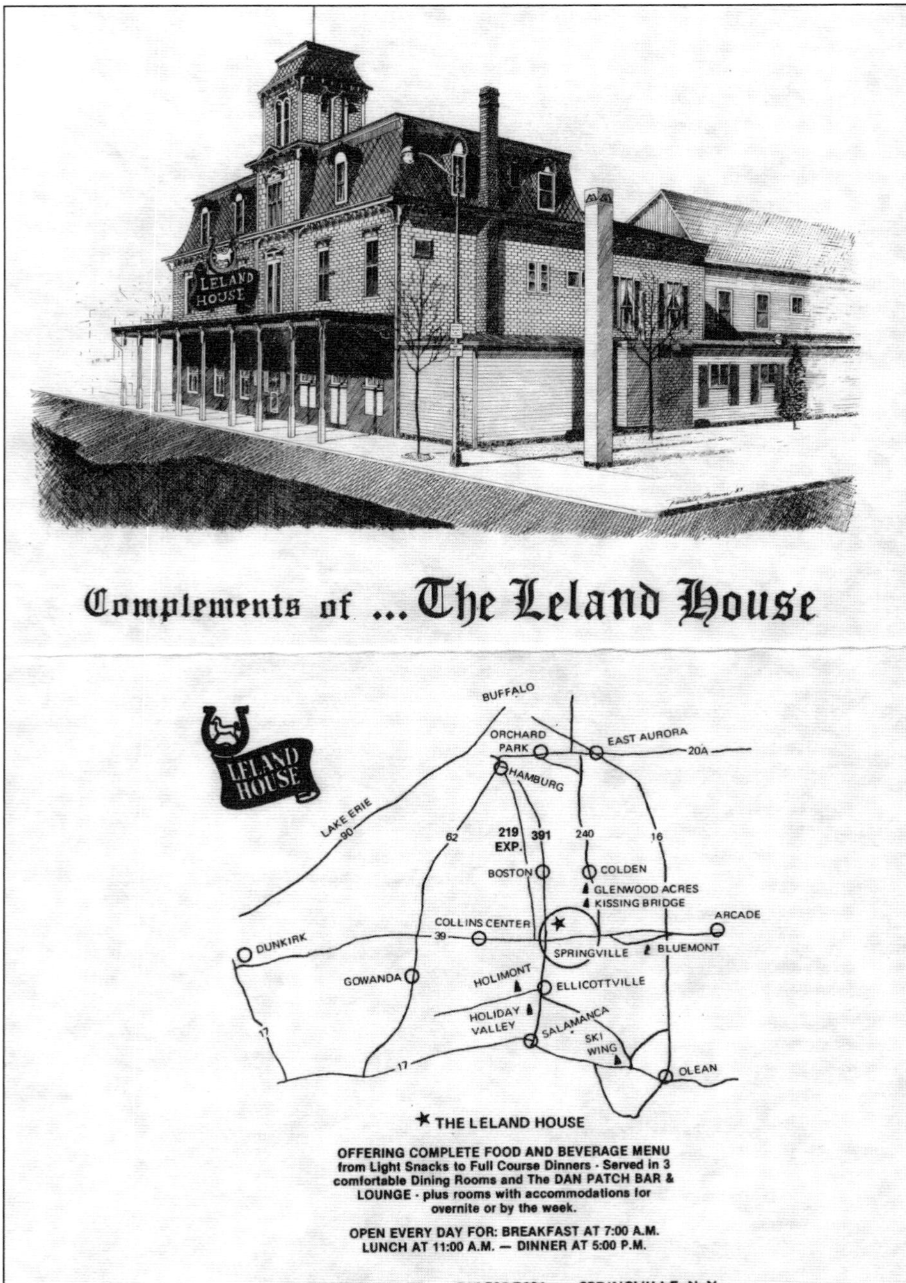

This is the front page of the Leland House menu from the 1970s. (Authors' collections.)

ON THE COVER: The south side of the East Main Street business district from Mechanic Street is pictured about 1930. The gasoline pump stands at the curb in front of longtime retailer J. Wilson Bement's store. An 1868 fire cleared this site, and only the Union Block (formerly Simon Bros.) was rebuilt in brick. Another fire leveled the block again in 1894, after which the structures seen to the east were built. (Courtesy of Concord Historical Society.)

IMAGES
of America

SPRINGVILLE

Alan V. Manchester and
David C. Batterson

ARCADIA
PUBLISHING

ISBN 978-0-7385-9157-5

Published by Arcadia Publishing
Charleston, South Carolina

Printed in the United States of America

Library of Congress Control Number: 2011940835

For all general information, please contact Arcadia Publishing:
Telephone 843-853-2070
Fax 843-853-0044
E-mail sales@arcadiapublishing.com
For customer service and orders:
Toll-Free 1-888-313-2665

Visit us on the Internet at www.arcadiapublishing.com

To a better understanding of the rich history of our community

Contents

ACKNOWLEDGMENTS

Without the foresight of those who came before us, efforts such as this book would not be possible. The Concord Historical Society is fortunate to have an exceptional collection of documents and images, which were assembled and identified by a number of individuals, most notably Lucy Bensley, and others like Grace Gentner and Elmer Ganschow, who created scrapbooks. In the late 1950s, Harry Richardson gathered a group of "old-timers" around a table and had Marie Seider transcribe their recollections. Town historians have also received and documented items for the collection. In recent years, historical society members have committed interviews to video. Each of us can contribute to future history-recording efforts by carefully labeling images in our possession, whether for our families or posterity. It is feared by some that a generation or more of image history will be lost in the hard drives of discarded computers. The authors have a long history of attic and cellar searching and auction and flea market attendance in the search for "Springville-Concord stuff," all of which would not be possible without the support and encouragement of their respective wives, Joyce Manchester and Pamela Batterson. Appreciation is also extended to Sarah and Deborah Owen for proofreading and word processing.

Unless otherwise noted, all images appear courtesy of the Concord Historical Society.

INTRODUCTION

Over time, certain structures or objects become a part of the fabric of the community. When they are removed, there is a sense of loss and sometimes resentment. Three examples from Springville come to mind.

The first is the chiming clock on the Farmers Bank (later Manufacturers and Traders Trust Company) building on the northeast corner of Main and Mechanic Streets, which was supposedly not repairable and was sold. The clock, however, found its way to a small town in western Pennsylvania and restoration. The second instance was the loss of "Old G.I." on Academy Street in 1973, when it fell to the wrecker's ball despite its structural integrity.

More recently, the loss of the Leland House, often described as "a witness to Main Street history," to a fire of suspicious origin in 2006 was painful. For those who might like a comprehensive pre-1883 history of the Springville area, Erasmus Briggs's *History of the Original Town of Concord* is recommended.

EXTENDING HOSPITALITY SINCE 1824

A silent witness to the history of Springville, New York, THE LELAND HOUSE, and its predecessor, the Springville House, date back to 1824.

The first residents of Springville, once known as Fiddler's Green, arrived by ox cart. Two of the earliest residents, Rufus C. Eaton Jr., and his brother, Elisha, erected a hotel and called it the Springville House. Their hotel was used as a post office, with Rufus serving as the first postmaster; it also provided meeting space for religious, fraternal, and political groups. At that time, "forest trees stood across the street," spreading from East Hill to Waverly Street. Banker H.G. Leland purchased the Springville House in 1878, replaced it in 1879 with the present structure, and gave it a new name - THE LELAND HOUSE. Regular stagecoach service had been available in Springville since the mid-1800's, and as Springville continued to prosper, in 1878, the Springville and Sardinia Railroad was built. Wide plank sidewalks extended from the "new" Leland House, allowing guests to meet trains at the Franklin Street Station, which stood on the site of the present fire hall.

The construction of the Buffalo, Rochester, and Pittsburgh Railroad (now Chessie) in 1883, with its depot on West Main Street, necessitated the "Leland House Bus," a stagecoach-type vehicle, which carried patrons to and from the depot. Stables for "bus" and guest horses were located on Mechanic Street.

On several occasions, great fires have almost destroyed the downtown area. In 1868, all buildings from the white brick "Blakeley House" across the street, east to Pearl Street, burned to the ground. Then in 1879, another fire leveled everything from the Blakeley House, west to Buffalo Street, including the stately opera house. Written accounts of this fire attribute providence and calm winds, together with the skill of the Hook and Ladder Company, to the sparing of this side of the street. Subsequent great fires occurred in 1894 and 1946.

In 1895, the Leland House was wired for electricity and the Village installed street lighting. Great numbers of migrating ducks and geese were drawn to the area by the lighting and one citizen bagged 23 birds from the night sky.

The Hotel has stood as a witness to numerous memorable moments in history. In 1900, the results of the presidential race between William McKinley and William Jennings Bryan were reported to our community via telegraph equipment located here. In later years, Bryan visited Springville on lecture circuit tours. Up until the construction of brick streets in 1912, fine area horses raced past here to the West Main Street Depot and back each New Year's Day.

Under Coach Glenn "Pop" Warner, Olympic Champion Jim Thorpe trained on our dusty village streets, while across the way in the Ralph B. Waite Building, products for painless dental surgery were being manufactured for worldwide distribution.

In the immediate downtown area, the Civil War era Blakeley House and Walters Pharmacy Building are the oldest structures. The Union Block, now Simon Bros., and the Springville Journal-Brown Shoe Store Building were built in 1868.

From 1904 through 1971, the Bernard F. Ferry and Emmett F. Ferry families operated the Leland House. Since 1971, your host, the Enser family, continues the long-established traditions of pride and service.

Witness to history, and an example of the splendor of earlier days, the Leland House continues to play an important part in a proud community that is entering a new era for business and a wholesome life for its residents.

Historical Ref.
Alan V. Manchester
Springville, New York
April 1983

This Leland House menu history insert reviews much of its history, as well as the history of its predecessor, Springville House, and of the town.

One

Schools

Springville Academy was organized in 1825, incorporated by the signature of DeWitt Clinton in 1827, and opened in the fall of 1830. It was the first high school in Erie County and the second in the Holland Land Purchase (all of New York State west of Batavia). Since 1867, it has been known as Griffith Institute because of a $10,000 scholarship—equal to nearly $150,000 today—given by Archibald Griffith, one of Springville Academy's original sponsors. The only condition of the scholarship was that the school maintain his gravesite, in East Concord's Evergreen Cemetery, in perpetuity.

Prior to the academy, early families held classes in their homes and built the first schoolhouse, a log structure where the parking lot of the First Presbyterian Church sits today. Later schools were at the corner of Franklin and Smith Streets and at the south end of Pearl Street. The academy received funding in many forms besides cash, including land, lumber, labor, and even goods—one pledge consisted of only boots and shoes. Citizen determination and dedication allowed the institution to survive and achieve its goals. Strict discipline and rules for good citizenship were enforced. Students were attracted from surrounding towns, boarding in village homes with strict curfews. That environment was not without its rewards, as it produced a remarkable list of significant contributions to society. Reorganization and centralization have made Springville-Griffith Institute Central School District the largest geographical school district in New York State. St. Aloysius School and the League for the Handicapped Preschool Learning Center have also served the area.

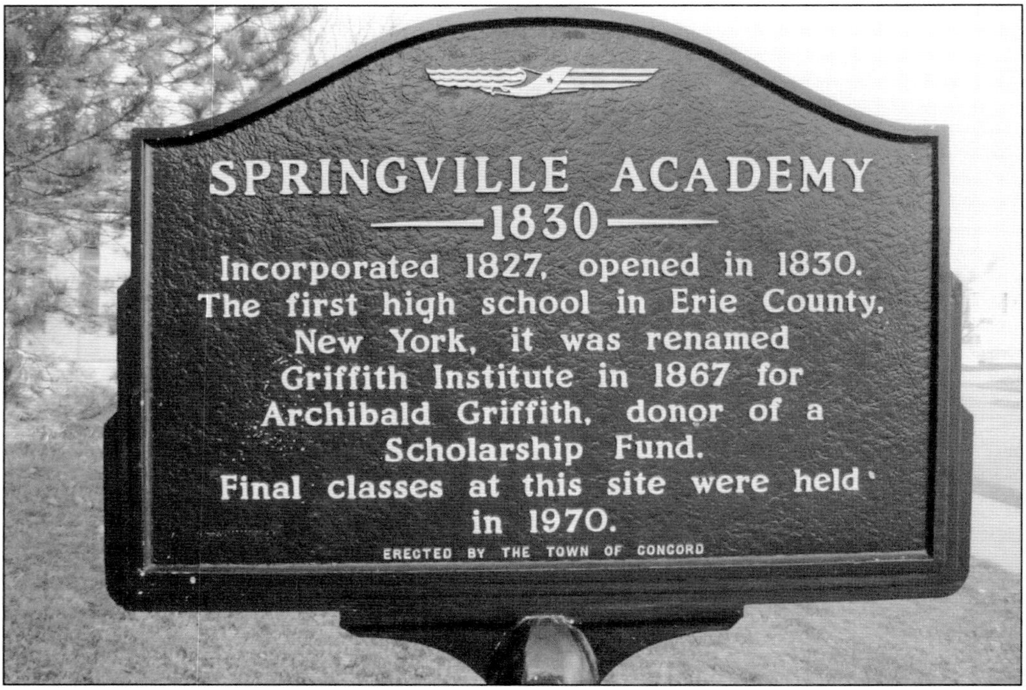

The bell from the Springville Academy tower has been preserved and is on display at the district office on Newman Street. It was last heard at the sesquicentennial of Springville Academy–Griffith Institute in 1980. The academy was fenced to keep unwelcome livestock, which roamed the village with limited restriction, off of the grounds. To eliminate the possibility of a forgetful or prank-minded student failing to close a gate, a stile (a set of stairs over the fence) was installed. In keeping with the times, separate ladies and gentlemen's school entrances were provided.

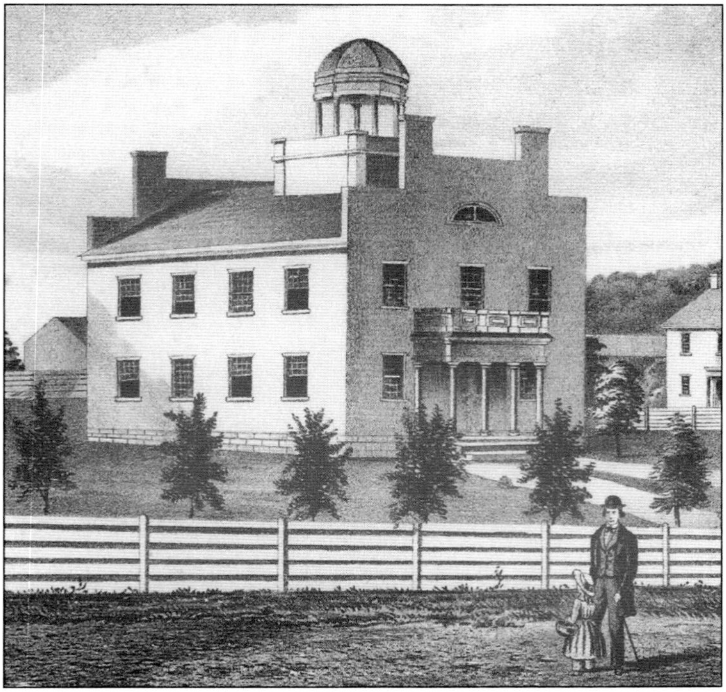

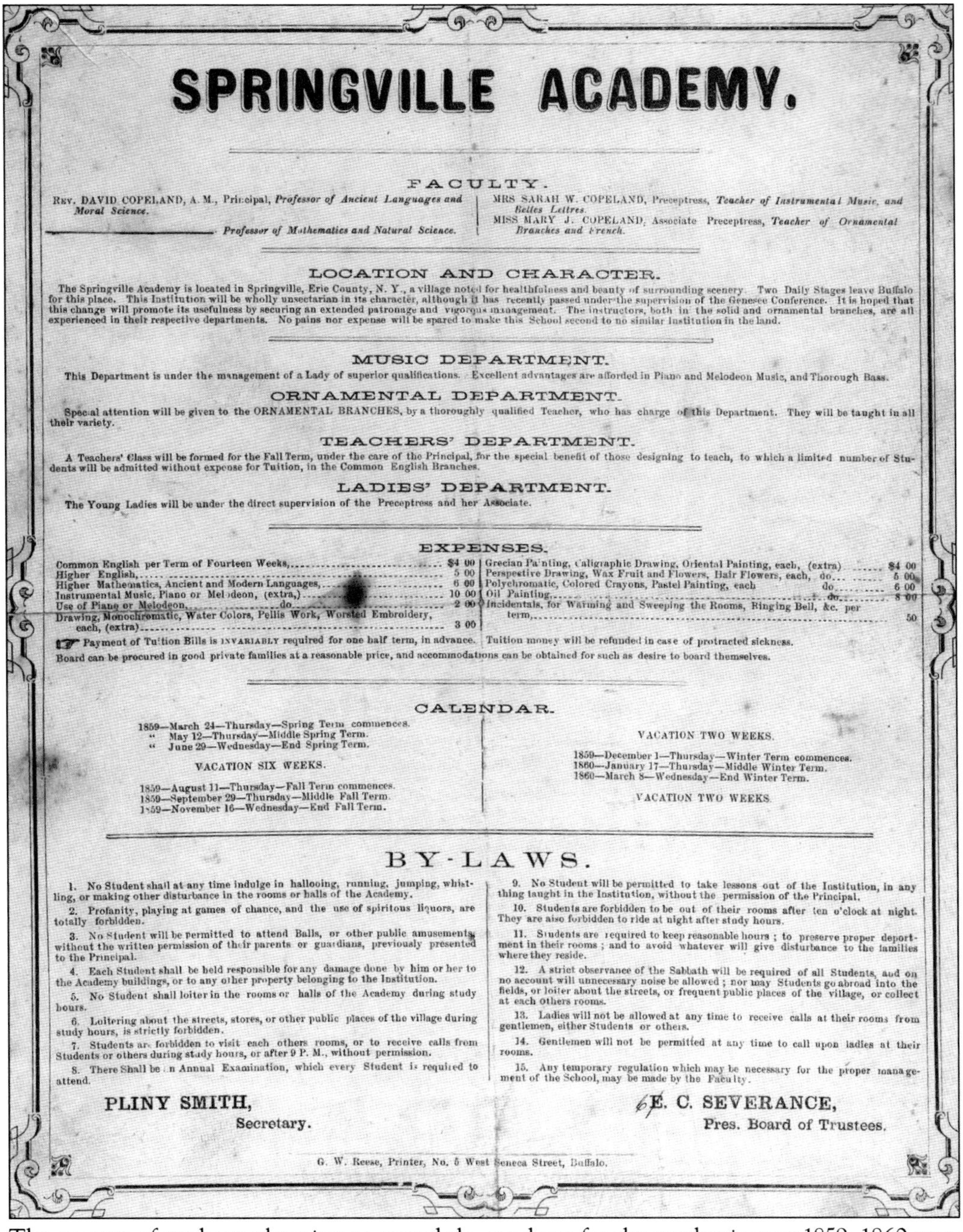

SPRINGVILLE ACADEMY.

FACULTY.

REV. DAVID COPELAND, A. M., Principal, *Professor of Ancient Languages and Moral Science.*

———————— *Professor of Mathematics and Natural Science.*

MRS SARAH W. COPELAND, Preceptress, *Teacher of Instrumental Music, and Belles Lettres.*

MISS MARY J. COPELAND, Associate Preceptress, *Teacher of Ornamental Branches and French.*

LOCATION AND CHARACTER.

The Springville Academy is located in Springville, Erie County, N. Y., a village noted for healthfulness and beauty of surrounding scenery. Two Daily Stages leave Buffalo for this place. This Institution will be wholly unsectarian in its character, although it has recently passed under the supervision of the Genesee Conference. It is hoped that this change will promote its usefulness by securing an extended patronage and vigorous management. The instructors, both in the solid and ornamental branches, are all experienced in their respective departments. No pains nor expense will be spared to make this School second to no similar Institution in the land.

MUSIC DEPARTMENT.

This Department is under the management of a Lady of superior qualifications. Excellent advantages are afforded in Piano and Melodeon Music, and Thorough Bass.

ORNAMENTAL DEPARTMENT.

Special attention will be given to the ORNAMENTAL BRANCHES, by a thoroughly qualified Teacher, who has charge of this Department. They will be taught in all their variety.

TEACHERS' DEPARTMENT.

A Teachers' Class will be formed for the Fall Term, under the care of the Principal, for the special benefit of those designing to teach, to which a limited number of Students will be admitted without expense for Tuition, in the Common English Branches.

LADIES' DEPARTMENT.

The Young Ladies will be under the direct supervision of the Preceptress and her Associate.

EXPENSES.

Common English per Term of Fourteen Weeks,	$4 00
Higher English,	5 00
Higher Mathematics, Ancient and Modern Languages,	6 00
Instrumental Music, Piano or Melodeon, (extra,)	10 00
Use of Piano or Melodeon, do.	2 00
Drawing, Monochromatic, Water Colors, Pellis Work, Worsted Embroidery, each, (extra)	3 00
Grecian Painting, Caligraphic Drawing, Oriental Painting, each, (extra)	$4 00
Perspective Drawing, Wax Fruit and Flowers, Hair Flowers, each, do.	5 00
Polychromatic, Colored Crayons, Pastel Painting, each do.	6 00
Oil Painting, do.	8 00
Incidentals, for Warming and Sweeping the Rooms, Ringing Bell, &c. per term,	50

☞ Payment of Tuition Bills is INVARIABLY required for one half term, in advance. Tuition money will be refunded in case of protracted sickness.

Board can be procured in good private families at a reasonable price, and accommodations can be obtained for such as desire to board themselves.

CALENDAR.

1859—March 24—Thursday—Spring Term commences.
" May 12—Thursday—Middle Spring Term.
" June 29—Wednesday—End Spring Term.

VACATION SIX WEEKS.

1859—August 11—Thursday—Fall Term commences.
1859—September 29—Thursday—Middle Fall Term.
1859—November 16—Wednesday—End Fall Term.

VACATION TWO WEEKS.

1859—December 1—Thursday—Winter Term commences.
1860—January 17—Thursday—Middle Winter Term.
1860—March 8—Wednesday—End Winter Term.

VACATION TWO WEEKS.

BY-LAWS.

1. No Student shall at any time indulge in hallooing, running, jumping, whistling, or making other disturbance in the rooms or halls of the Academy.
2. Profanity, playing at games of chance, and the use of spiritous liquors, are totally forbidden.
3. No Student will be permitted to attend Balls, or other public amusements, without the written permission of their parents or guardians, previously presented to the Principal.
4. Each Student shall be held responsible for any damage done by him or her to the Academy buildings, or to any other property belonging to the Institution.
5. No Student shall loiter in the rooms or halls of the Academy during study hours.
6. Loitering about the streets, stores, or other public places of the village during study hours, is strictly forbidden.
7. Students are forbidden to visit each others rooms, or to receive calls from Students or others during study hours, or after 9 P. M., without permission.
8. There Shall be an Annual Examination, which every Student is required to attend.
9. No Student will be permitted to take lessons out of the Institution, in any thing taught in the Institution, without the permission of the Principal.
10. Students are forbidden to be out of their rooms after ten o'clock at night. They are also forbidden to ride at night after study hours.
11. Students are required to keep reasonable hours; to preserve proper deportment in their rooms; and to avoid whatever will give disturbance to the families where they reside.
12. A strict observance of the Sabbath will be required of all Students, and on no account will unnecessary noise be allowed; nor may Students go abroad into the fields, or loiter about the streets, or frequent public places of the village, or collect at each others rooms.
13. Ladies will not be allowed at any time to receive calls at their rooms from gentlemen, either Students or others.
14. Gentlemen will not be permitted at any time to call upon ladies at their rooms.
15. Any temporary regulation which may be necessary for the proper management of the School, may be made by the Faculty.

PLINY SMITH,
Secretary.

E. C. SEVERANCE,
Pres. Board of Trustees.

G. W. Reese, Printer, No. 5 West Seneca Street, Buffalo.

The parents of students planning to attend the academy for the academic year 1859–1860 were assured that the village was noted for healthfulness and surrounding beauty. Further, "No pains or expense will be spared to make this school second to no institution in the land." The bylaws made quite clear the expectations placed on students who planned to attend.

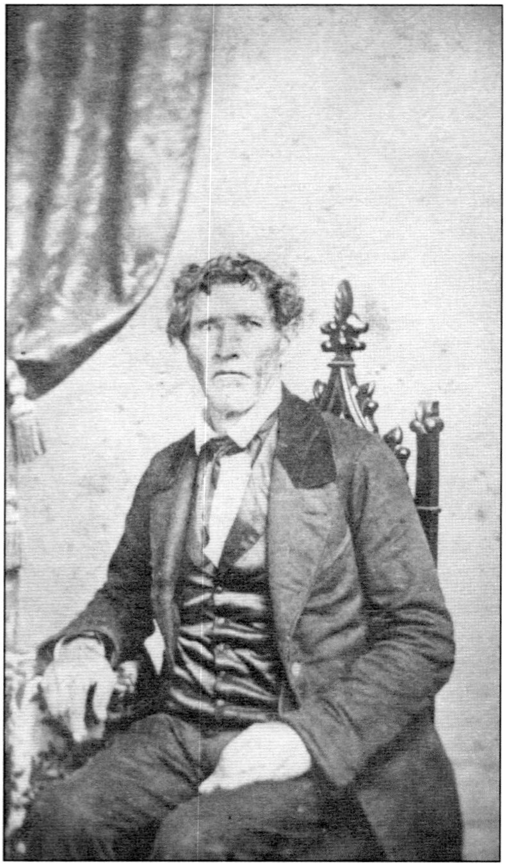

It is assumed that Archibald Griffith could smile, but early photographic plates were slow to capture images and recorded motion as a blur, so he was instructed to pose with a serious expression. Early photographers also employed a steel brace, out of sight behind the subject, to prevent movement. An iron fence surrounds the Griffith family plot at East Concord.

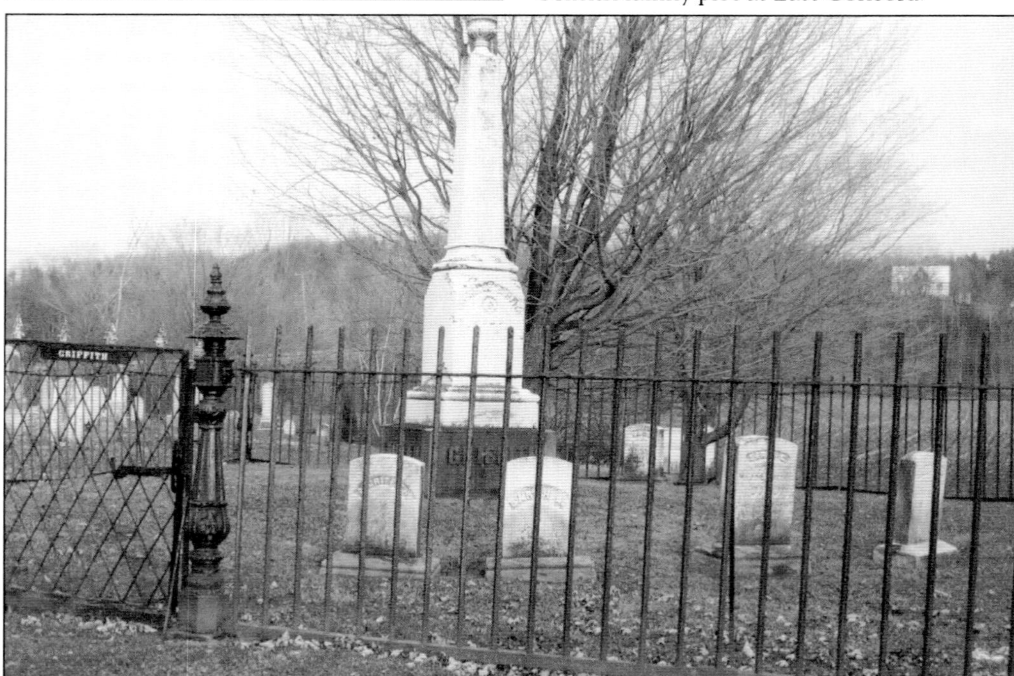

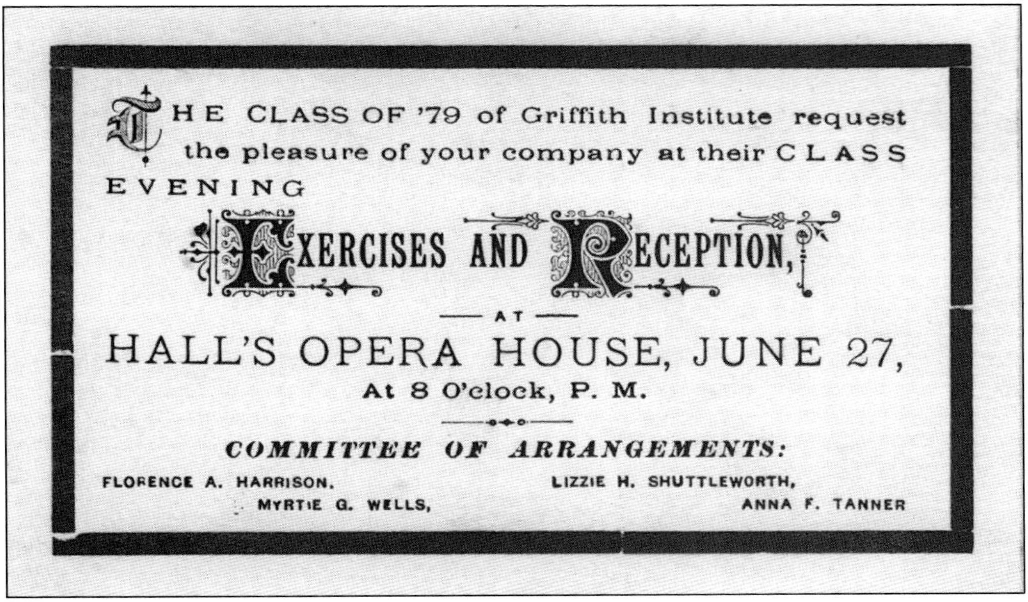

THE CLASS OF '79 of Griffith Institute request the pleasure of your company at their CLASS EVENING

EXERCISES AND RECEPTION,

— AT —

HALL'S OPERA HOUSE, JUNE 27,

At 8 O'clock, P. M.

COMMITTEE OF ARRANGEMENTS:

FLORENCE A. HARRISON. MYRTIE G. WELLS, LIZZIE H. SHUTTLEWORTH, ANNA F. TANNER

Attendees of Springville Academy or Griffith Institute included Elon Howard Eaton, a distinguished ornithologist who inspired a youthful Roger Tory Peterson; Edwin Walker, an inventor who held the majority of patents on the mechanical ice cream disher (scoop); Gen. Eugene Asa Carr, a Civil War veteran and commander of Fort Apache who fought Indians with his personal guide, "Buffalo Bill" Cody; Clark Ezra Carr, who helped plan the Gettysburg cemetery and who rode in the procession and sat on the platform during the Gettysburg Address; Addison C. Gibbs, governor of Oregon; Supreme Court justice Truman C. White, who presided at the trial of Pres. William McKinley's assassin, Leon Czolgosz; Buffalo mayor Timothy T. Lockwood; Thomas M. Reynolds and a number of other congressmen; Glenn Scobey "Pop" Warner; Ralph Britton Waite; Bertrand Chaffee; Lt. Gen. Eric Fiel; and countless other individuals who have served the nation's military.

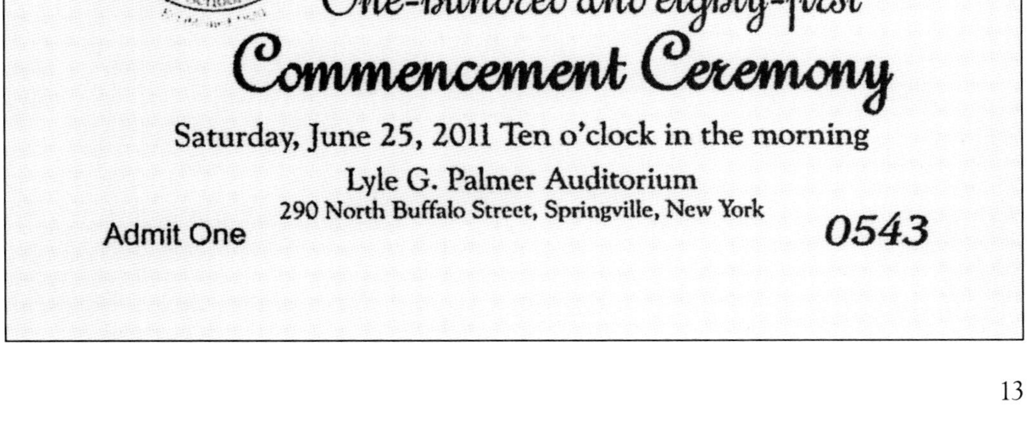

Springville-Griffith Institute Central School District

One-hundred and eighty-first

Commencement Ceremony

Saturday, June 25, 2011 Ten o'clock in the morning

Lyle G. Palmer Auditorium

290 North Buffalo Street, Springville, New York

Admit One 0543

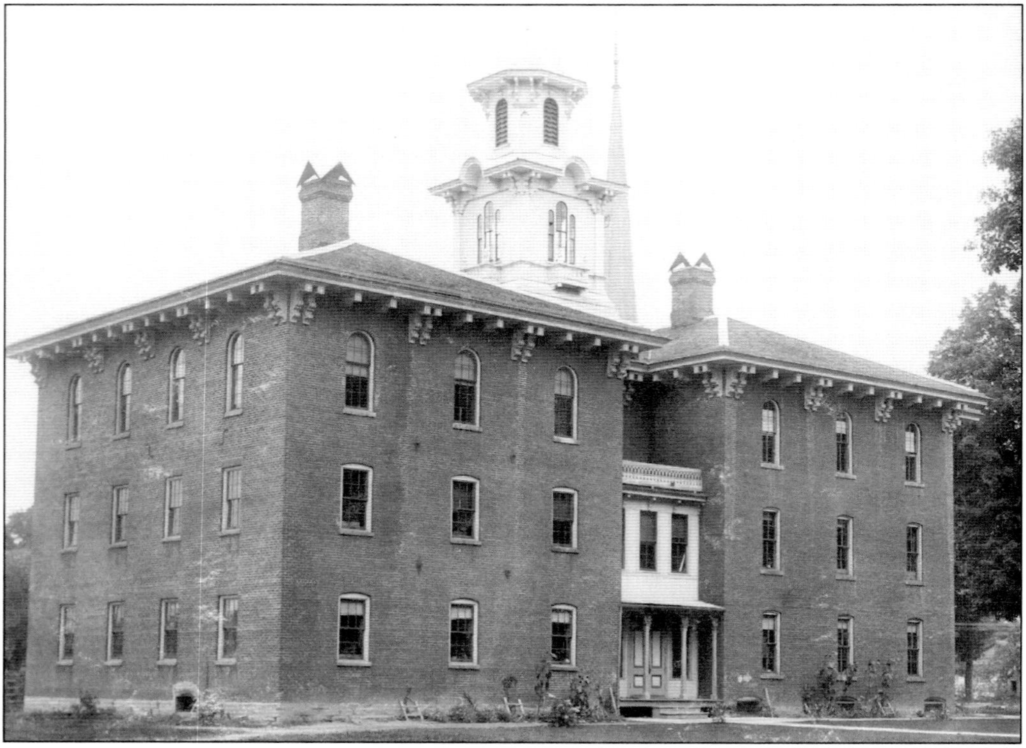

An 1885 addition to Griffith Institute, designed by Louise Blanchard Bethune of Buffalo, who is considered America's first professional female architect, doubled the size of the school. Here the building is viewed from Academy Street.

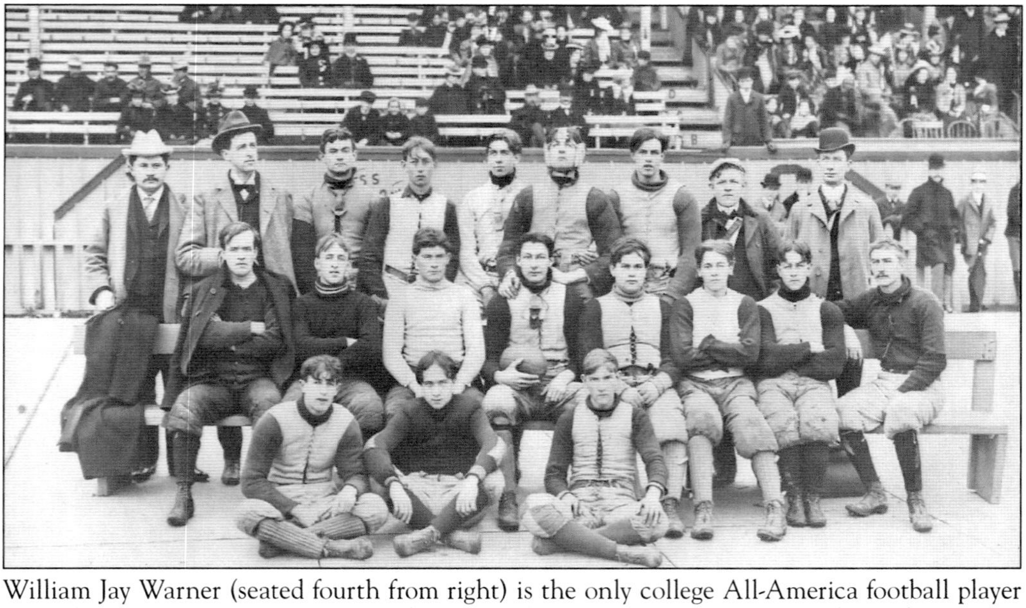

William Jay Warner (seated fourth from right) is the only college All-America football player to graduate from Griffith Institute, which he did in 1898. Like his older brother, Glenn "Pop" Warner, he studied law at Cornell. The grandstand behind the team was located on John Dygert's Elk Street farm. Seated third from left is Charles Tefft, the grandfather of the donor of this photograph, Carol Wohlheuter.

NOTICE!

Any marking or defacement of this building, inside or outside, or of any of its desks, seats or other furnishings, is ABSOLUTELY PROHIBITED. This order will be strictly enforced, and any person violating the same will be required to pay all damage, and in addition, will be subject to a fine or suspension or expulsion from school.

By Order of the

BOARD OF EDUCATION

Dated at Springville, N. Y., June 19th, 1909.

Around the Main Street corner, built at a cost of $75,000, sits one of the finest school buildings in New York State. The framed notice was removed before the wrecking ball arrived in 1973. The great steel beams that framed the gymnasium ceiling and supported the second-floor auditorium had been towed down Main Street by steam tractors from the railroad at the time of construction.

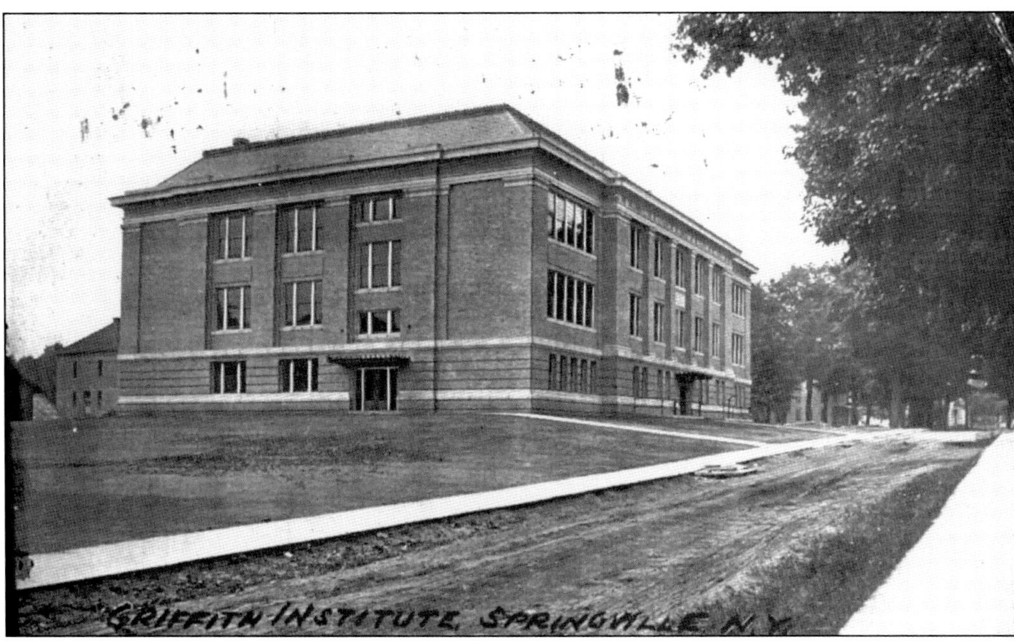

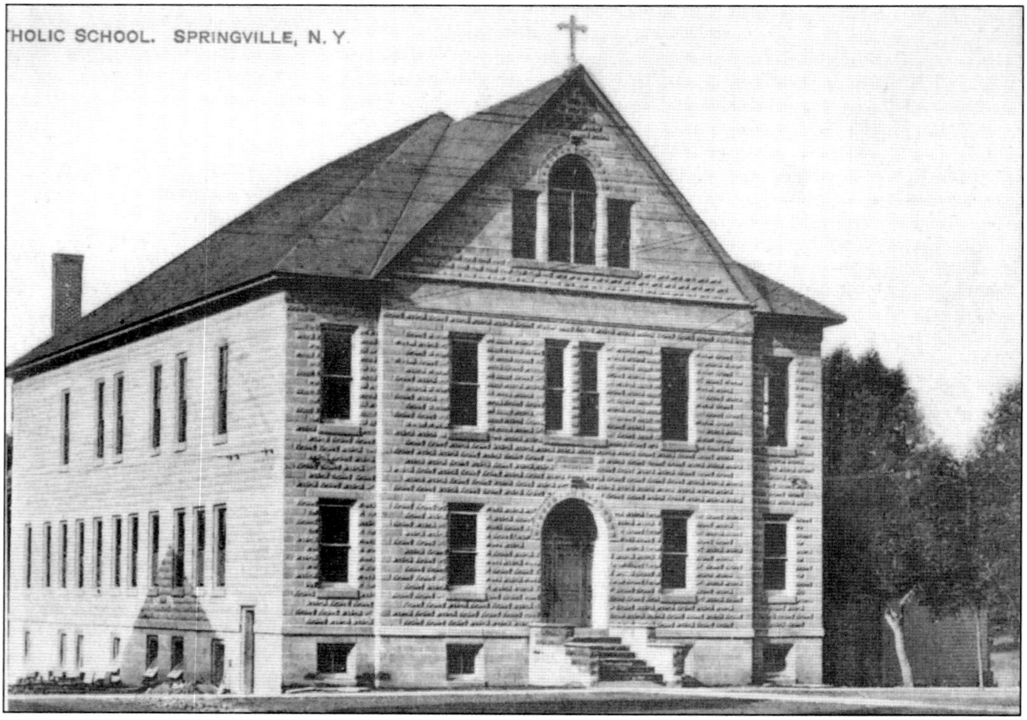

St. Aloysius School opened its doors in 1883 with an enrollment of 76 students. The Sisters of St. Francis were the original teachers and staffed the school until 2007. Before 1905, classes were held in the brick building on the corner of Franklin and Smith Streets. In 1996, St. Aloysius became a regional school serving 10 parishes, and it celebrated 125 years of Catholic education in 2008.

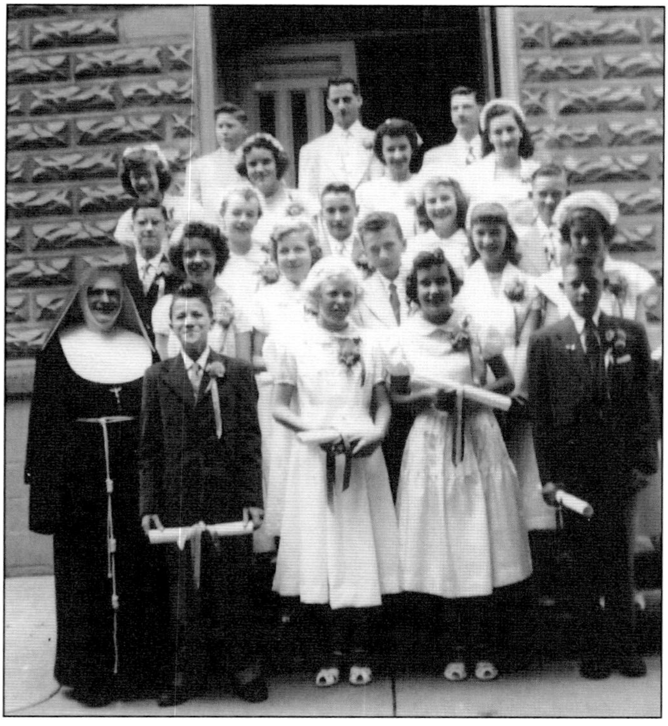

The 1952 graduating class of the St. Aloysius School is pictured here. In no particular order are Sister Richard, Jean Gentner, Nancy Gentner, Claudia Wolniewicz, Barbara Mrugala, Theresa Gernatt, James Kraft, Timothy Trost, Richard Rogers, Mary Harrington Tolan, Charles "Ike" Krezmien, Richard Germain, Frank Lerminiaux, Sheila Hemmerling, Jean Schweickert, Jean Fox, Margaret Shimburski, Nancy Ellis, Dennis Smith, Thomas Kazmark, Nancy Bennet, Marjorie Gentner, and Gerald Salzler. (Courtesy of Claudia Wolniewicz.)

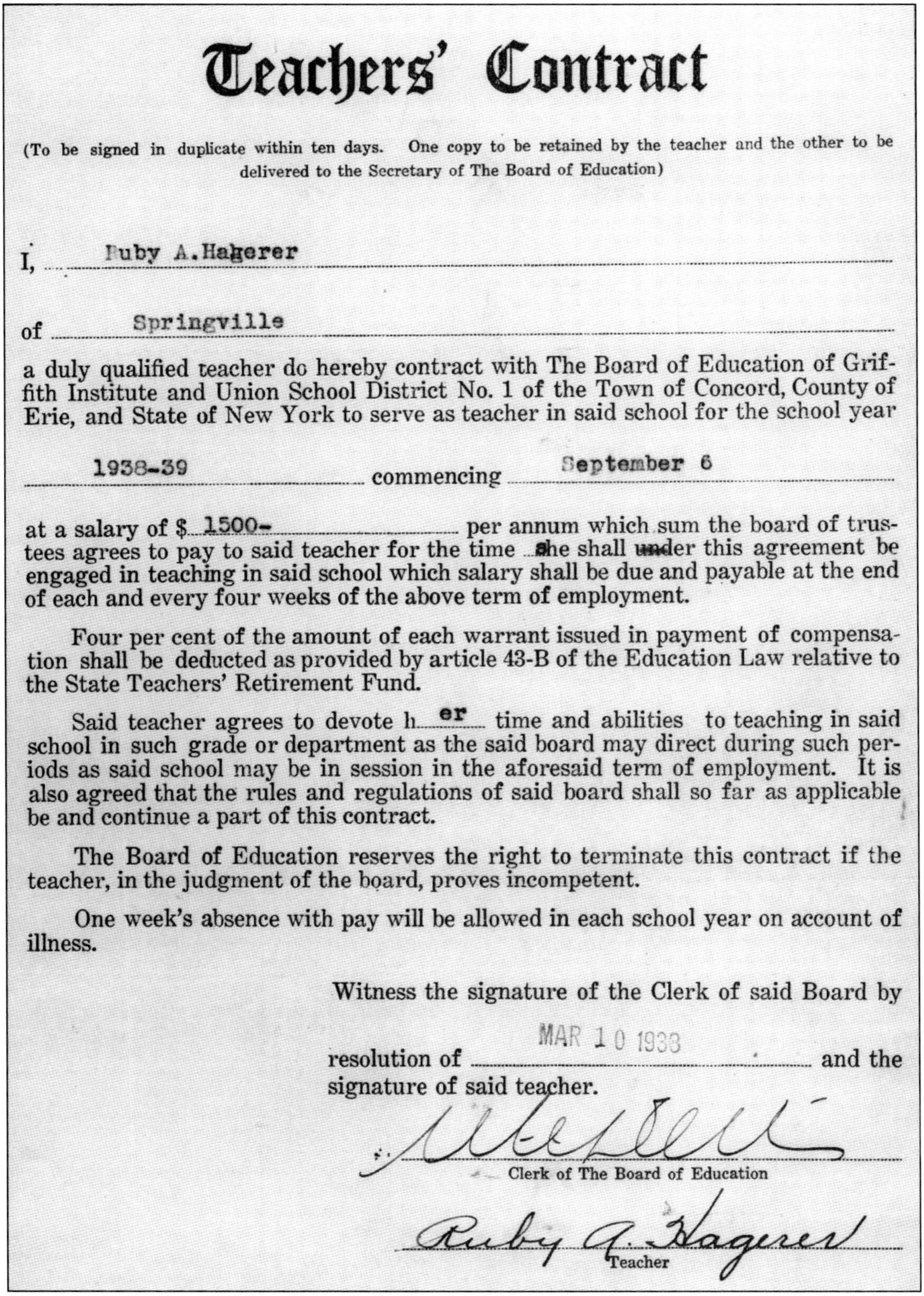

Teachers' Contract

(To be signed in duplicate within ten days. One copy to be retained by the teacher and the other to be delivered to the Secretary of The Board of Education)

I, Ruby A.Hagerer

of Springville

a duly qualified teacher do hereby contract with The Board of Education of Griffith Institute and Union School District No. 1 of the Town of Concord, County of Erie, and State of New York to serve as teacher in said school for the school year

1938-39 commencing September 6

at a salary of $ 1500- per annum which sum the board of trustees agrees to pay to said teacher for the time she shall under this agreement be engaged in teaching in said school which salary shall be due and payable at the end of each and every four weeks of the above term of employment.

Four per cent of the amount of each warrant issued in payment of compensation shall be deducted as provided by article 43-B of the Education Law relative to the State Teachers' Retirement Fund.

Said teacher agrees to devote her time and abilities to teaching in said school in such grade or department as the said board may direct during such periods as said school may be in session in the aforesaid term of employment. It is also agreed that the rules and regulations of said board shall so far as applicable be and continue a part of this contract.

The Board of Education reserves the right to terminate this contract if the teacher, in the judgment of the board, proves incompetent.

One week's absence with pay will be allowed in each school year on account of illness.

Witness the signature of the Clerk of said Board by resolution of MAR 10 1938 and the signature of said teacher.

Clerk of The Board of Education

Ruby A. Hagerer
Teacher

This teachers' contract from an earlier era specifically forbids marriage by a teacher during the life of the contract. J. Leland Anderson and Lucille Anderson chuckled years later as they recalled how they and others had been secretly married and continued their teaching careers.

Griffith Institute Alma Mater

Just Around The Main Street Corner
On Academy Street
Stands Our Noble Alma Mater
Says She Can't Be Beat

Lift The Chorus, Speed It Onward
Loud Her Praises Cry
Hail To Thee, Our Alma Mater
Hail, Oh Hail G.I.

Many Years Our School Has Welcomed
Students To Its Halls
Oh, The Ties Of Love And Friendship
Found Within Its Walls.

Lift The Chorus, Speed It Onward
Loud Her Praises Cry
Hail To Thee, Our Alma Mater
Hail, Oh Hail G.I.

Known to thousands, "Old G.I." can still bring a tear to its graduates. In an earlier time, in front of an earlier building, Glenn Warner and his friends played football utilizing an inflated pig's bladder as a ball. There was no school football team at the time. Later, a blacktopped playground with a street lamp for first base and ice for winter lunch-hour skating were added. One day in the 1940s, Miss Hagerer moved Dennis Corsette to another desk for disciplinary reasons, just seconds before a football shattered the window above where he had been sitting, showering down shards of glass.

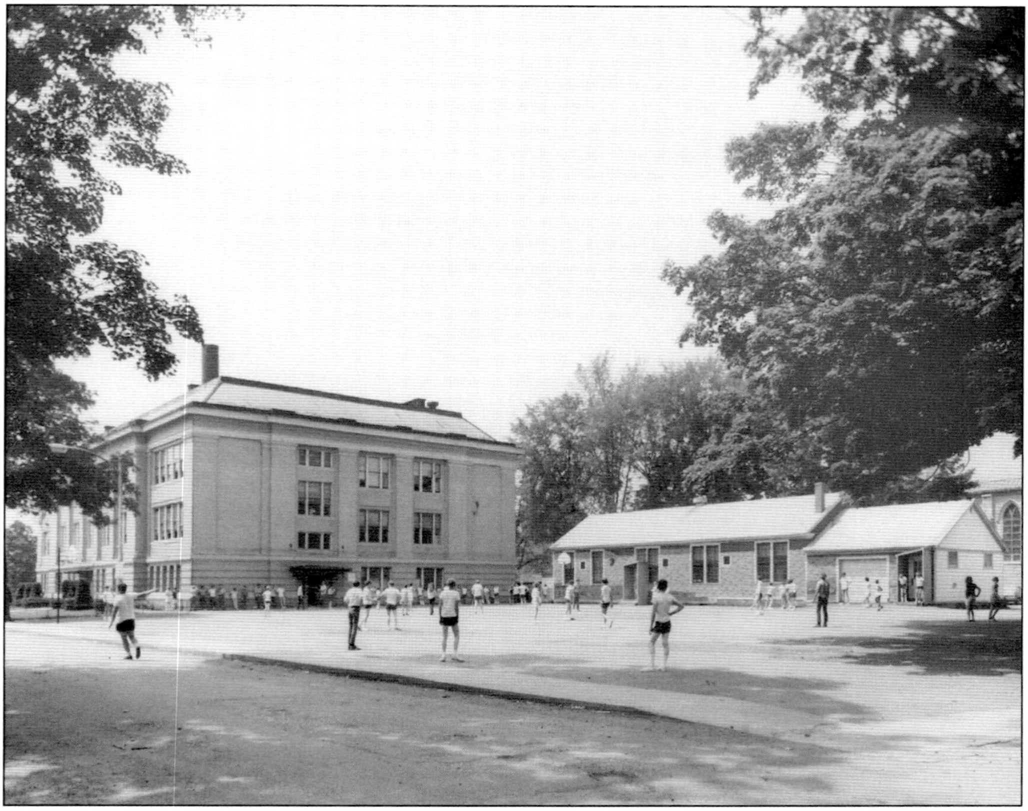

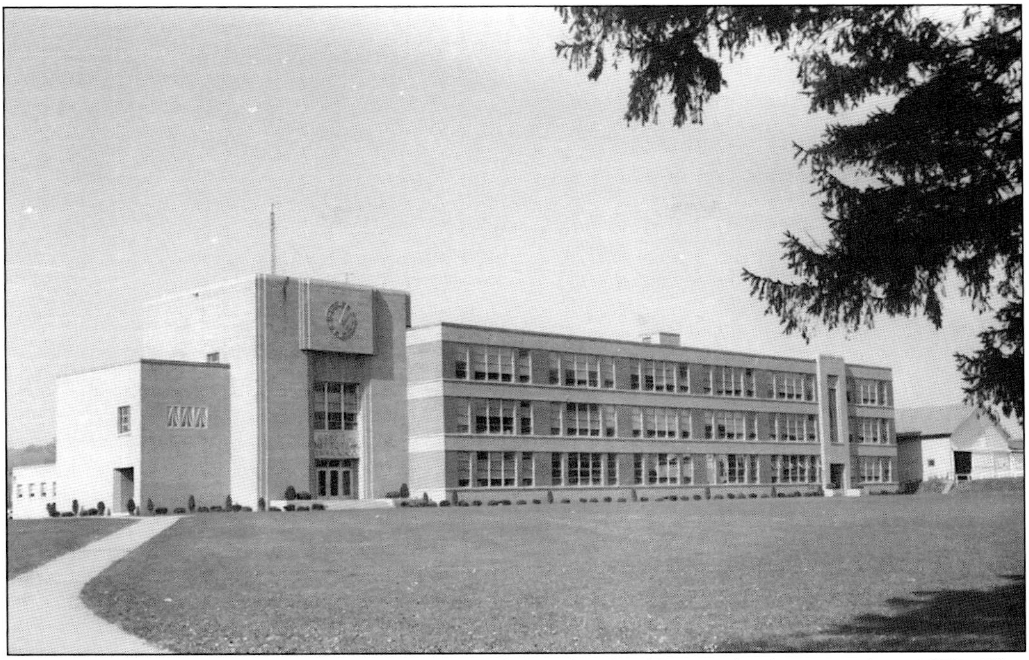

In 1949, a $990,000 bond issue was proposed for this building, which opened in 1952. The structure to the right was the Smith Farm barn, which was adapted to use for bus maintenance and a bus storage facility. The new building was needed to relieve crowding and to end the use of rented classrooms.

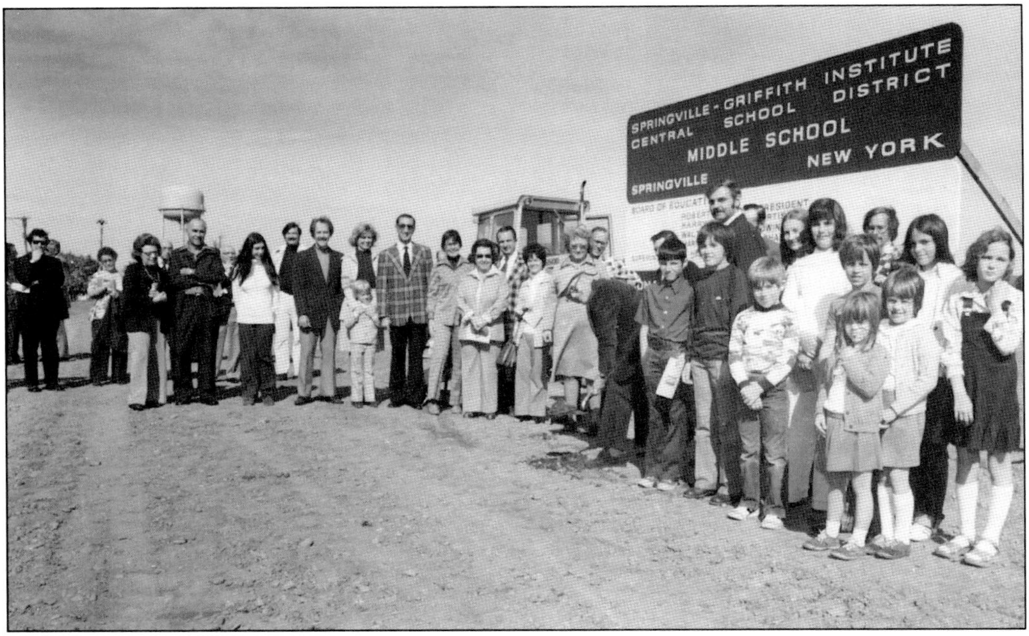

On October 5, 1975, the ground on Newman Street was broken for construction of a middle school. Its completion ended a half-dozen years of "double sessions," where high school classes met mornings and middle school met in the afternoon. This was necessitated by the closing of the Academy Street "Old G.I." building in 1970. Famed mathematics teacher A. Sanford Kenyon is at the shovel.

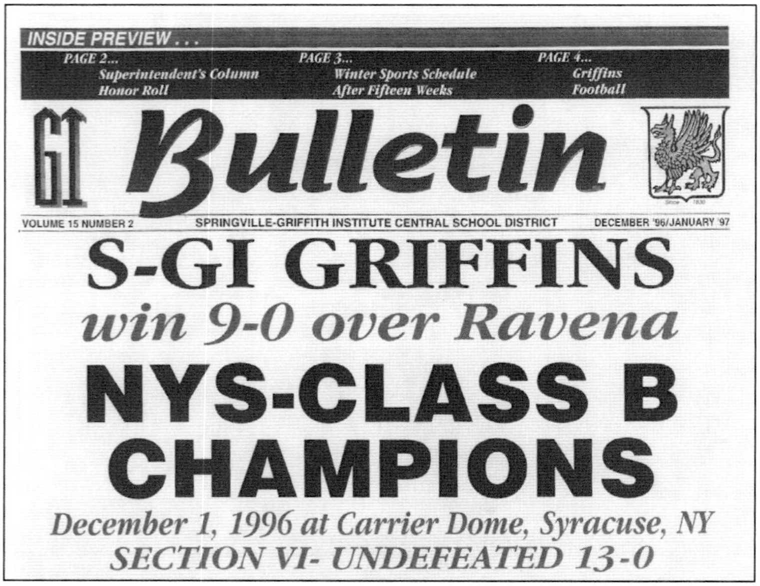
INSIDE PREVIEW . . .

PAGE 2... Superintendent's Column, Honor Roll

PAGE 3... Winter Sports Schedule, After Fifteen Weeks

PAGE 4... Griffins Football

GI Bulletin

VOLUME 15 NUMBER 2 SPRINGVILLE-GRIFFITH INSTITUTE CENTRAL SCHOOL DISTRICT DECEMBER '96/JANUARY '97

S-GI GRIFFINS

win 9-0 over Ravena

NYS-CLASS B CHAMPIONS

December 1, 1996 at Carrier Dome, Syracuse, NY

SECTION VI- UNDEFEATED 13-0

The school district bulletin proudly proclaims S-GI's championship status.

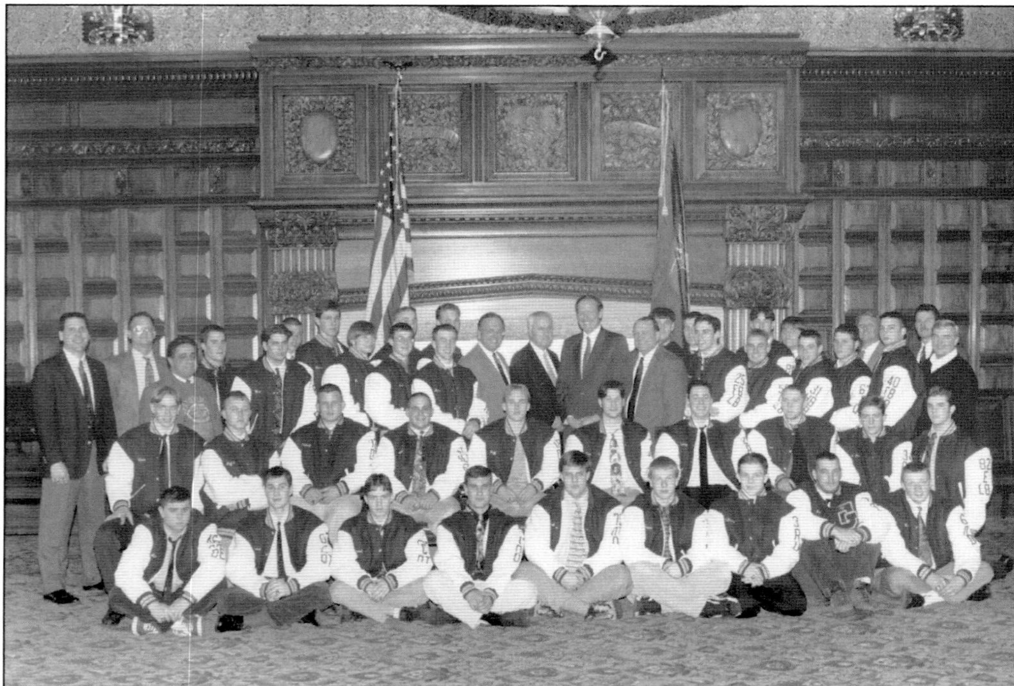

From left to right are (first row) Joel Lux, Aaron Godert, Todd Conrad, Jeff Leavell, Luke Wockensky, Justin Jones, Mark DeGeorge, Mark Aul, and Bruce Robinson; (second row) Eric Lunser, Jeff Greene, Mark Aldstadt, Mike Amodeo, Jeff Piscitelli, Mark Rendell, Ben Garvey, Daryl Pierce, Paul Salzler, and Mike Pinelli; (third row) Larry Amodeo, Don West, Ben Butzer, Dan Stuart, Brian Blesy, Assembly Leader Thomas M. Reynolds, New York State senator Dale Volker, New York governor George Pataki, coach James Duprey, Axel Neff, Dusty Strianese, Matt Amodeo, Tom Baker, Scott Kearns, and coach Thomas O'Brien; (fourth row) Benjamin Halsey, coach Ronald Tamraz, Shea Hannon, Bill Horn, Chris Walczyk, Mike Capella, Mike Brady, Darin Johnson, William Baker, Mike Oatman, James Kearns, and Rick Adamczak. (Courtesy of James Duprey.)

Two

Railroad Town

It is almost impossible to imagine Springville as a railroad town; for that matter, it is difficult to picture stagecoaches on dusty streets either.

The first attempt to establish a rail connection was the formation of the Buffalo & Springville Railroad in 1871, a venture that did not materialize. It was decided that a more affordable option was to build 11 miles east and connect with the Buffalo, New York & Philadelphia Railroad at what later became Chaffee, a name suggested by Carl Chaffee for the rail hub and future metropolis. The Springville & Sardinia Railroad served briefly, from 1878 to 1886, delivering freight and passengers. The emerging Rochester & Pittsburgh Railroad (later Buffalo, Rochester & Pittsburgh Railway, or BR&P) used standard-gauge (4 feet, 8.5 inches) rail spacing, which meant the end of the three-foot narrow-gauge line that was auctioned off in 1886.

Millions of tons of coal and freight passed through Springville on the BR&P. Great steam locomotives were still in use during World War II and, in addition to coal, pulled war-effort trucks, jeeps, tanks, and big guns north. The Buffalo & Susquehanna Railway operated briefly from 1906 to 1916. A Buffalo, Rochester & Pittsburgh Railway ownership change, a drop in freight volume due to competing trucks, and roadbed damage all contributed to the end of the era.

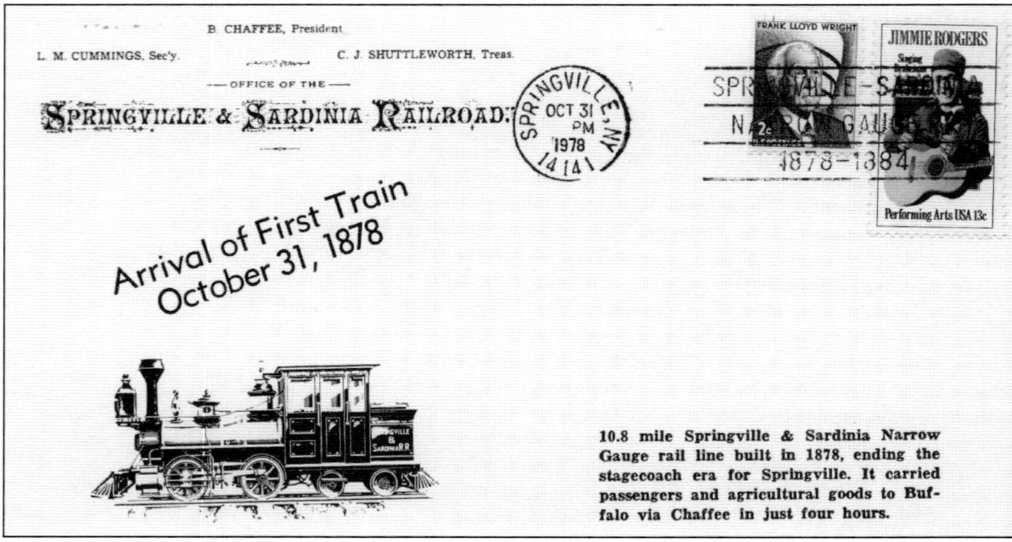

The Concord Historical Society sought the cooperation of the postal service in the creation of a special cancellation for Springville mail celebrating the arrival of the first train. Army colonel Clare Rogers, a former area resident, researched the history of the Springville & Sardinia Railroad for a book on narrow-gauge railroads.

Arrival of the First Train

On a windy, snowy, chilly day, at 5:13½ in the afternoon of the 31st of October, 1878, the "Rock City" entered Springville for the first time. The Springville "Journal and Herald" was quite beside itself. "Out of the Woods!" it shouted, "Springville a Railroad Town!" President Bert Chafee was carried in triumph up and down Main Street. At 7:45 that same evening Bert re-entered Springville on the line's own locomotive "Little Darling," a Brooks 10-ton "Forney" type double-ender (0-4-4T). He was accompanied by the president of the Brooks Locomotive Works of Dunkirk, none other than Horatio Brooks himself, who had come in person to see the wonders of Springville.

Col. Clare Rogers, Railroad Historian
Arlington, Va.

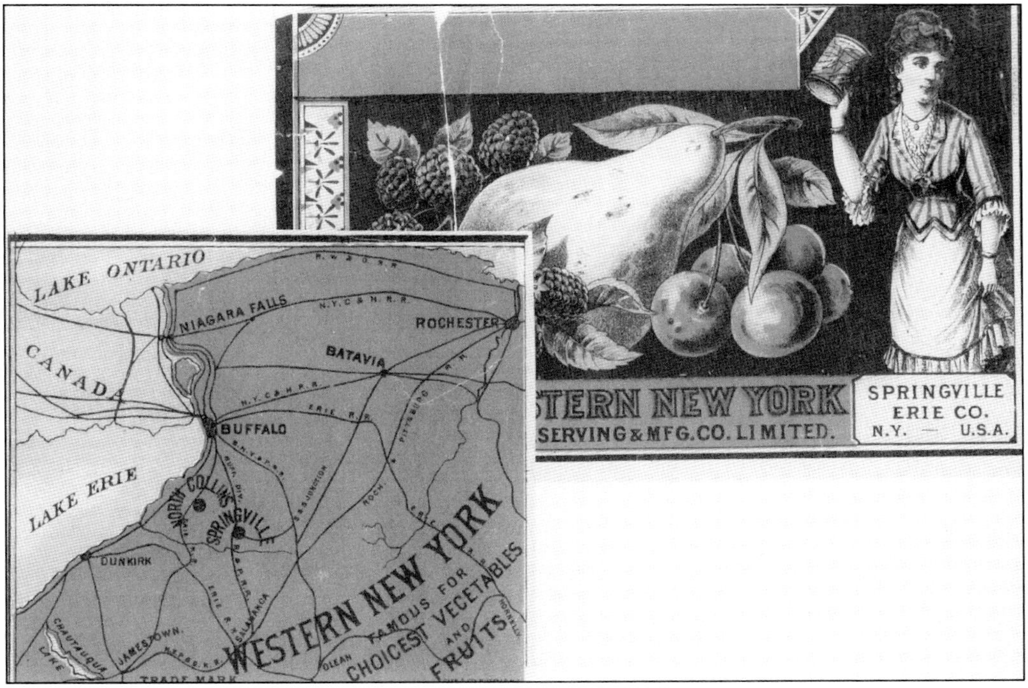

Western New York Preserving and Manufacturing Company, known as the canning factory, was located between Franklin Street and Maple Avenue. One remnant of the factory remains and was renovated as the Boys and Girls Club. The factory proudly displayed its railroad access to the world on its 1883 can labels, showing the Rochester & Pittsburgh Railroad and the soon-to-be defunct Springville & Sardinia Railroad. This Springville Book Store advertisement projects the excitement of retailers when the Springville & Sardinia Railroad line opened in 1878. (Below, courtesy of Robert Ruhlman.)

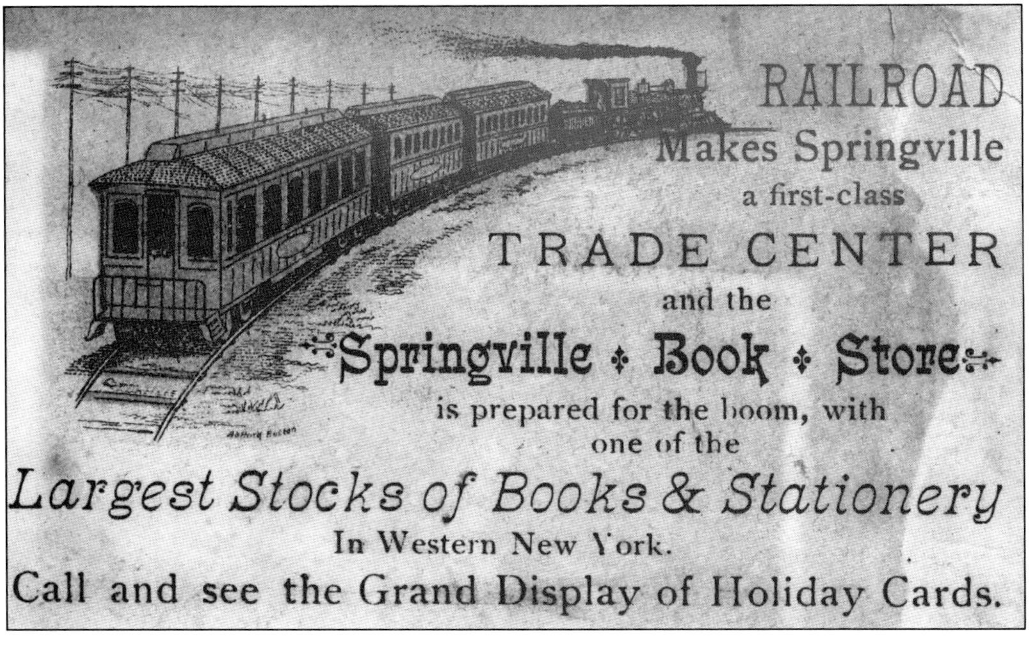

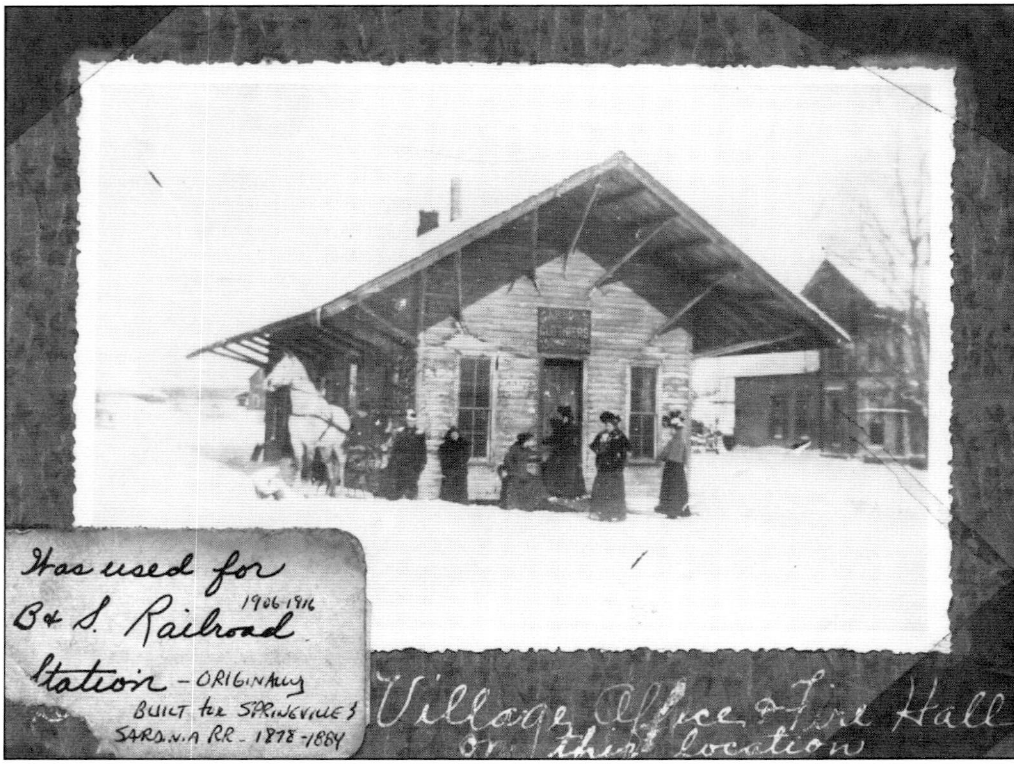

The Springville depot of Springville & Sardinia Railroad on Franklin Street would later have its roof trimmed back to serve as the Buffalo & Susquehanna Railway passenger station. At its peak, the Springville & Sardinia Railroad had two locomotives—the *Rock City* and the *Little Darling*—as well as two boxcars, six flatcars, a baggage car, and a passenger car. The 11.5-mile trip to Sardinia Junction (Chaffee) took just one hour (it traveled at 11.5 miles per hour). The trip to Buffalo was not as fast, covering about 40 miles in four hours, or 10 miles per hour. Bertrand "Burt" Chaffee, still not sure whether to spell his last name with one *F* or two, joins other railroad executives in giving out courtesy over-the-line passes. (Below, courtesy of George Geiger.)

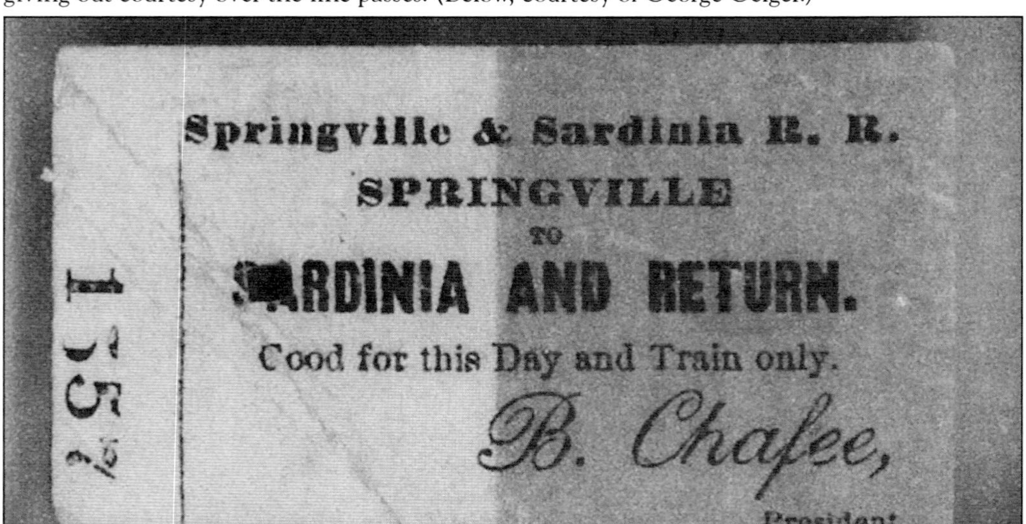
Springville & Sardinia R. R.
SPRINGVILLE
TO
SARDINIA AND RETURN.
Good for this Day and Train only.
B. Chafee,
President.

Pictured is the Springville & Sardinia Railroad (S&S) trestle. While the train waited, Burt Chaffee, president of S&S, strode to the center of this brand-new 61-foot-high 1878 trestle, leaped into the air, and landed his nearly 300-pound body safely, proclaiming, "It's safe, bring the locomotive and cars across." This brave act placated the terror-stricken passengers on their first train ride out of Springville.

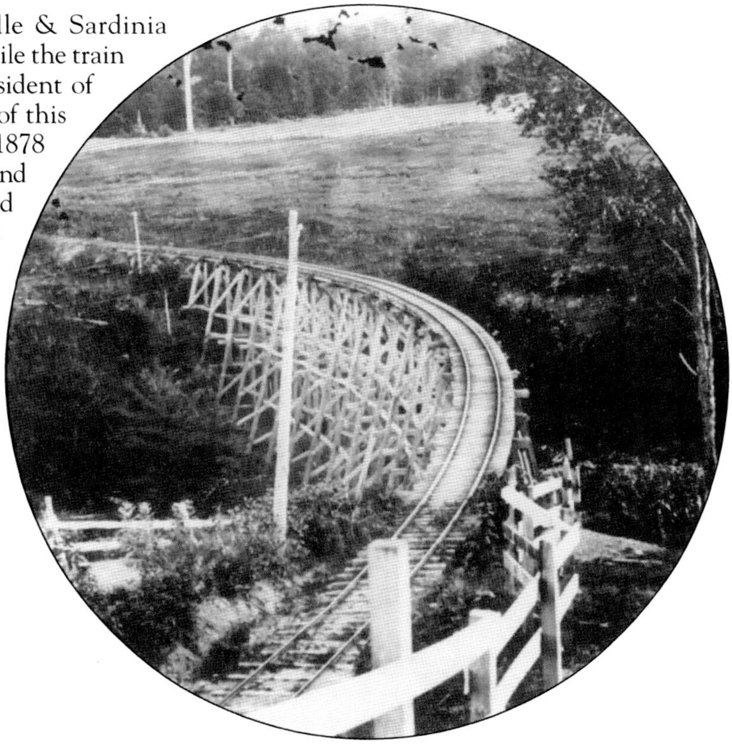

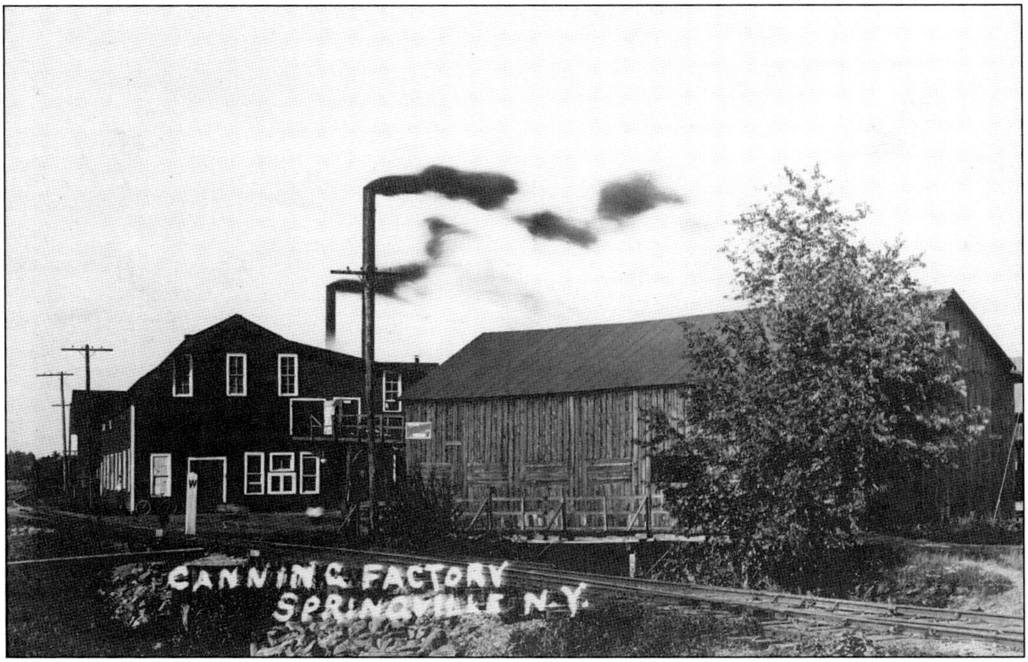

The canning factory operated into the 1940s, leaving memories of flatbed trucks with pea vines trailing behind. When the trucks slowed for a railroad crossing or stopped at an intersection, excited children would grab and pull handfuls of vines from the truck and retire to the curb to crack open the pods and get to the sweet individual peas within. When finished, they would return to play, listening for the next truck.

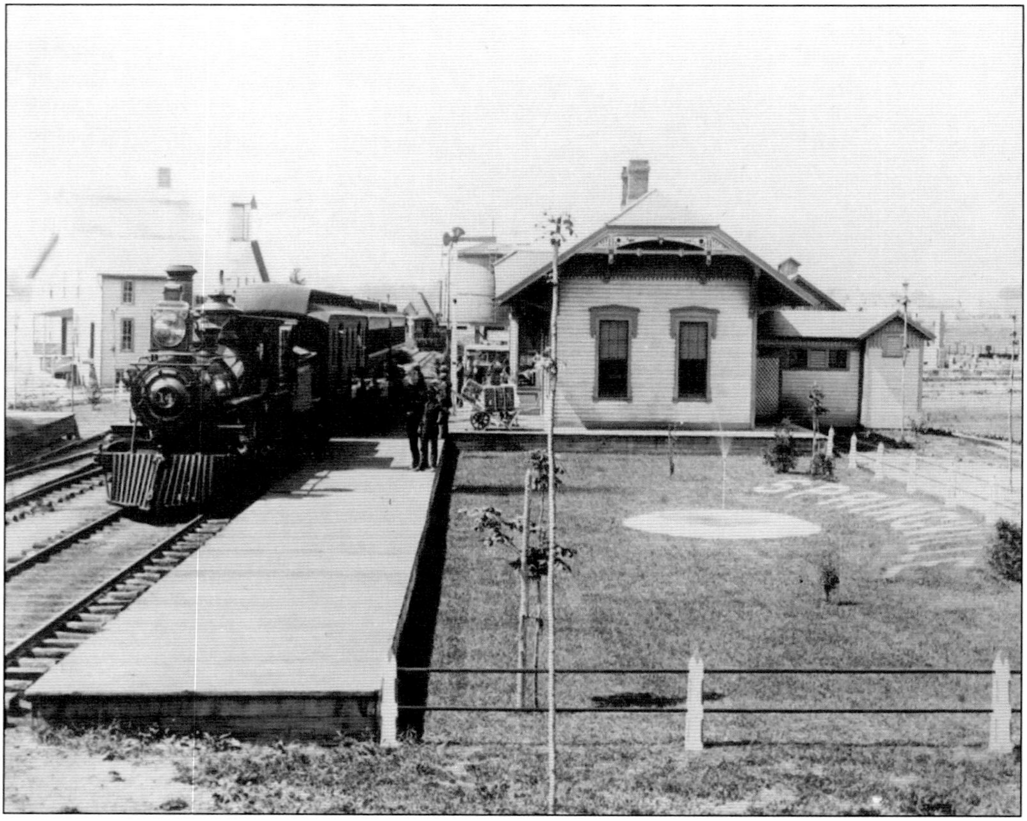

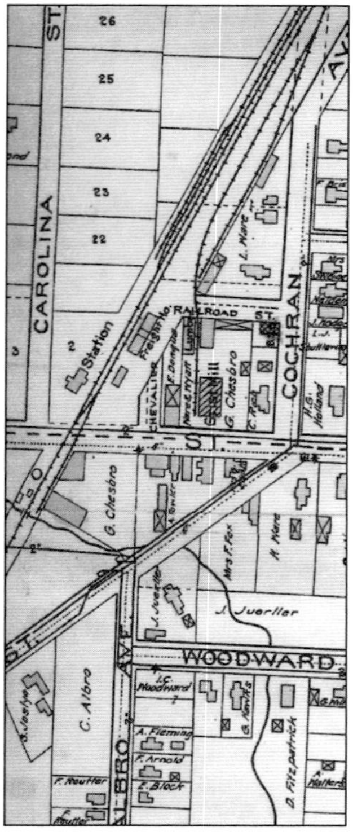

On November 19, 1883, the first passenger train on the Buffalo Division of the Buffalo, Rochester & Pittsburgh Railway arrived at the station, located on the west side of the track. The nearby water tank across Main Street was used for delivery of water to thirsty steam locomotives. The building at left is a mill, last known as Gramco, which has since burned. Railroading was not glamorous, and on February 17, 1893, two freight trains on the Buffalo, Rochester & Pittsburgh Railway collided near Springville. Engineer Hermon Reck of Buffalo had his arm pinned between two pieces of iron and could not be pulled out. The steam was pouring over him, literally cooking his flesh, when Dr. MacFarland of Springville picked up an axe and chopped the arm off near the shoulder. Reck was taken to Springville, where he later died. (Left, courtesy of 1909 *New Century Atlas*.)

DELIGHTFUL DAY'S OUTING

AT

NIAGARA FALLS

Friday, August 10th, 1894,

UNDER THE AUSPICES OF THE

Ladies' Society of the Springville Presbyterian Church

VIA

Buffalo, Rochester & Pittsburgh Railway.

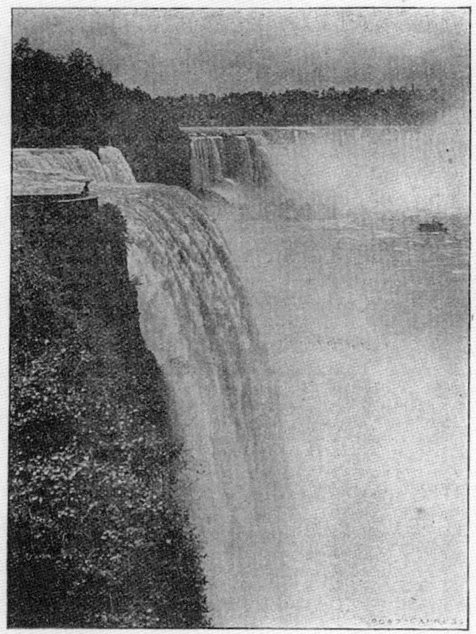

Buffalo, Rochester & Pittsburgh Railway.

Low Rates, Excellent Service and Ample Accommodations for Everybody.

SEE THE MIGHTY AVALANCHE OF WATERS.

MILLIONS have Gazed upon the Falls in Rapture

And thousands have unsuccessfully attempted to describe them. Invite your friends to join you in a pleasure trip to

"The Grandest of Nature's Wonders."

SPECIAL TRAIN OF THROUGH COACHES WILL RUN AS PER FOLLOWING SCHEDULE:

STATIONS.	TIME.	FARE.	STATIONS.	TIME.	FARE.
ELLICOTTVILLE, -	7.30 A. M.	$1.25	GLENWOOD, - - -	8.45 A. M.	$0.90
ASHFORD, - - -	7.45 "	1.00	COLDEN, - - - -	8.50 "	.90
WEST VALLEY, -	8.00 "	1.00	WEST FALLS, - -	9.00 "	.85
SPRINGVILLE, - -	8.25 "	1.00	JEWETTVILLE, - -	9.05 "	.85
EAST CONCORD, -	8.35 "	1.00	ORCHARD PARK, -	9.15 "	.75

Arrive at Niagara Falls, 10.45 A. M. Returning, leave the Falls at 6.00 P. M.

For Further Information Consult Agents at Stations Named.

R. G. MATHEWS, Acting Gen'l Supt. A. J. JOHNSON, Acting Div. Supt. E. C. LAPEY, Gen'l Pass. Agt.

6116-7, 25, '94-3 M. The Post Express Printing Company, Rochester, N. Y.

Boarding at Springville or East Concord, a $1 fare got riders a round-trip seat on a through-train to Niagara Falls. The schedule allowed visitors seven hours to view the scenic wonder and share the day with friends or relatives from neighboring towns.

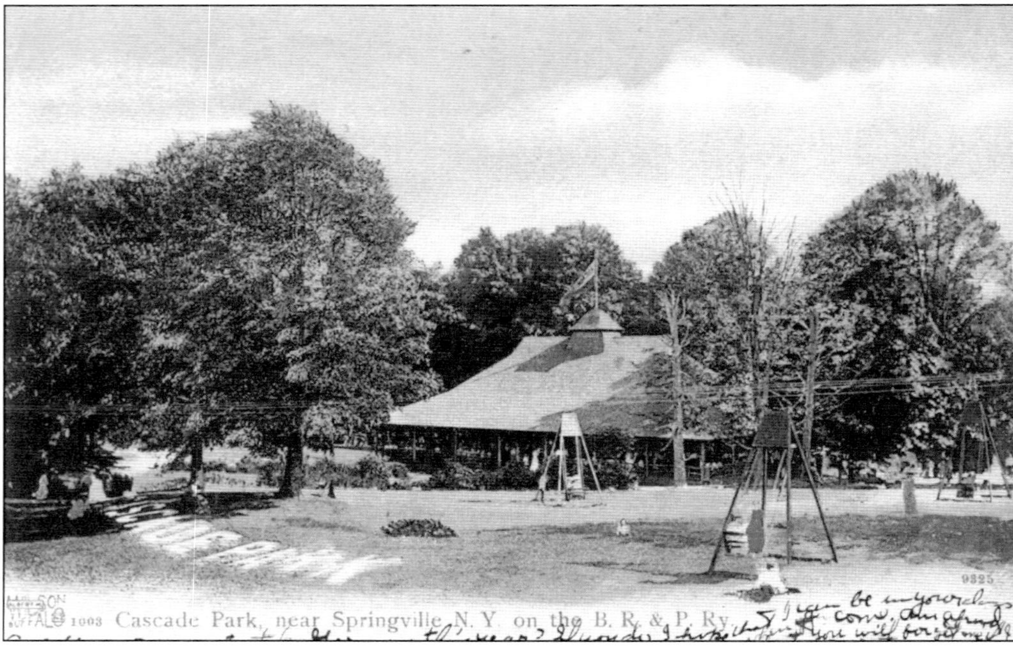

Anxious to serve the traveling public, many excursions were planned by local organizations. One destination that appealed to Buffalo-area residents was Cascade Park, developed by the Buffalo, Rochester & Pittsburgh Railway on the grounds of what is now the Springville Country Club. The park consisted of a dance hall, a dining hall, picnic pavilions, rustic paths, and access to the Cattaraugus Creek at the base of the 200-foot-high banks. During summer months, special trains of 10 to 15 passenger coaches departed daily from Buffalo for the park. The facility was operated by the railroad until 1921, when the country club acquired it, as the automobile gave people new travel options.

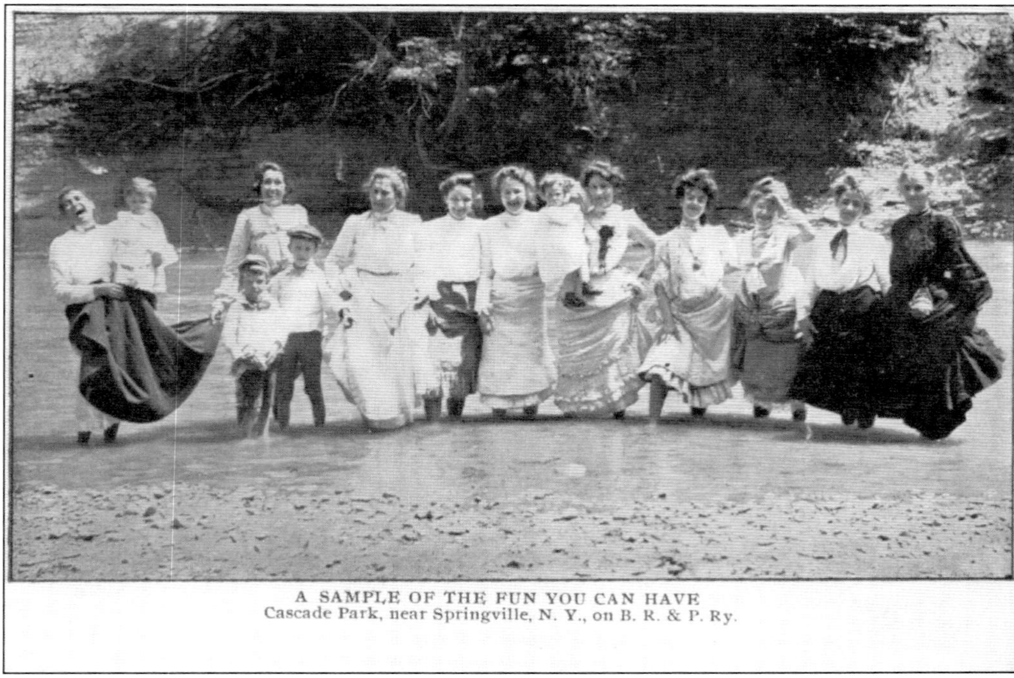

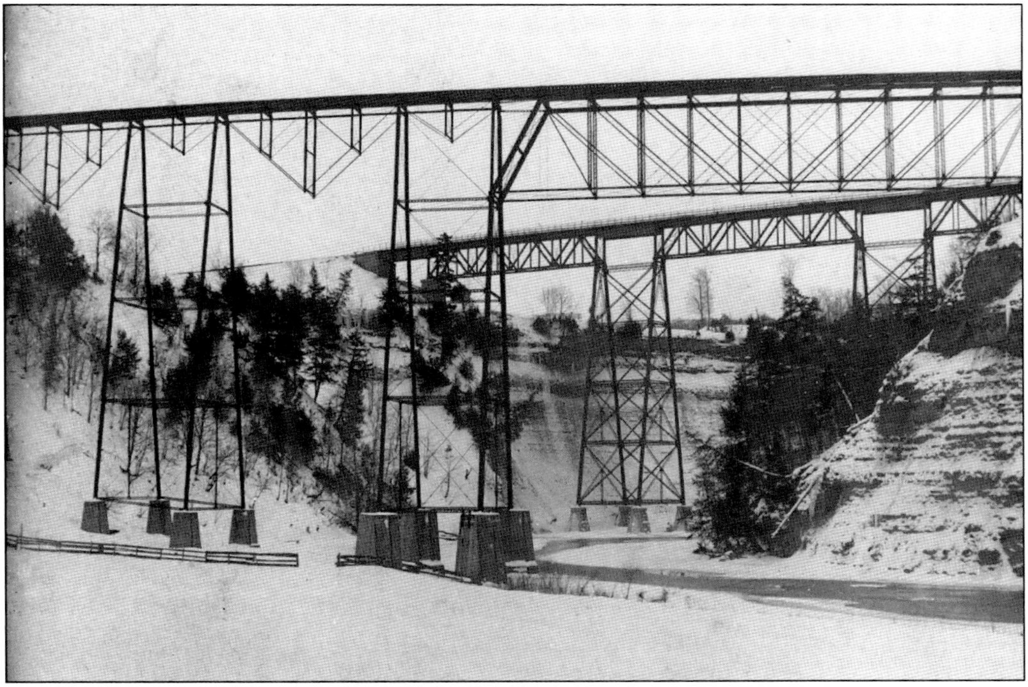

Traffic continued on the older, lighter bridge in the foreground while a new, heavier structure was being built. The land cuts for the old bridge roadway can still be seen across the Mill Street Bridge at the top of the hill.

CASCADE PARK BRIDGE

"The Rochester and Pittsburgh Railroad, predecessor of Buffalo, Rochester and Pittsburgh Railway, was constructed through this section from Buffalo, N. Y., to Ashford, N. Y., in 1882 and 1883, and crossed Cattaraugus Creek on an iron bridge, upstream from the present location. This bridge, erected in 1882 by the Keystone Bridge Company, was 540 feet long, and the track was 145 feet above bed of stream. The bridge was supported on stone abutments and pedestals, and was strengthened about 1887, at which time also the pedestals were encased with 'Beton,' as concrete was then known.

This structure was removed in 1898 after the Buffalo, Rochester and Pittsburgh Railway's line and grade had been changed to its present location and elevation in 1897, at which time a new steel structure was erected by the Pencoyd Iron Works. This structure is 780 feet long, and the track is 190 feet above bed of stream. The bridge is supported on stone and concrete abutments and pedestals. In 1915 the entire structure was reinforced by the American Bridge Company to carry the Railway Company's heaviest locomotives."

This detailed information sheet was included with an early Citizens National Bank calendar.

SPRINGVILLE, N. Y.

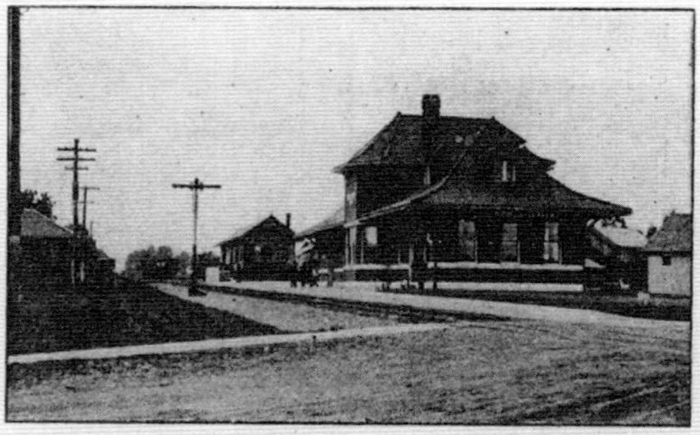

SPRINGVILLE is acknowledged to be one of the best kept and most attractive villages in the Empire State and enjoys the distinction of occupying the loftiest elevation in Erie County, being 800 feet higher than Buffalo and 1,300 feet above sea level. Its principal streets rival Buffalo's most beautiful residential avenues and the pleasing diversity in the architecture of the houses and the prevailing air of luxury and refinement command this really attractive town to the seeker for a suburban home. Rents are low; real estate is reasonable, and farm and dairy produce is much cheaper than in Buffalo.

This is an incorporated village of 2,500 people, it has a finely equipped fire department, municipal water works, unlimited supply of natural gas, and a municipal electric light plant furnishes power and light at prices lower than any other known place. The Griffith Institute, occupying a new $75,000 building, is classed with the leading High schools of the United States. There is an up-to-date free library of 6,000 volumes, eight beautiful churches, representing as many different denominations, and a dozen fraternal lodges and well-founded clubs.

Springville enjoys a mild and healthful climate; the atmosphere is fresh, dry and exhilarating and is wholly free from any miasmatic or disease producing conditions. There has not been a typhoid case in over twenty years traceable to the water supply, and the vital statistics for the past few years speak volumes for the general good health of this community.

WHY NOT combine your business in Buffalo with suburban life?

Railroads often publicized the communities through which they passed, like this glowing promotion of Springville, as a way to build passenger traffic.

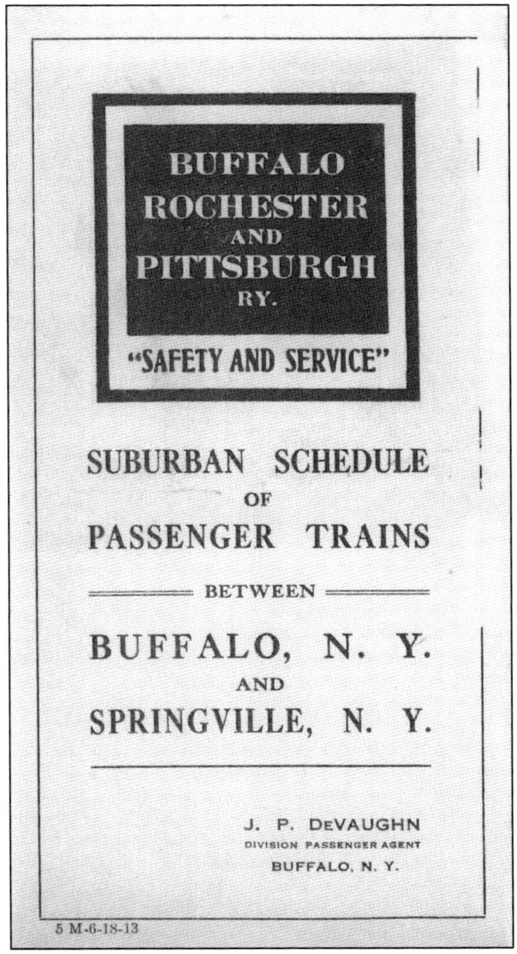
BUFFALO
ROCHESTER
AND
PITTSBURGH
RY.

"SAFETY AND SERVICE"

SUBURBAN SCHEDULE
OF
PASSENGER TRAINS
BETWEEN
BUFFALO, N. Y.
AND
SPRINGVILLE, N. Y.

J. P. DeVAUGHN
DIVISION PASSENGER AGENT
BUFFALO, N. Y.

5 M-6-18-13

The c. 1900 view below looks north toward Main Street (opposite of the view on page 26). At left is a section-car storage building. Section cars were light motorized track vehicles for transporting workers to work sites on the section of track they maintained. The water tank, with a capacity in the thousands of gallons, utilized gravity to quickly fill the locomotive tender tank. Seen between the tanks in the distance across Main Street are the wooden 1883 depot and the Gramco mill to the right.

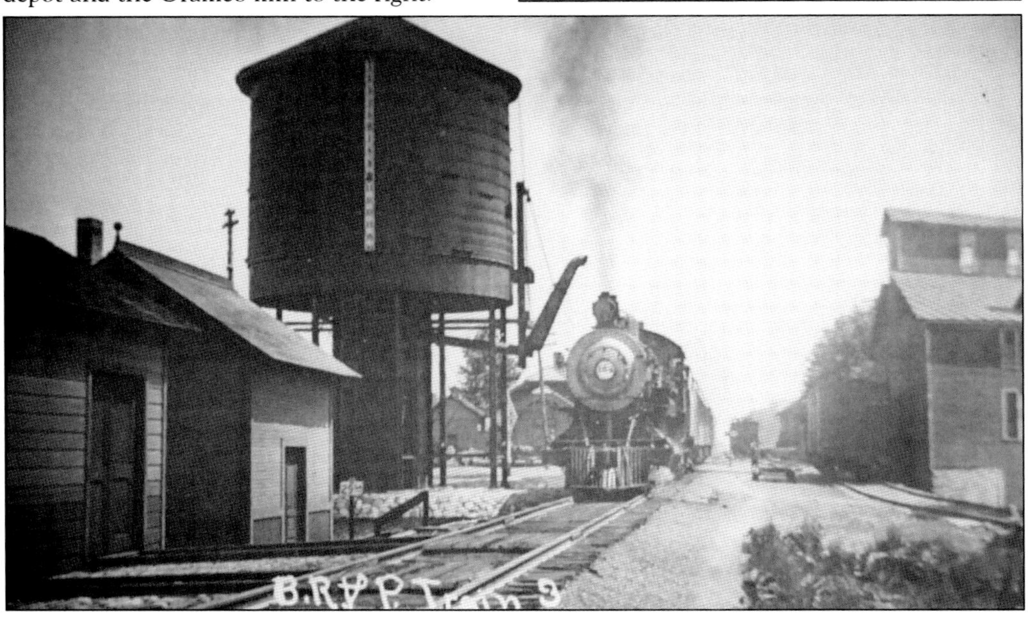

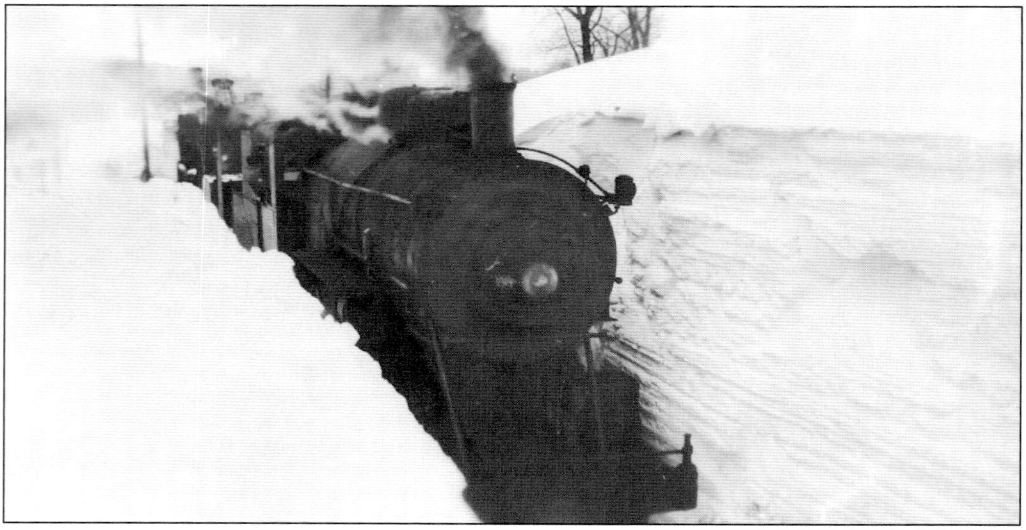

The S&S was shut down for 45 days in 1878–1879 because of snow. In 1906, the Goodyears expanded their railroad from Wellsville to Buffalo, passing through Arcade, Springville, and the Boston Valley. The roadbed is today's power line route near North Street and Dowd Road, across Middle Road and Sharp Street, and then across Genesee Road to the north. The roadbed, minus power lines, is seen near Maple Avenue as a trail. The Buffalo & Susquehanna Railway (B&S) hauled coal, coke, lumber, agricultural products, and passengers prior to its 1916 financial failure. In 1912, Springville boasted that it was served by 16 daily passenger trains. The B&S utilized the old Springville & Sardinia Railroad depot on Franklin Street near the village municipal building. Passengers await a train in this south-facing photograph. At center is a boxcar at the mill, which burned in 1946. Immediately to the right is Springville Hardware, where, due to present-day grading, the bottom row of windows is now underground.

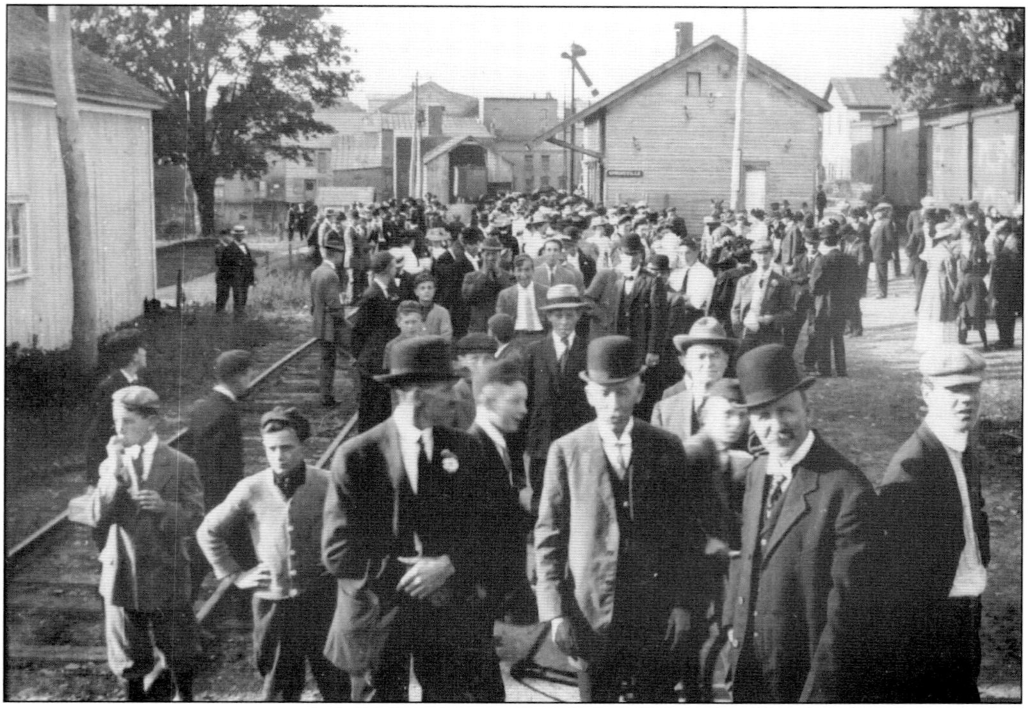

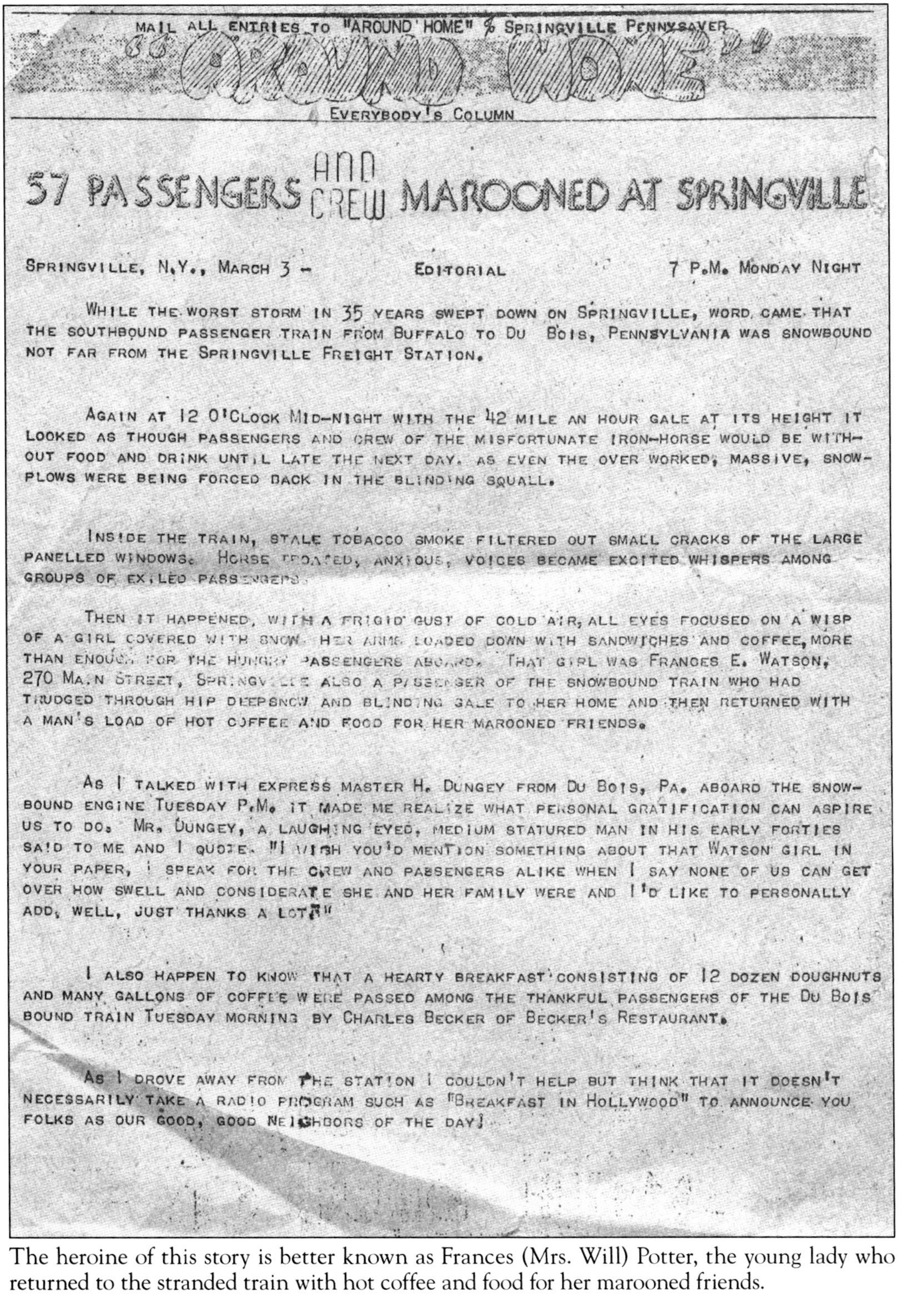

Mail all entries to "Around Home" % Springville Pennysaver

"Around Home"

Everybody's Column

57 Passengers and Crew Marooned at Springville

Springville, N.Y., March 3 - Editorial 7 P.M. Monday Night

While the worst storm in 35 years swept down on Springville, word came that the southbound passenger train from Buffalo to Du Bois, Pennsylvania was snowbound not far from the Springville Freight Station.

Again at 12 O'Clock Mid-night with the 42 mile an hour gale at its height it looked as though passengers and crew of the misfortunate Iron-Horse would be with-out food and drink until late the next day, as even the over worked, massive, snow-plows were being forced back in the blinding squall.

Inside the train, stale tobacco smoke filtered out small cracks of the large panelled windows. Horse troated, anxious, voices became excited whispers among groups of exiled passengers.

Then it happened, with a frigid gust of cold air, all eyes focused on a wisp of a girl covered with snow. Her arms loaded down with sandwiches and coffee, more than enough for the hungry passengers aboard. That girl was Frances E. Watson, 270 Main Street, Springville also a passenger of the snowbound train who had trudged through hip deep snow and blinding gale to her home and then returned with a man's load of hot coffee and food for her marooned friends.

As I talked with express master H. Dungey from Du Bois, Pa. aboard the snow-bound engine Tuesday P.M. it made me realize what personal gratification can aspire us to do. Mr. Dungey, a laughing eyed, medium statured man in his early forties said to me and I quote. "I wish you'd mention something about that Watson girl in your paper, I speak for the crew and passengers alike when I say none of us can get over how swell and considerate she and her family were and I'd like to personally add, well, just thanks a lot!"

I also happen to know that a hearty breakfast consisting of 12 dozen doughnuts and many gallons of coffee were passed among the thankful passengers of the Du Bois bound train Tuesday morning by Charles Becker of Becker's Restaurant.

As I drove away from the station I couldn't help but think that it doesn't necessarily take a radio program such as "Breakfast in Hollywood" to announce you folks as our good, good neighbors of the day!

The heroine of this story is better known as Frances (Mrs. Will) Potter, the young lady who returned to the stranded train with hot coffee and food for her marooned friends.

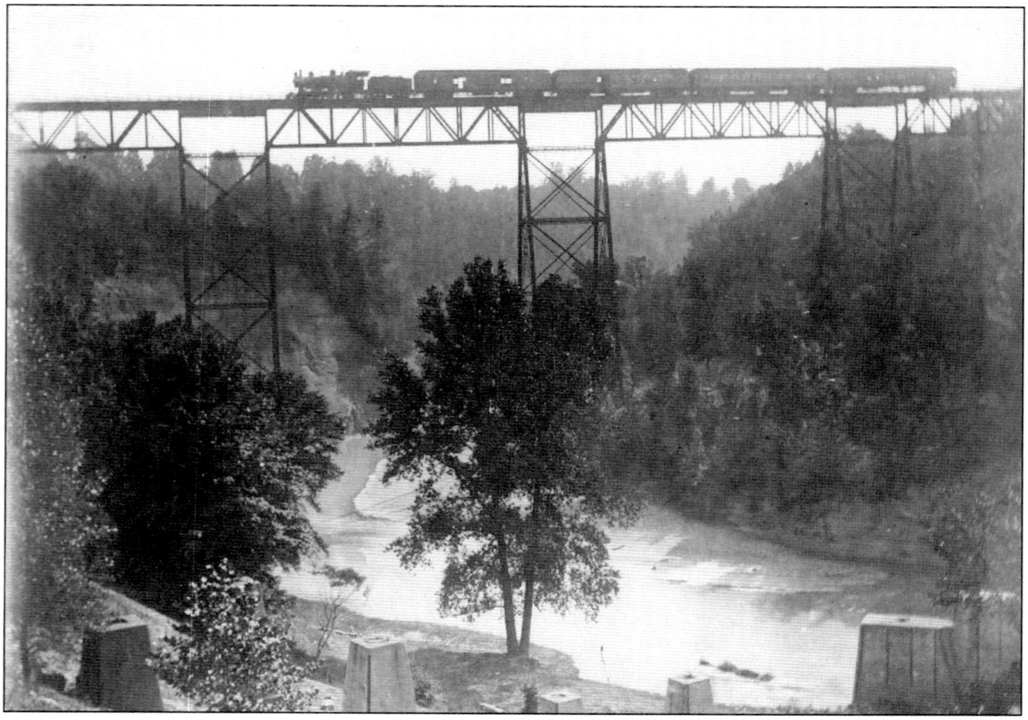

This southbound "Pittsburgh Flyer" is pictured on the Cascade Park viaduct with the abutments from the earlier bridge in the foreground. A fast train north was called a "Buffalo Flyer." The Baltimore & Ohio Railroad removed steam locomotives and passenger trains from service on October 15, 1955, ending an era that had lasted 72 years. Freight service remained and was diesel powered. Steam would return one more time on June 15, 1996, when the 230-ton Milwaukee No. 261 pulled a passenger train of dignitaries from Buffalo to Ellicottville, stopping at Orchard Park and Springville.

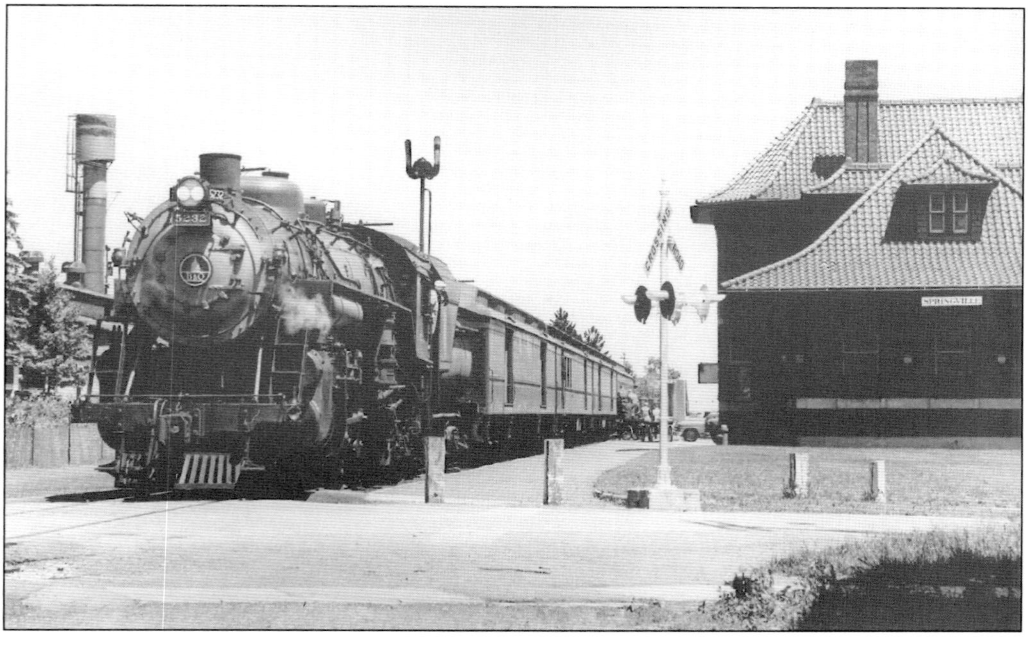

Three

Early Churches

Church steeples served two purposes: directing attention upward to focus on the heavenly aspect, and architecturally improving the symmetry and balance of the structure. Not all were adorned with crosses, but all were grounded with lightning cable. In the 1800s, wood and labor were readily available, making steeple maintenance affordable. As costs rose, steeples fell into disfavor. As seen on page 36, every church had a steeple equipped with a bell to call worshippers, celebrate an occasion, or mourn a loss. Although there is a similarity, for the most part, in the architecture of Springville churches, the denominational makeup has changed over time, likely reflecting the differences in backgrounds of new arrivals.

The very substantial First Baptist Church on Church and Buffalo Streets closed in the early 1900s, merging with the Free Baptist Church on the corner of Franklin Street, which has since closed. Some churches have moved, such as the Methodist church, which moved from Chapel Street to the corner of Buffalo and Franklin Streets and then to East Main Street. The Episcopal church was, at one time, at the corner of Park Street and Central Avenue. The Lutheran church moved to West Main Street from Spring Street. The Assembly of God outgrew its Smith Street facility and built on Transit Line Road.

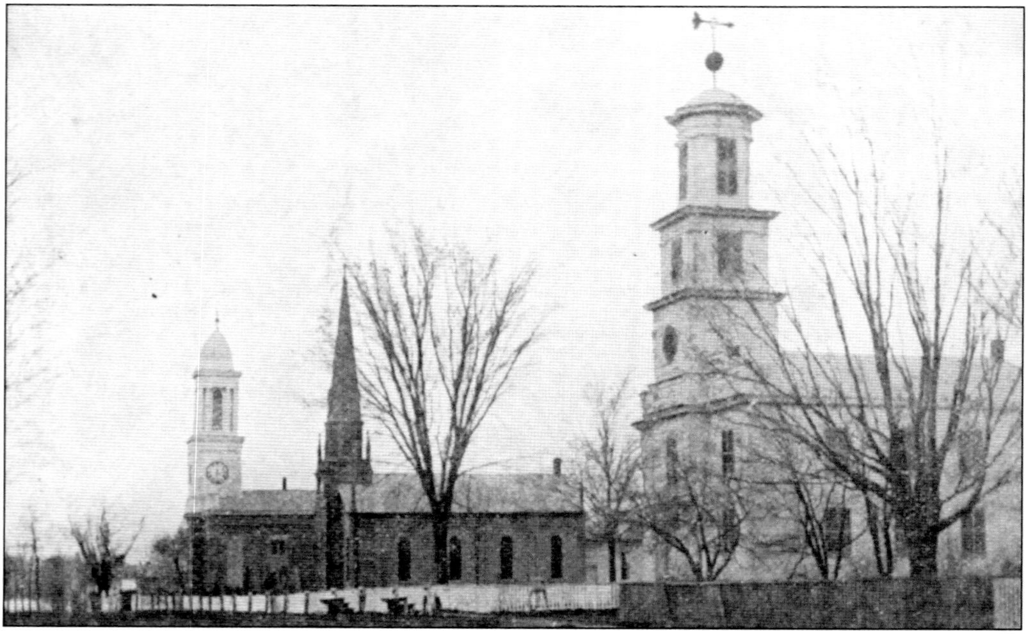

Looking south, the Presbyterian church sits on the left. The town clock tower was removed in 1875, and the roof was given a greater pitch with a built-over roof, which may have contributed to the inability to control the 1921 fire that destroyed it. At center in this photograph is the Methodist Episcopal church with its steeple, which was later removed. At right is the First Baptist Church with a bell tower and weather vane.

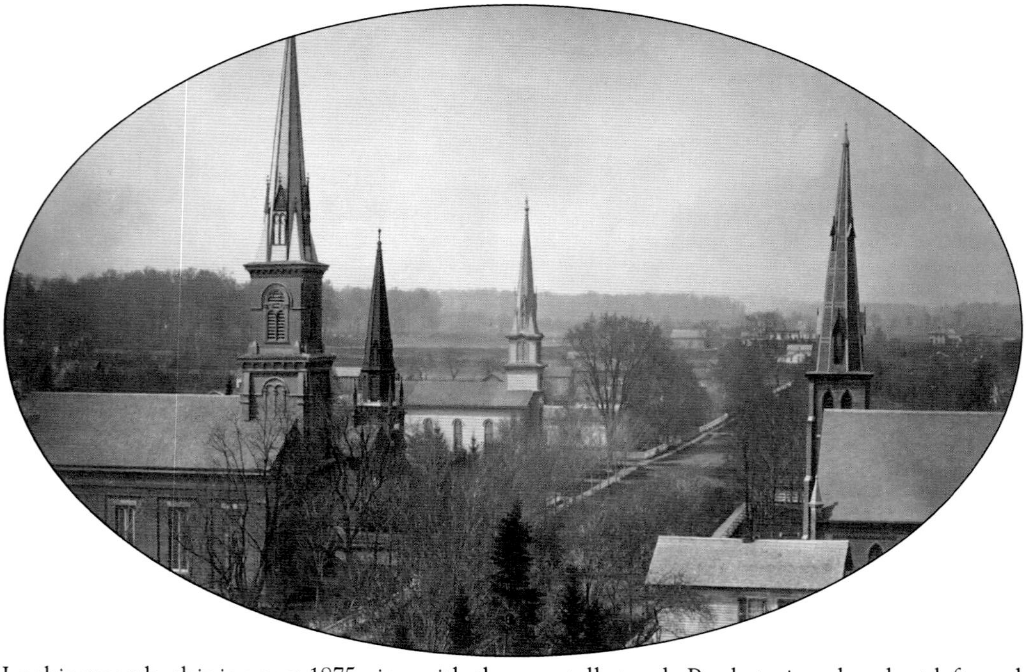

Looking north, this is a post-1875 view with the new tall-steeple Presbyterian church at left, and at left center is the still unchanged Methodist Episcopal church. At center right is the new tall steeple on the First Baptist Church. And on the far right is the Free Baptist Church with a tall steeple, which is missing today.

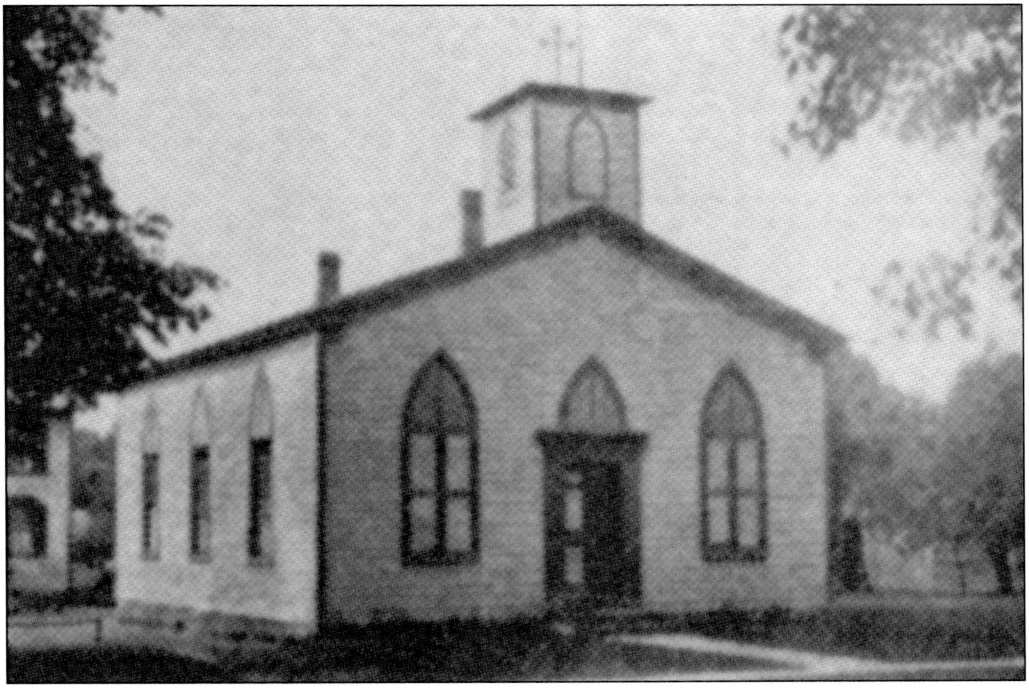

Built at a construction cost of $1,200 in 1832, this is both the oldest Presbyterian church in Western New York and the first Catholic church in Springville (1853). It is now a private home at 70 Smith Street. In 1947, to celebrate the centennial of the new Presbyterian church, wood was removed from this building and fashioned into a gavel for use in meetings of the Presbytery of Western New York. The present First Presbyterian Church was organized as a Congregational church.

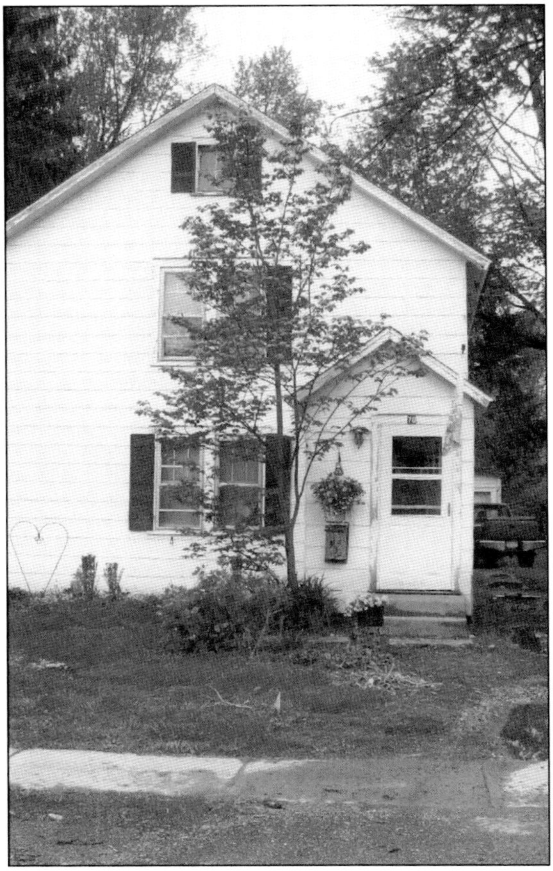

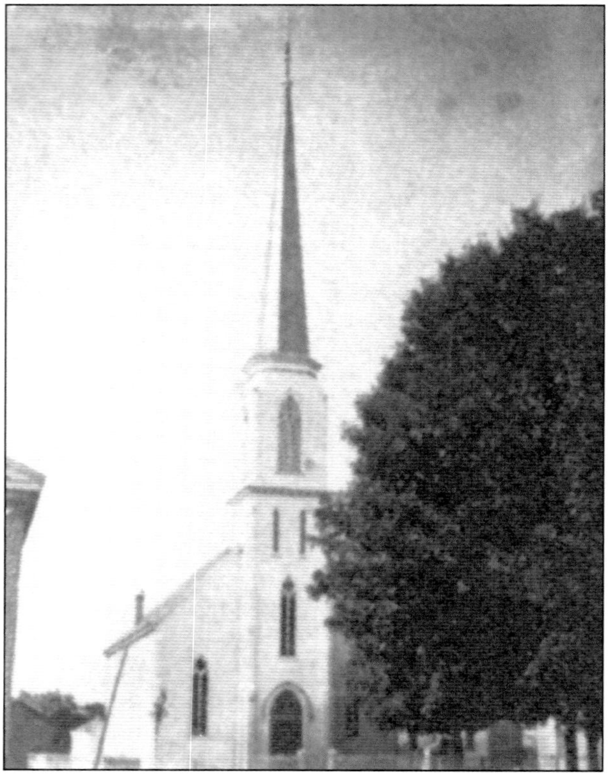

This 1879 view shows St. Aloysius Parish Church, with a steeple reportedly three feet taller than the Presbyterian church steeple. It was designed by local architect Americus Lincoln, who lived at 100 North Central Avenue and greatly exaggerated his kinship to the martyred president. The construction cost was about $7,000, and about 100 families attended. That number grew to 500 families when ground was broken in 1953 for the current structure. Salem Lutheran Church, dedicated August 28, 1887, at the corner of Spring Street and Maple Avenue, is shown with a tall steeple in this 1906 photograph. The congregation moved to a new building at the corner of Main Street and Central Avenue in 1951. The old structure has been converted to apartments.

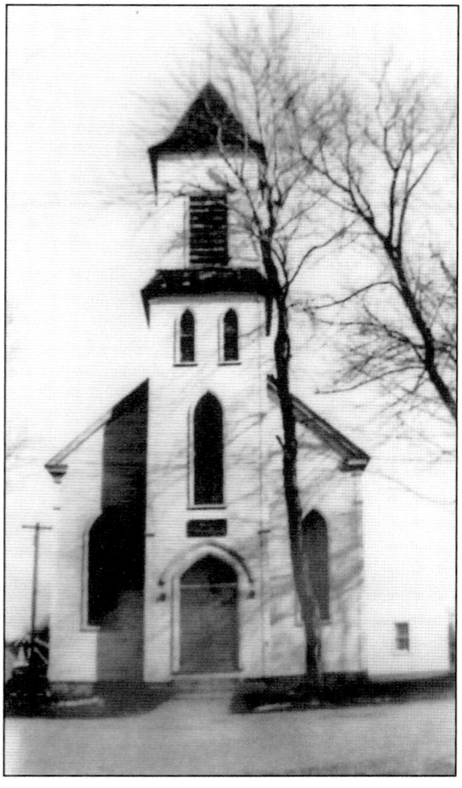

Four

Fire

It looks like a polished black boot—minus the foot—and its capacity is not much over a gallon. It can be seen at the Warner Museum and is likely all that remains of Springville's bucket brigade firefighting days. According to an account of one Springville fire, "Hook and Ladder Company [organized in 1842] arrived within five minutes with their carriage, raised the ladder, and buckets commenced flying." A group of citizens would form a line from a pond or stream to the fire site and pass along water-filled buckets to the person closest to the fire, who would dump the remaining contents into the flames.

Numerous fires dot Springville's history. The "Great Fire" occurred on June 7, 1868, claiming all structures from Blakeley House to Pearl Street and destroying all town clerk records. Shuttleworth Foundry on Franklin Street between Main and Mechanic Streets was lost in 1875, prompting Charles J. Shuttleworth to move to Mill Street, acquire the pond, and raise Buffalo Street 10 feet to increase pond volume. It was useful to his new foundry and supplied water for subsequent firefighting efforts.

September 5, 1879, saw a second "Great Fire" that destroyed everything from Blakeley House to Buffalo Street. The fire company became Fountain Hose Company on February 1, 1882, and a hand pumper fire engine was purchased. Equipped with 400 feet of hose, it could shoot a stream of water 73 feet into the air and required 16 to 20 men to pump 220 gallons a minute. In 1892, a fire hall was built next to the South Buffalo Street log cabin that remained in use until 1936, when the department moved to Franklin Street, next to the post office. On February 28, 1894, the owners of the Union Block were rewarded for their wise use of brick in rebuilding after the 1868 fire. Everything was destroyed between the Union Block and Pearl Street, where all the buildings were wooden.

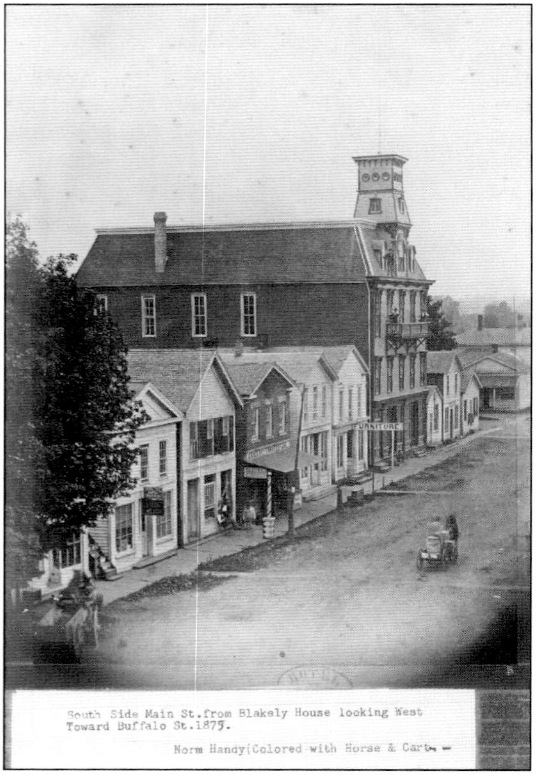

The photograph at left shows the stores and opera house that were lost in the 1879 "Great Fire," looking west from Leland House.

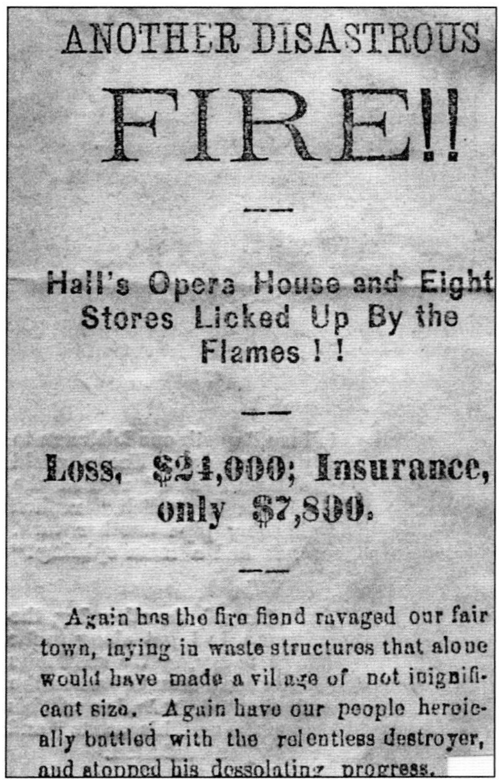

ANOTHER DISASTROUS

FIRE!!

Hall's Opera House and Eight Stores Licked Up By the Flames ! !

Loss, $24,000; Insurance, only $7,800.

Again has the fire fiend ravaged our fair town, laying in waste structures that alone would have made a village of not insignificant size. Again have our people heroically battled with the relentless destroyer, and stopped his dessolating progress.

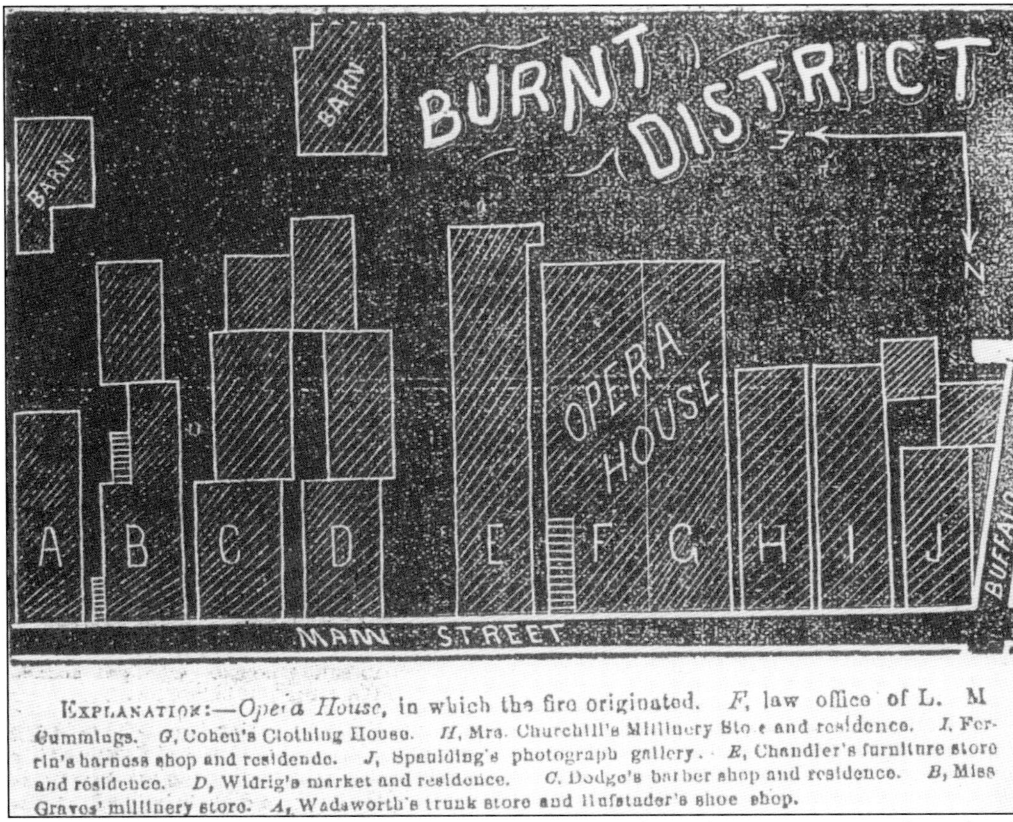

This is a map of the fire-ravaged district, and a view of charred remains as seen from South Buffalo Street is below.

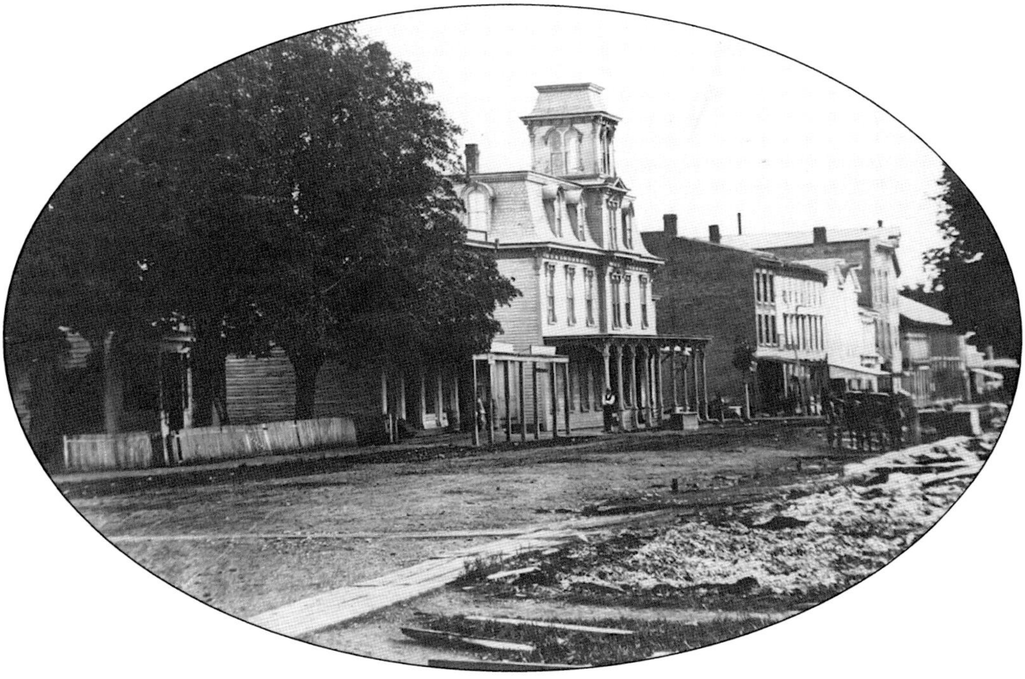

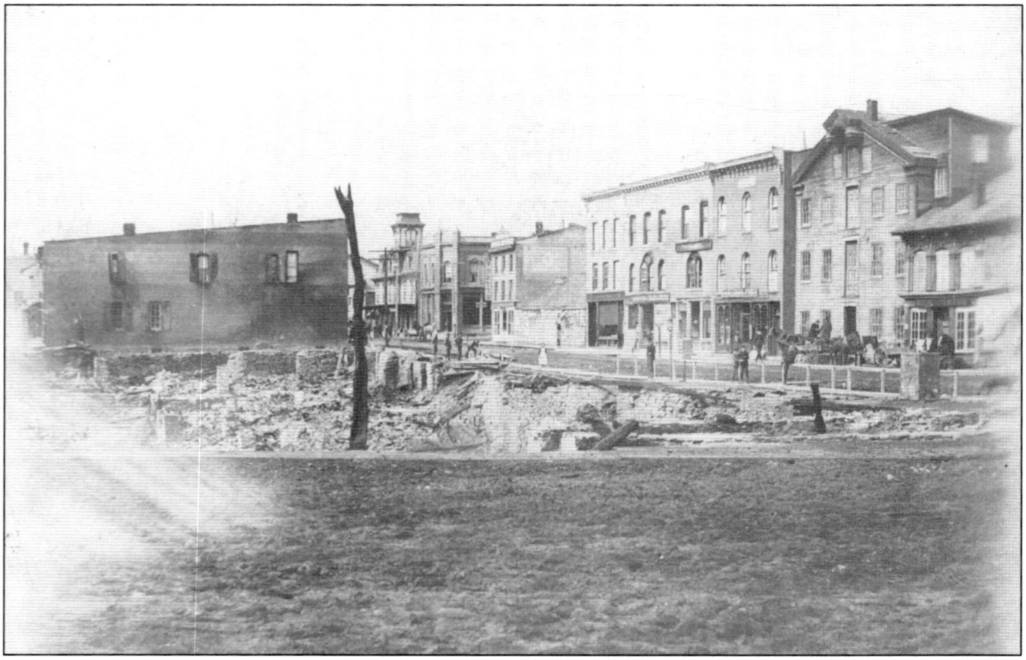

The fire of 1894 is pictured from Pearl Street, looking west toward the Union Block.

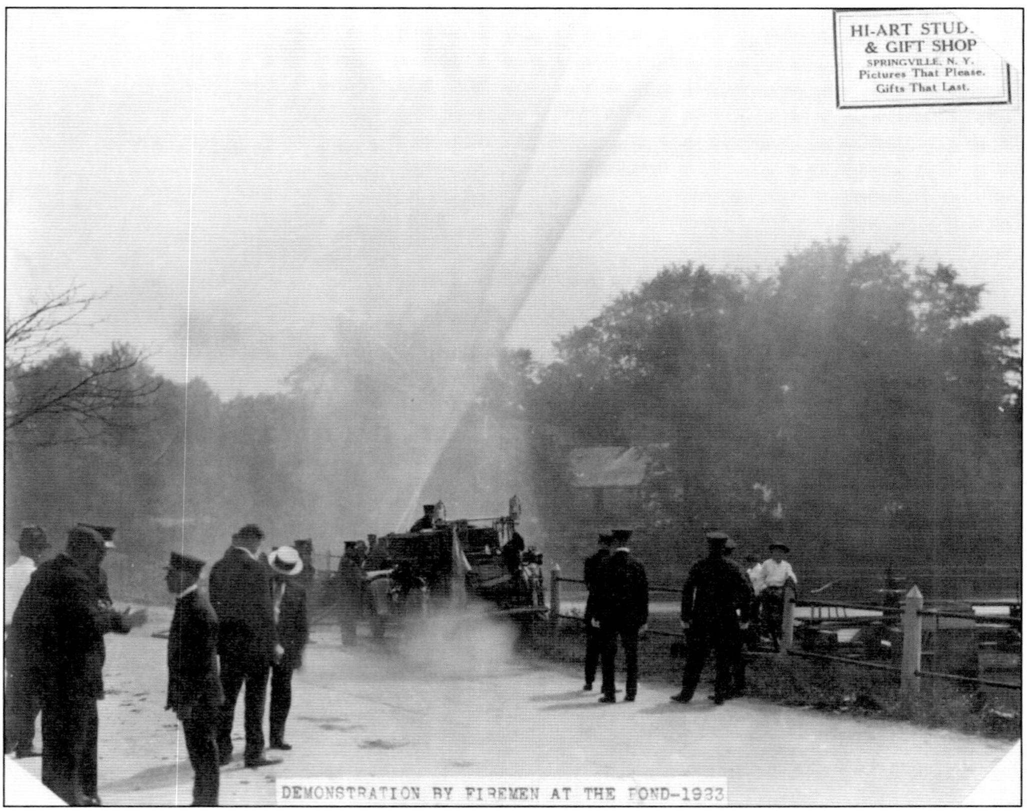

Shown here is a pump testing of the newly arrived motorized fire truck in April 1921, a couple of months after the destructive fire at the Presbyterian church.

On Monday morning, February 21, 1921, at about 6:30 a.m., the Baptist pastor across the street saw flames in the steeple of the Presbyterian church and sounded the alarm. Firemen arrived quickly but were fearful of the steeple falling, which it did at 7:00 a.m., igniting the double roof and ultimately destroying the sanctuary. The pulpit was saved and is in use to this day.

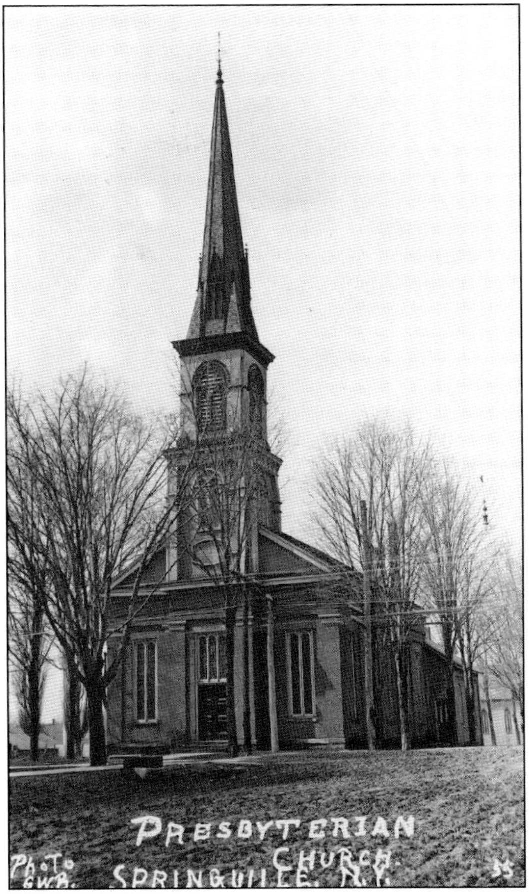

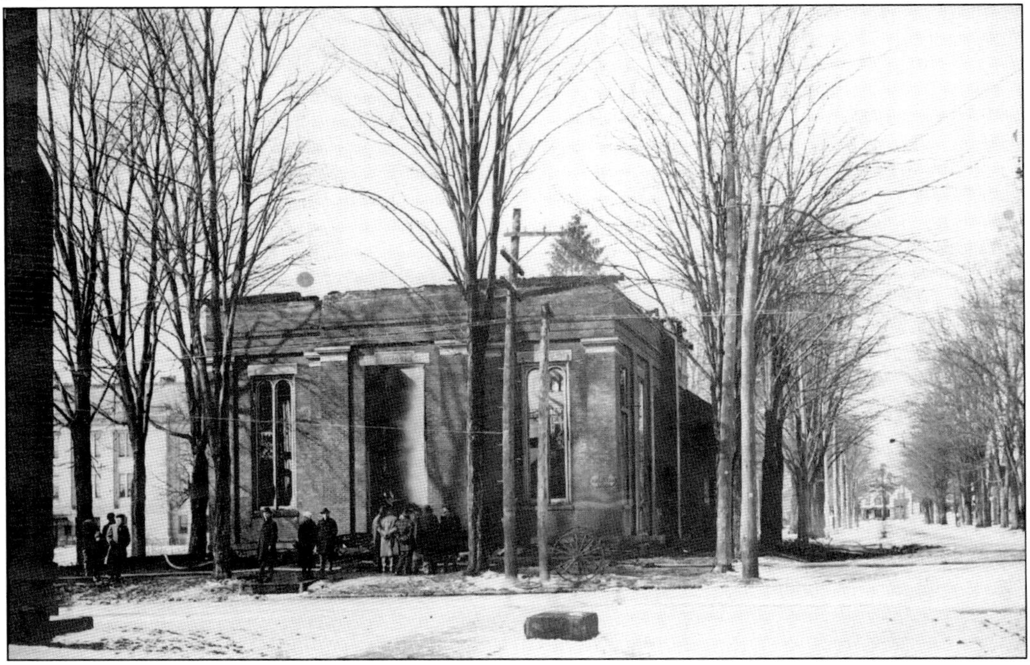

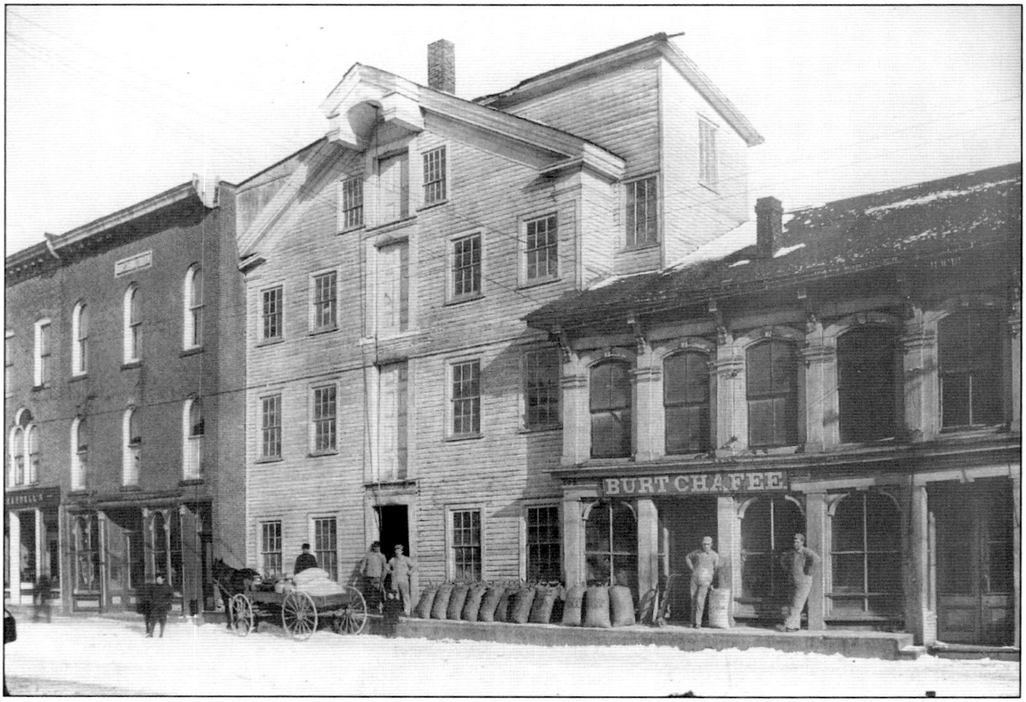

At 3:08 a.m. on Friday, September 13, 1946, the first alarm was sounded at the Springville Roller (animal feeds) Mills. The building, built in 1835, was on fire. Located at what is now 56 East Main Street, its destruction threatened the entire business district. The brick-walled Masonic Building prevented westward progression of the inferno, which brought 19 sister fire departments and 500 men to join Springville volunteer firemen under Chief Gordon Rouse. Water from hydrants, Spring Brook, and the Shuttleworth Pond, now the site of the municipal parking lot, extinguished the last of the embers at 8:00 p.m. on Sunday, September 15, 1946. The damage was $250,000, or nearly $3 million in today's dollars.

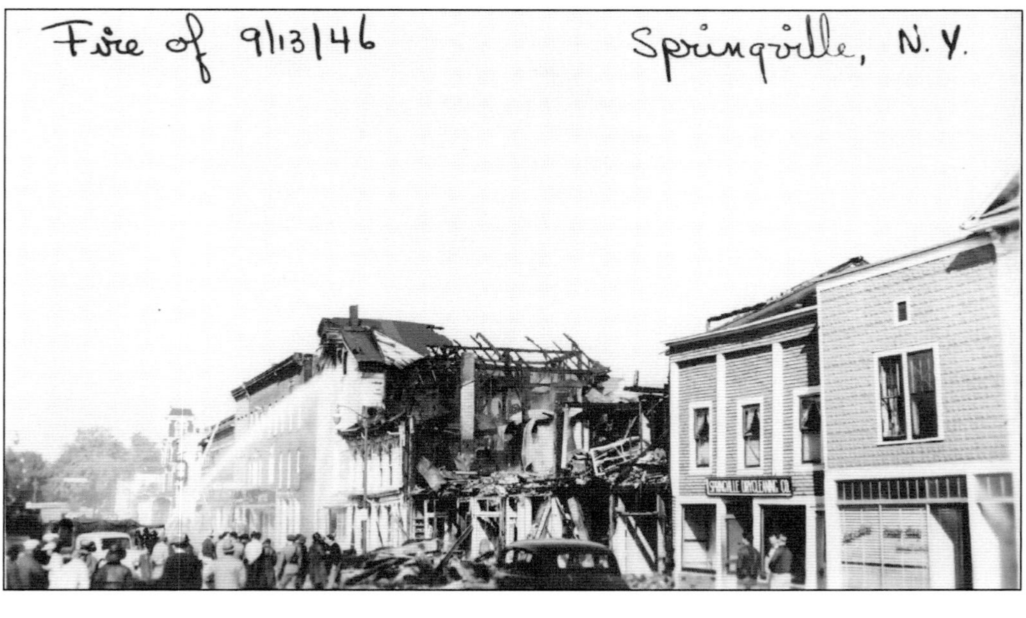

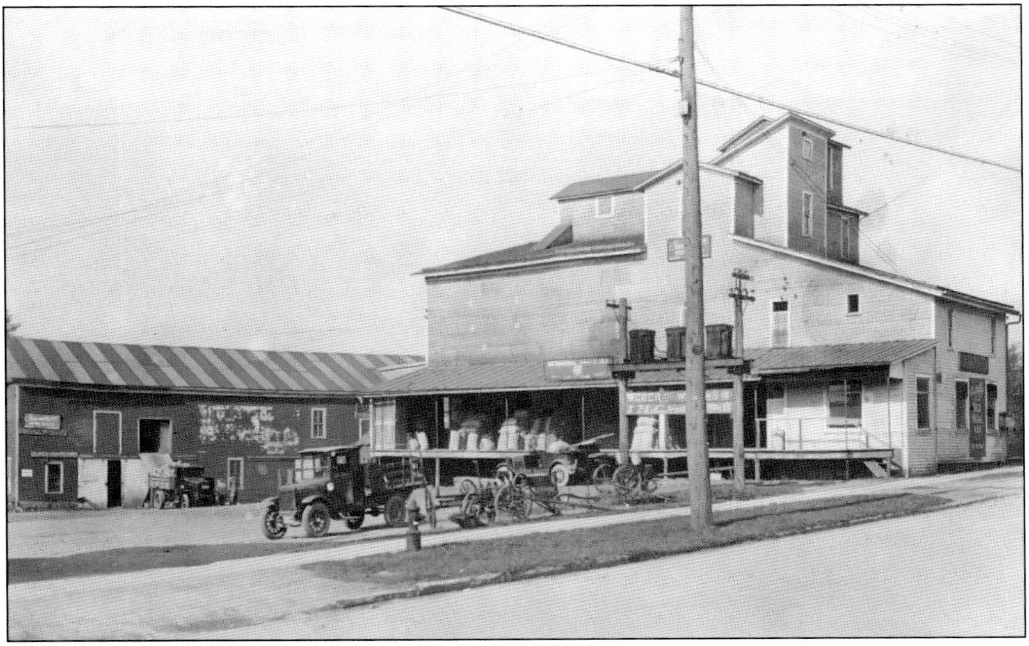

This is a 1929 view of the James H. Gray Milling Company near the Buffalo, Rochester & Pittsburgh Railway tracks, across from the depot on West Main Street. It was last owned by Gramco, which had abandoned it in favor of an efficient new plant on Waverly Street. The building is suspected to have attracted youths, who likely kindled it. The fire of March 11, 2003, threatened the Western House and showered down debris on Bob Johnson Motors nearby. Mutual aid, modern equipment, and trained firefighters confined the fire to the mill site. (Above, courtesy of Bob and Jan Mattison; below, courtesy of Judy Wright.)

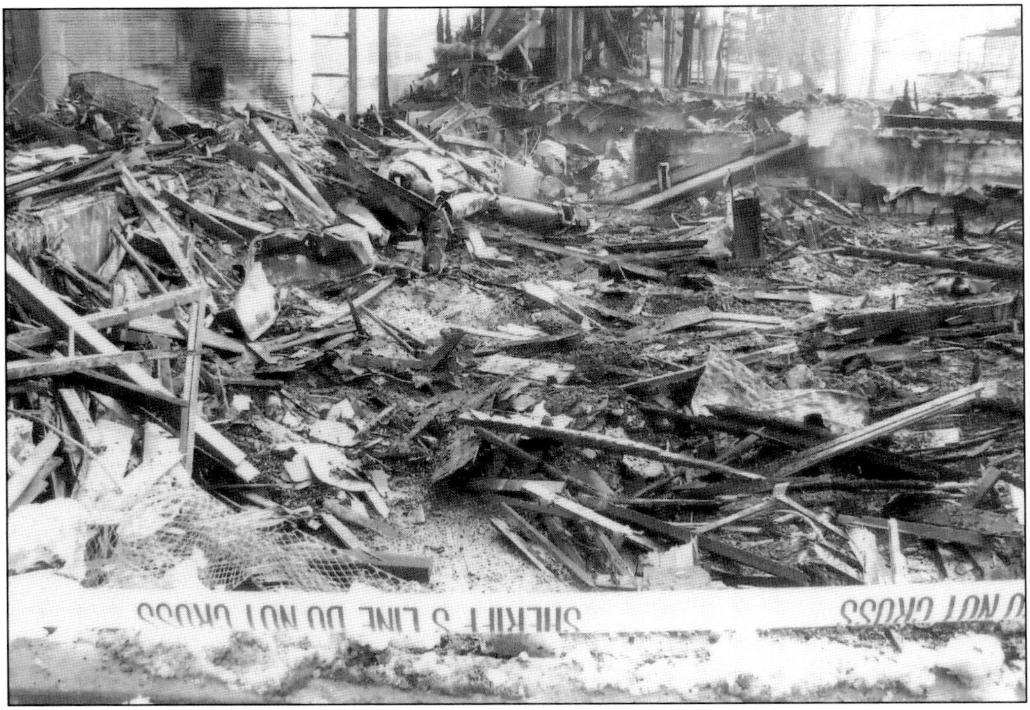

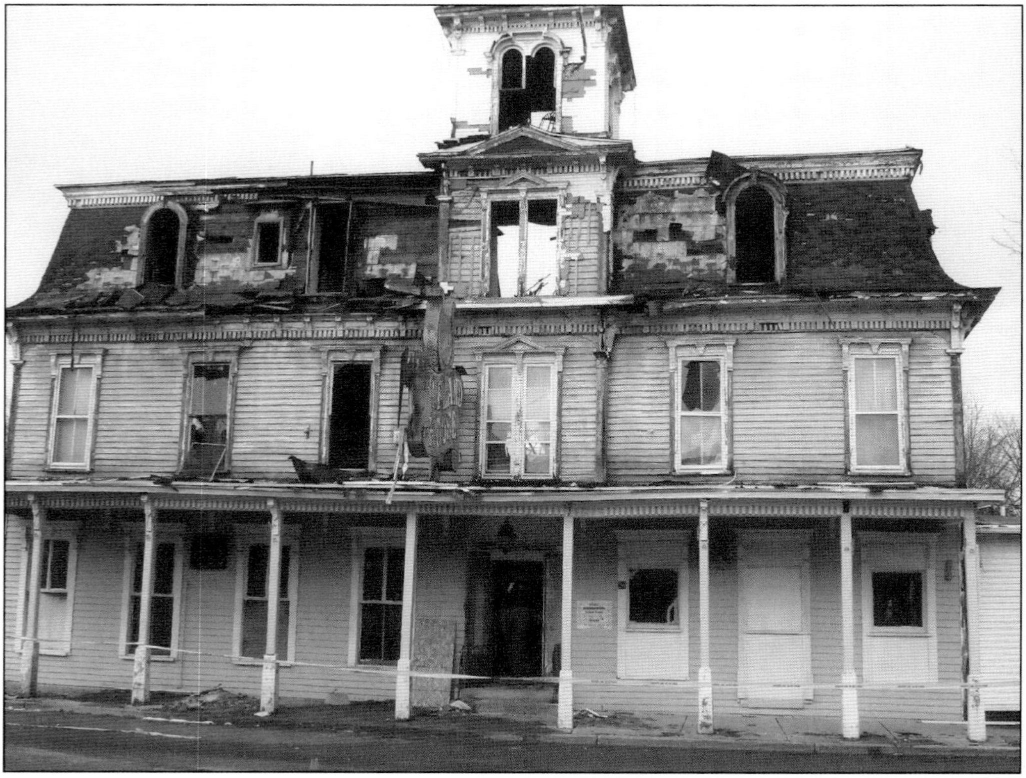

The Leland House, the "Grand Old Lady of Main Street," is no more, lost to a conflagration of suspicious origin on January 18, 2006. Seven fire companies quickly responded to prevent a burn-to-the-ground event. The haunting remains of the 1879 building stood for hours as options played out. Would an interested party purchase and restore the building? Would the owner respond to demands for a "plan" to guarantee public safety? Finally, Mayor William Krebs made the decision to demolish the structure, stating, "I certainly empathize with the sadness of village residents, however, this decision was made after careful review of the emergency situation." Hundreds stood silently as the demolition began and machinery picked away at and crushed its remnants, which were then quickly trucked away. The Leland House is dead; long live its memory. (Above, courtesy of Tyler Owen.)

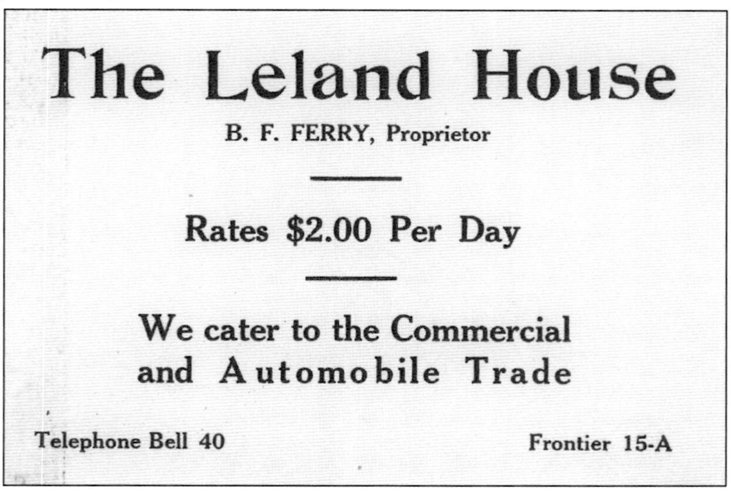

Five

People and Places

In 2004, the Concord Historical Society, envisioning a concept to share more of the area's history, purchased the building last known as "the Fish Bowl." The dream, a country store, was to be called Concord Mercantile.

Years of primarily volunteer effort have gone into the construction of this beautiful facility, which saw its guest book signed, between January and October 2011, by 3,000 visitors. In the interest of history, it should be noted how it was accomplished. Projects do not just happen; they require a driving force to keep them on track and to bring in and encourage volunteers. Joel Maul, Peter Mueller, and Donald Tober were that force who, in turn, consulted professional builder, historian, and coauthor David Batterson. A new, not-to-be seen concrete slab was poured, and stairs to the second floor were built. Painting was accomplished by volunteers under the leadership of trustee Mel Miller. General stores from 1880 to 1920 did not have concrete floors, and they did not have building inspectors like Michael Kaletta, who said, "You must have a restroom, and, no, your customers may not use the vintage privy behind the 'Pop' Warner Museum." The newly poured concrete floor was covered with a two-inch layer of foam that became the bed for a beautiful hemlock floor. The mercantile in-store post office display discreetly contains the code-required restroom.

Why all the excitement over a mere replica of a country store? It has become the focal point for a wave of enthusiasm and cooperation for sharing the incredible history of the people of this small, seemingly insignificant community.

In the pages that follow are highlighted the accomplishments of Dr. Ralph Britton Waite, Jack Yellen, Jud Strunk, Thomas Reynolds, Eric Fiel, and others. The contributions of leaders Stanley A. Krezmien, Lloyd Lamb, Arthur Benson, Betty Cooke, Edie Palmer, and others are noted, with a vision for a better community.

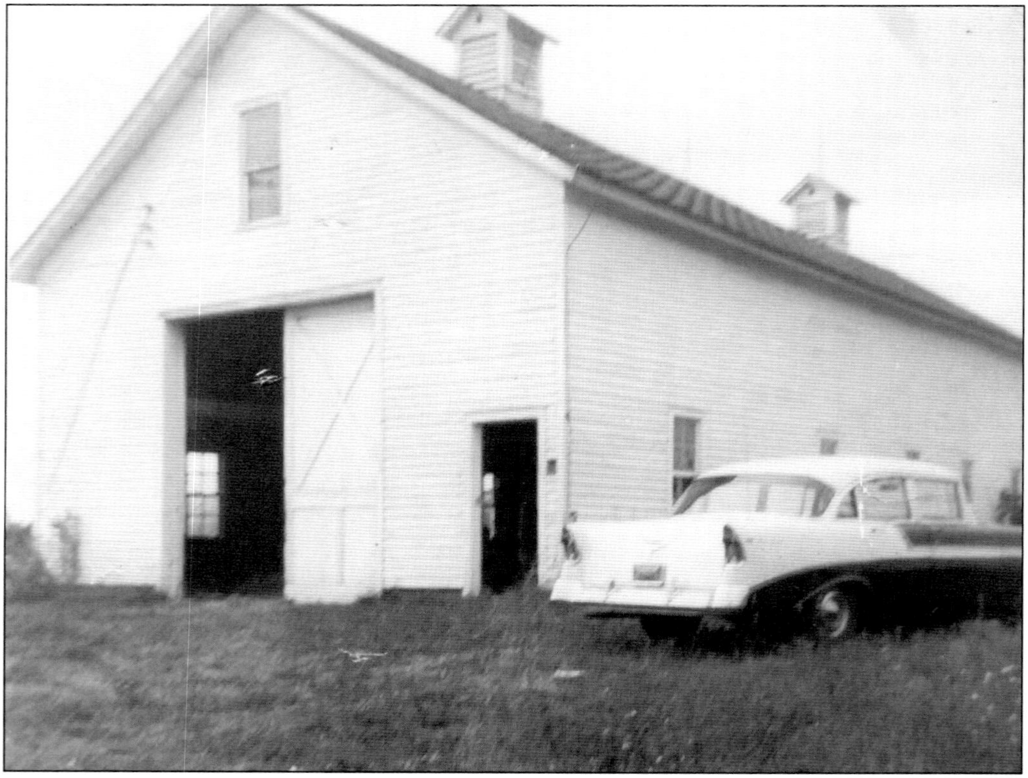

A visionary named Lloyd Lamb saw Springville as the agricultural hub of Western New York and proceeded to build a business at the corner of Routes 219 and 39 to serve that facet of the economy. In 1960, he partnered with Austin Webster to form Lamb and Webster International Harvester dealership, which has grown from a staff of two to 85 today. This barn, pictured around 1956, was the first building in a complex that is now one of the four location of the company.

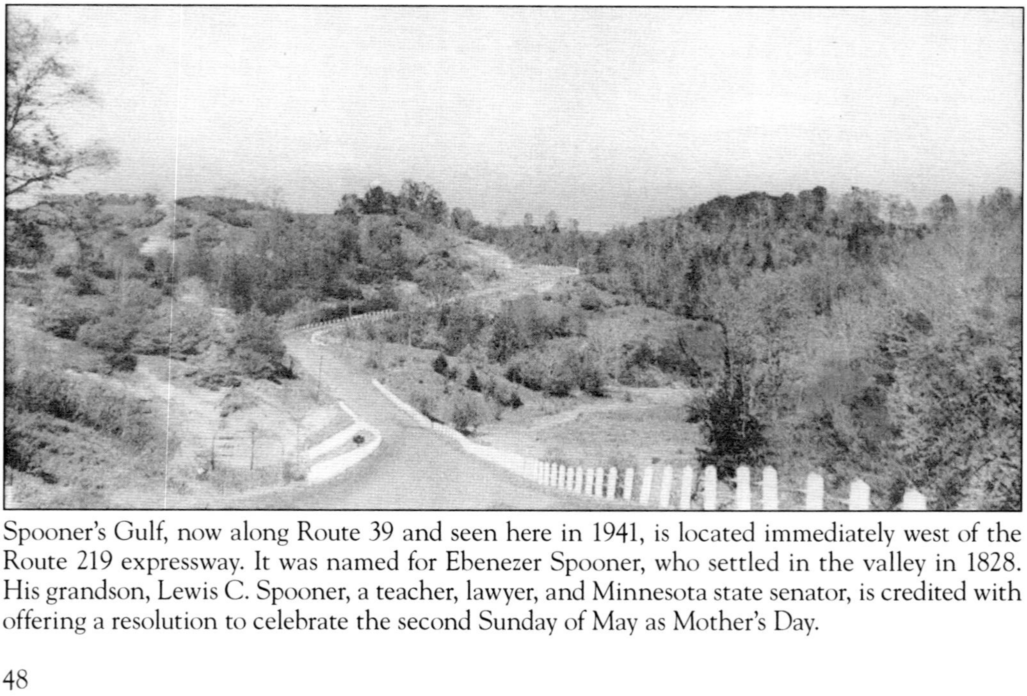

Spooner's Gulf, now along Route 39 and seen here in 1941, is located immediately west of the Route 219 expressway. It was named for Ebenezer Spooner, who settled in the valley in 1828. His grandson, Lewis C. Spooner, a teacher, lawyer, and Minnesota state senator, is credited with offering a resolution to celebrate the second Sunday of May as Mother's Day.

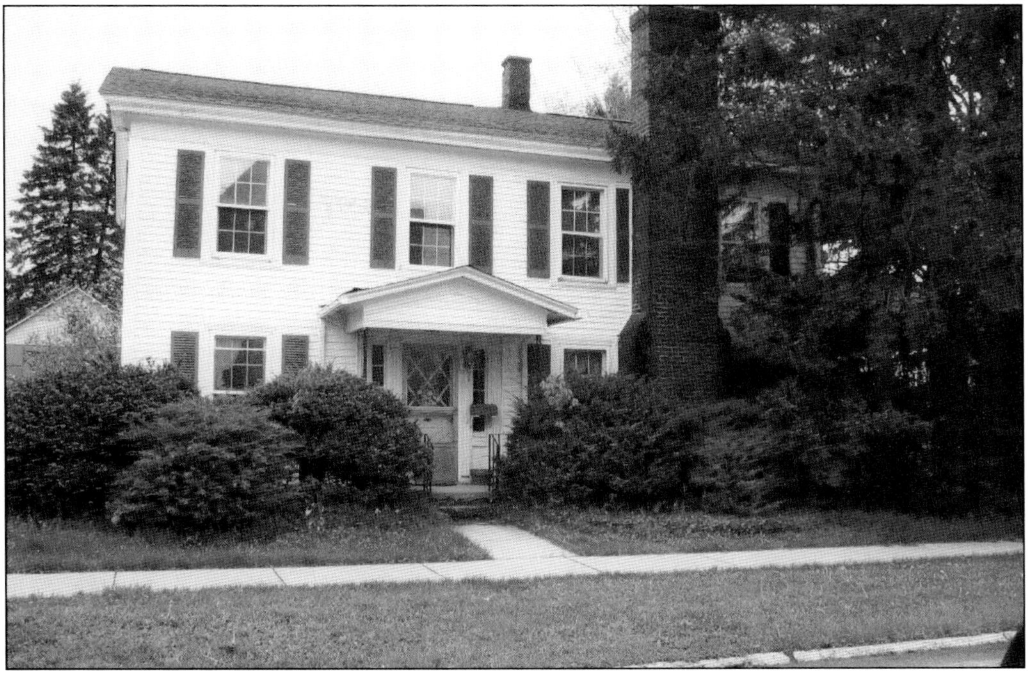

This is the Franklin Street home of Peter and Kathy Swales, where William Jennings Bryan was once a guest. Bryan was a participant on the Lyceum Circuit, traveling from town to town and giving lectures. He appeared at Godard Hall on three occasions. He is remembered for his 1896 "Cross of Gold" speech, as a candidate for president (1896, 1900, and 1908), and for his participation in the famed Dayton, Tennessee, antievolution "Scopes Trial" of 1925.

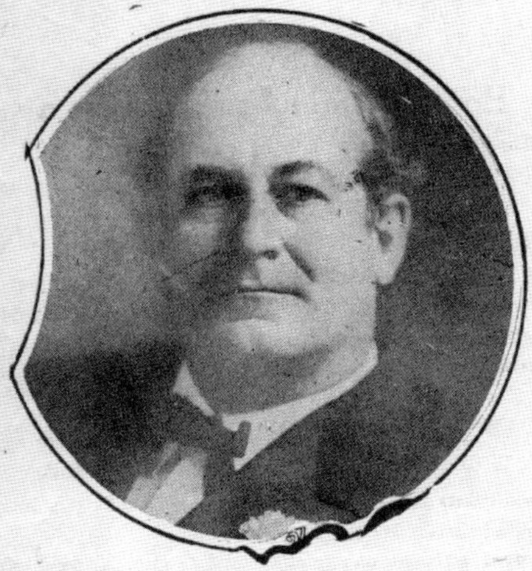

WILLIAM JENNINGS BRYAN

The Great Commoner

Three times the nominee of the Democratic party for the Presidency

A lecturer whose drawing power is unsurpassed in United States today.

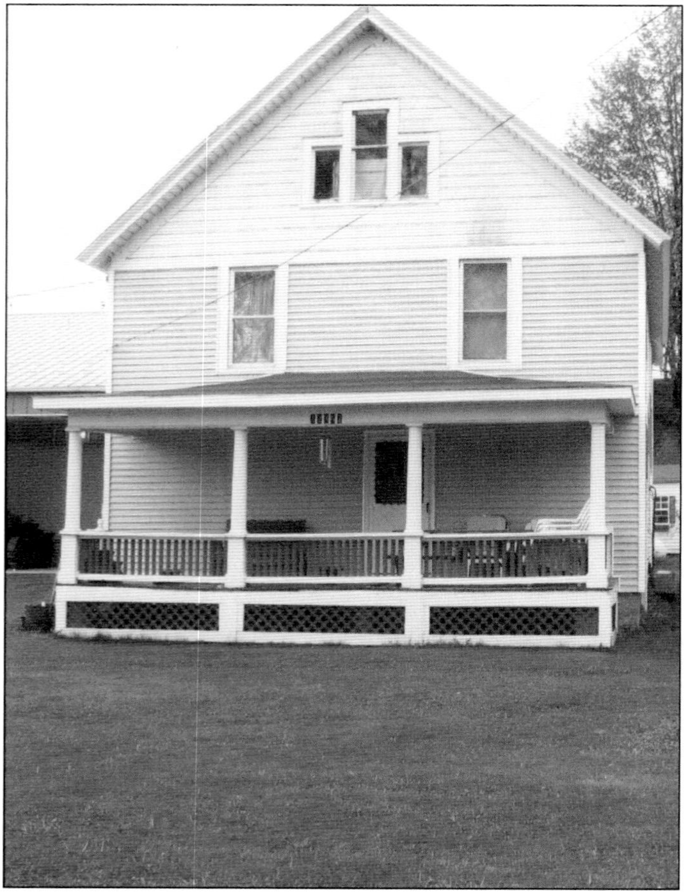

The home of Jack and Beverly White on Sharp Street was formerly owned by Ross (1874–1965) and Cora (1884–1974) Ingalls, who returned to New York State because of Ross's health. He was the son of Aaron Ingalls and brother of Lansford Ingalls, who had nine children and a granddaughter named Laura, who was later known as Laura Ingalls Wilder of *Little House on the Prairie*. "Cousin Ross" was an old-time fiddler who entertained at area homes and barn dances. His great-grandchildren include the talented Sullivan family triplets, born April 2, 1963. The triplets played in the 1980s and 1990s with an eight-member family instrumental group called the Reflections. They are, from left to right, David, Duane, and Dennis. (Below, courtesy of the Sullivan family.)

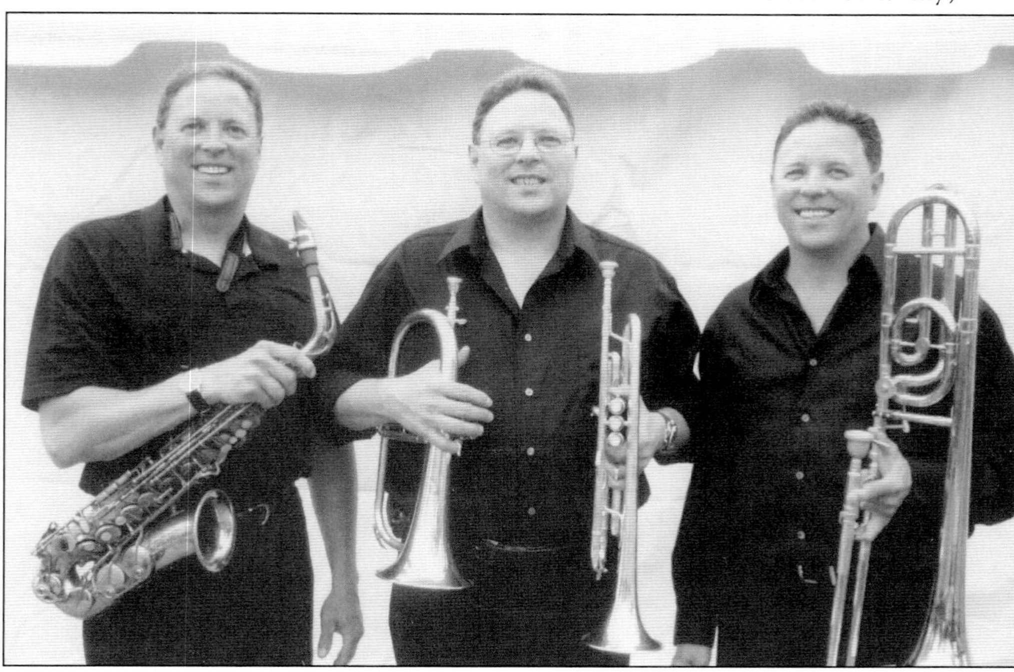

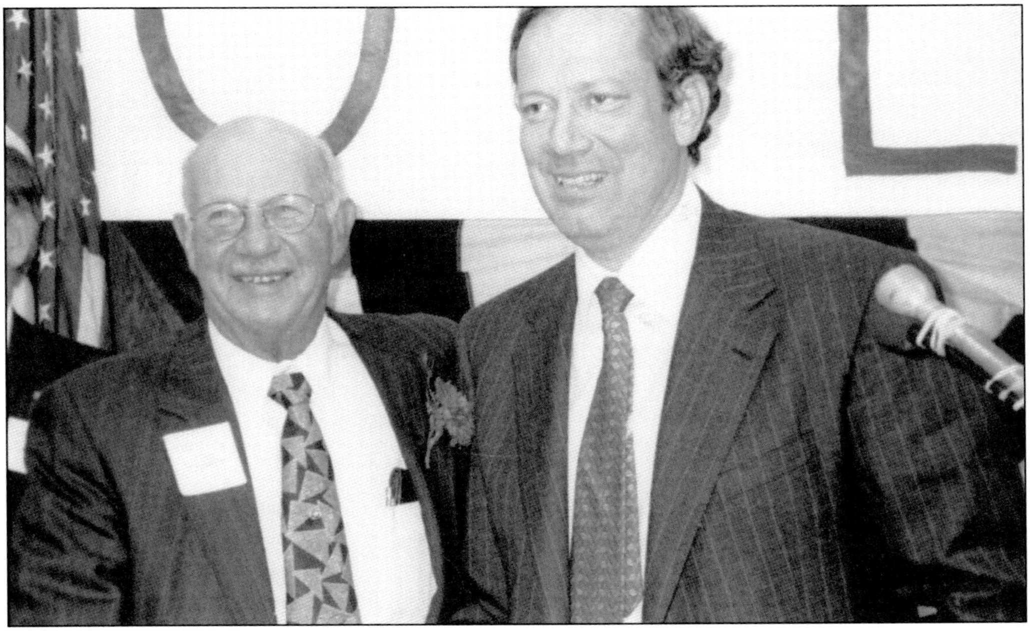

New York governor George E. Pataki (right) presents Stanley A. Krezmien (1920–2011), known as "Stosh," with the prestigious Citizen of the Year Award from the Springville Area Chamber of Commerce on February 23, 1995. Krezmien, a decades-long Main Street businessman, was the president of Witter-Davis Furniture Company. Witter-Davis succeeded A.L. Pingrey on the north side of Main Street and later moved to the corner of Pearl Street, acquiring the premises long occupied by furniture dealers Weismantel Bros. Like most old-time furniture dealers, Weismantel Bros. were also undertakers. In addition, they operated an ambulance service. (Both, courtesy of James Krezmien.)

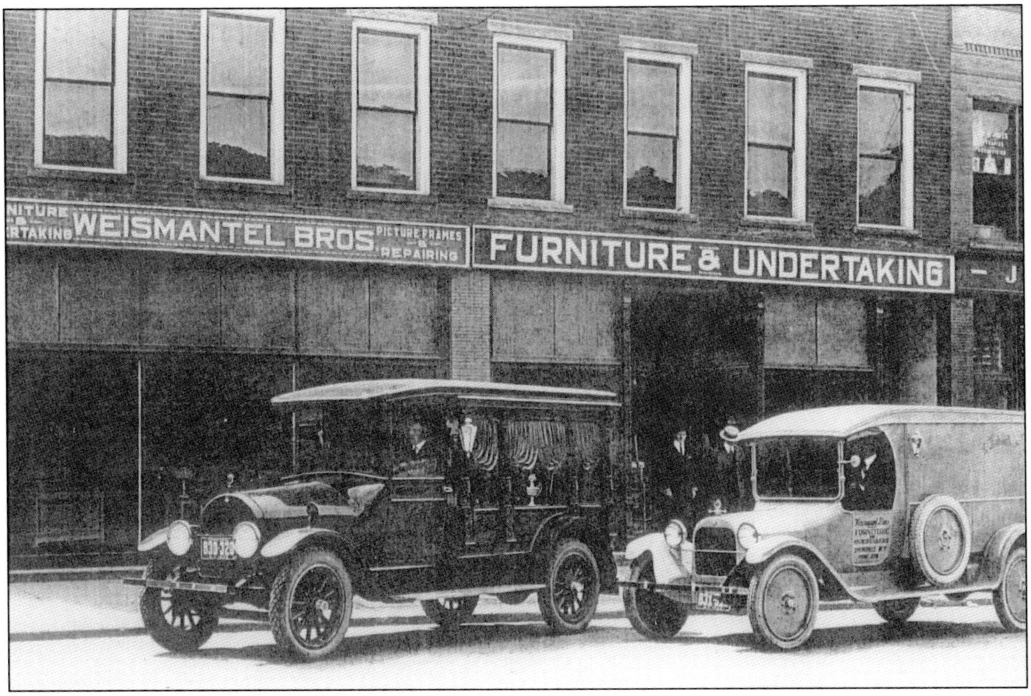

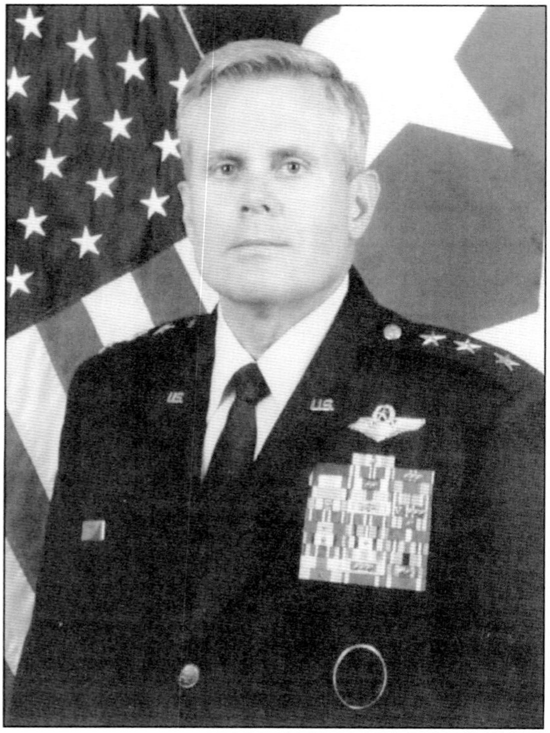

Three-star lieutenant general Eric E. Fiel, the son of Dr. Robert and Elizabeth Fiel and 1976 Griffith Institute and 1980 University of Buffalo graduate, took command of the US Air Force Special Operations Command, Hulbert Field, Florida, on June 24, 2011. Fiel holds two master's degrees and has extensive training in business and management. His command has over 16,000 personnel. He commanded a special operations squadron during Bosnia and Kosovo operations and was forward-deployed and a task commander in Operations Enduring Freedom and Iraqi Freedom. In the air, he is a master navigator, with more than 2,000 flight hours. Included among his awards and decorations are the Legion of Merit; the Distinguished Flying Cross; Kosovo, Iraq, and Afghanistan Campaign Medals; and the Global War on Terrorism Expeditionary Medal. (Both, courtesy of Carl and Sandra Emerling.)

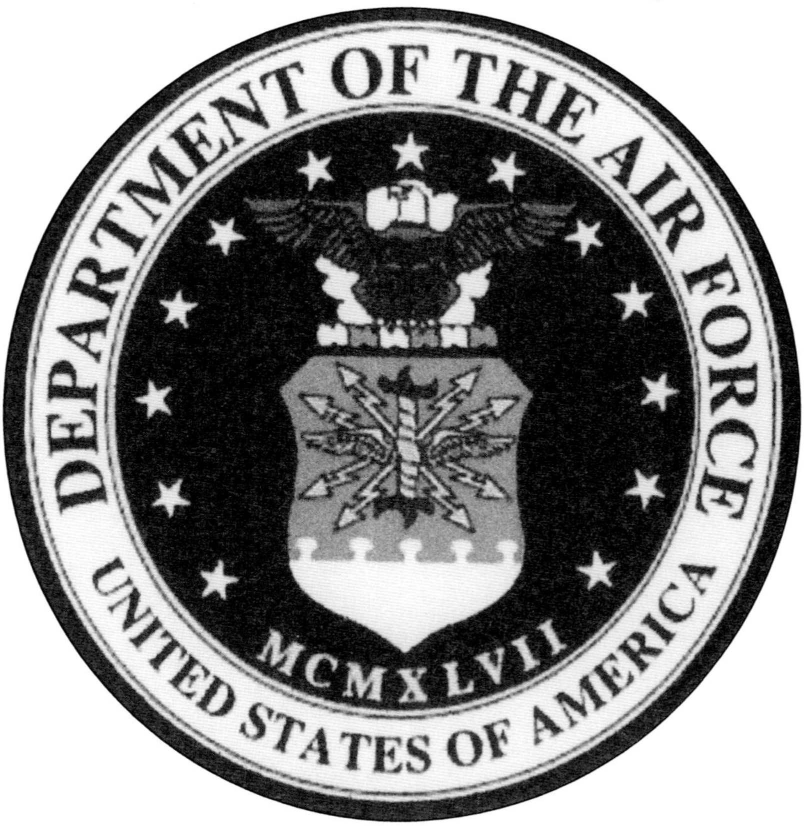

Below is what young Glenn Warner saw as he looked south on Sharp Street from the one-room school he attended at the corner of Genesee Road. Note the privy to the left. Privies were still common until the end of the 1940s and were targets of Halloween tricksters who tipped them over, sometimes with an occupant inside. The property on which this barn sat was developed by "Cheese King" Stephen R. Smith, who owned three cheese factories and in 1871 manufactured a 2,975-pound "Springville Giant" cheese using 30,105 pounds of milk, for display at Buffalo's International Industrial Exhibition. The 213-foot-long barn had a high walkway wide enough to accommodate a team of horses and a wagon of hay running the entire length of the barn to discharge hay for storage. The barn, under ownership of Homer and Laura Klein, was lost to fire in September 1957. (Below, courtesy of 1880 F.W. Beers Atlas.)

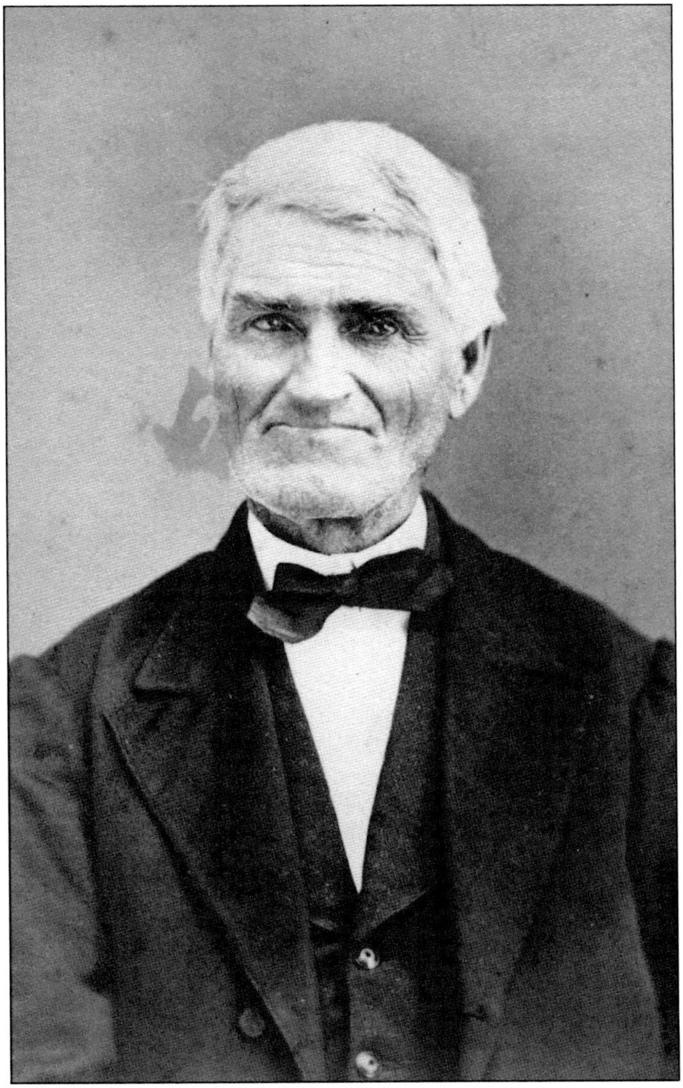

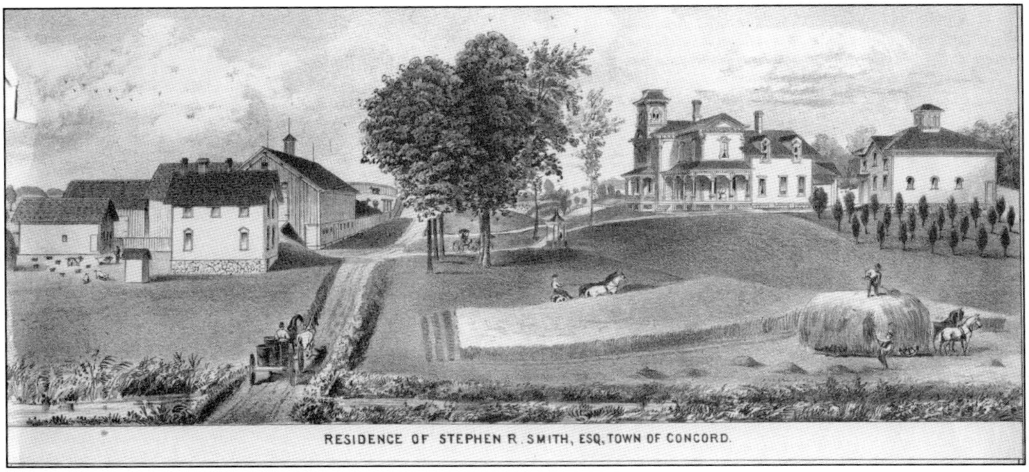

RESIDENCE OF STEPHEN R. SMITH, ESQ, TOWN OF CONCORD.

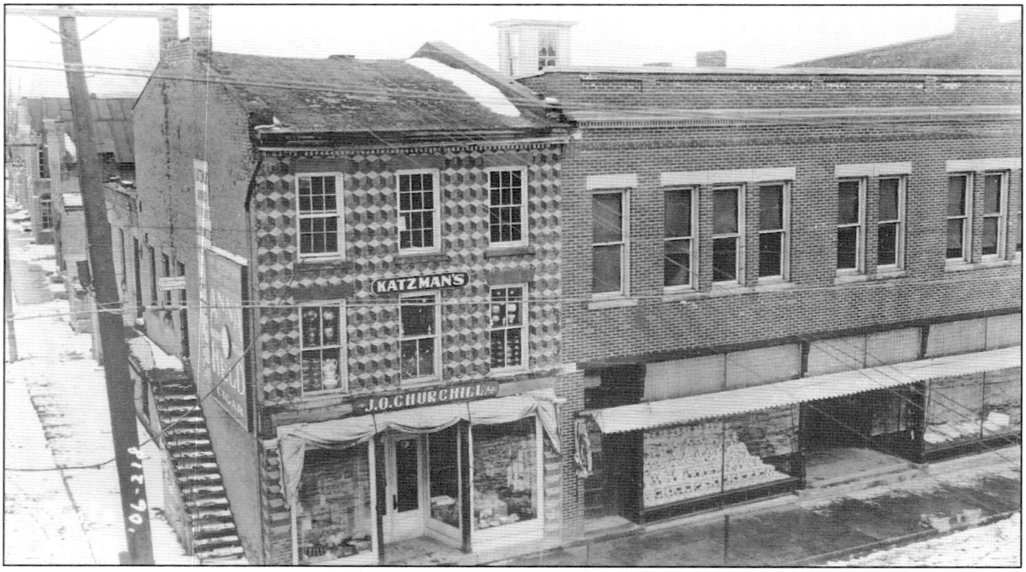

Katzman's (now Carolsel Shop) is one of downtown's oldest buildings, across the street from the Blakely House. The second floor was once the dentist's office of Dr. Carlos Waite, father of painless-dentistry pioneer Dr. Ralph B. Waite. The newer, 1904 building to the right housed the H.D. Smith Store. These 1921 workers are, from left to right, Charles Hopper, Florence Weismantel, Charles Thurber, and Lagarda Barton Salzler.

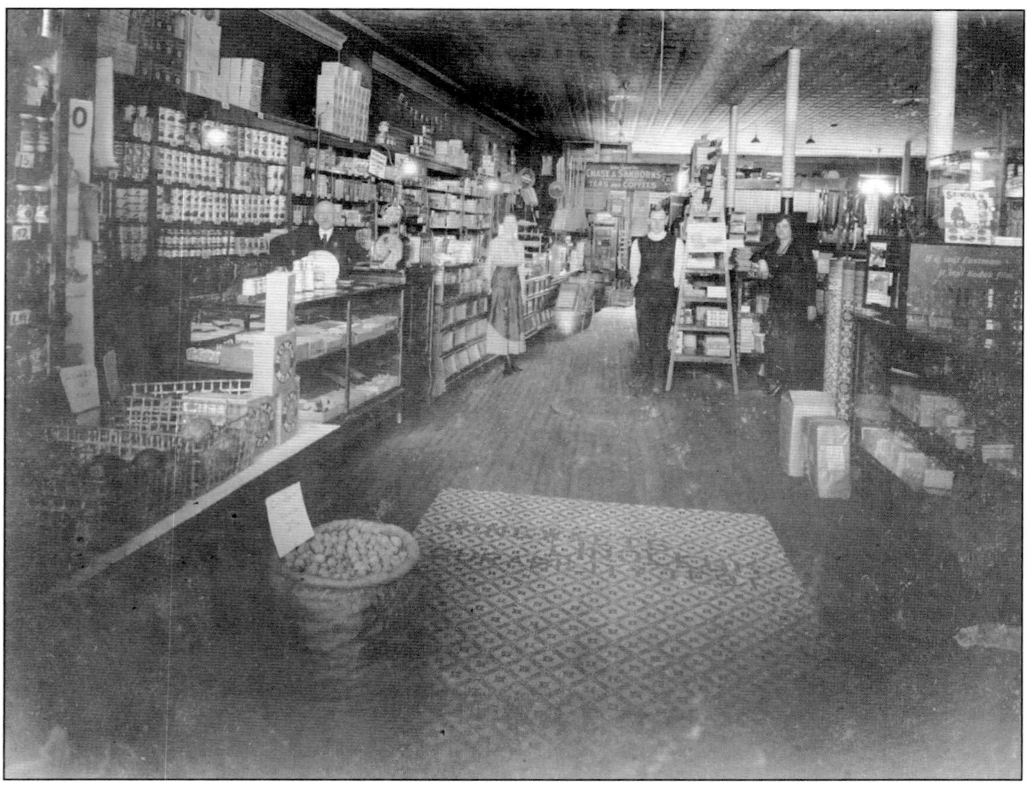

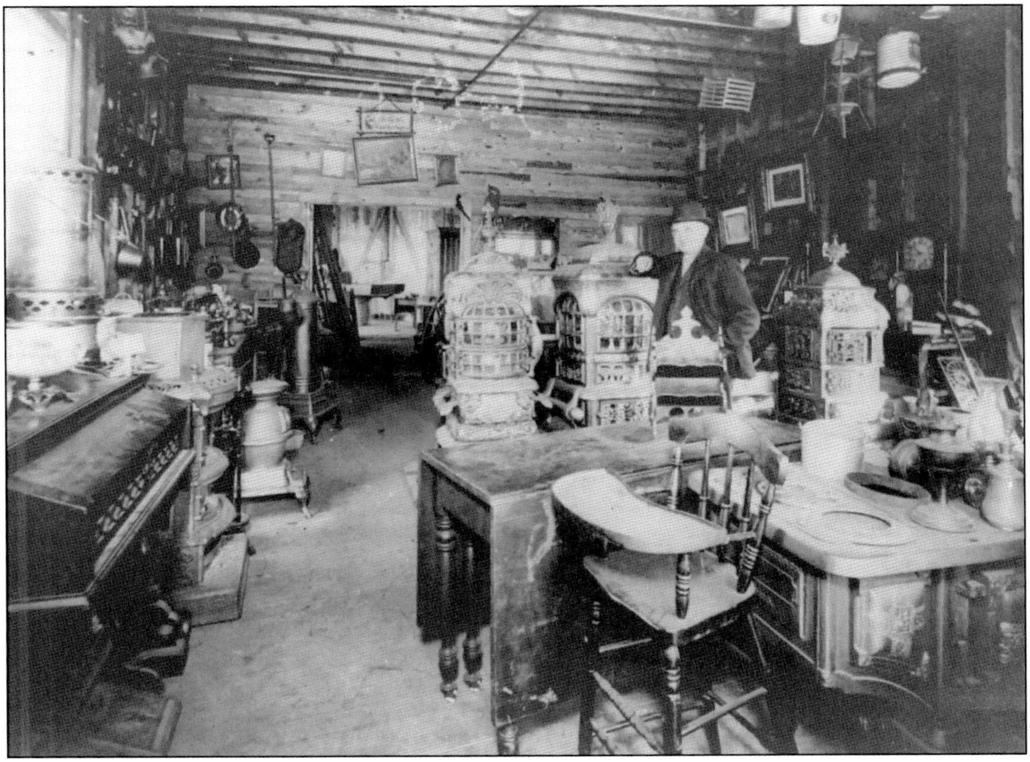

Levi Prior is pictured in his store, the Old Curiosity Shop, located on Franklin Street near Factory Street. This 1907 statement lists painting supplies and six pounds of lead.

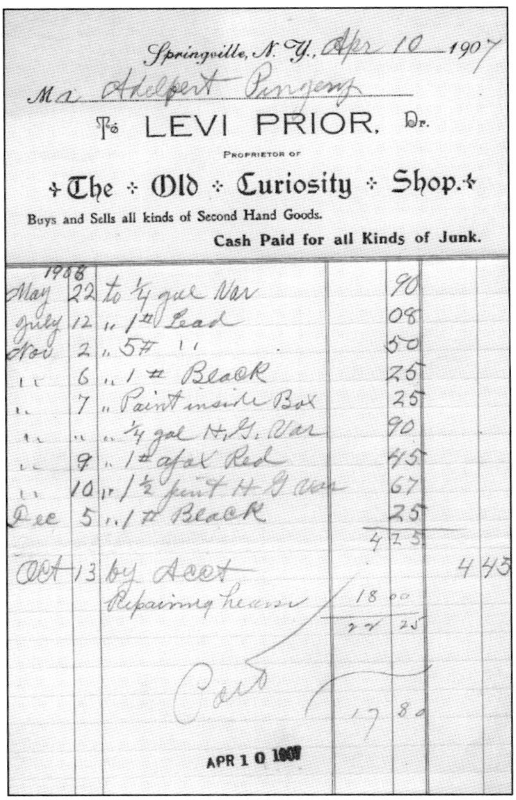

Springville, N. Y., Apr 10 1907

Mr Adelpert Pingery

To LEVI PRIOR, Dr.

PROPRIETOR OF

The Old Curiosity Shop.

Buys and Sells all kinds of Second Hand Goods.

Cash Paid for all Kinds of Junk.

1906			
May	22	to ¼ gal Var	90
July	12	" 1# Lead	08
Nov	2	" 5# "	50
"	6	" 1# Black	25
"	7	" Paint inside Box	25
"	"	" ¼ gal H. G. Var	90
"	9	" 1# afat Red	45
"	10	" ½ pint H G var	67
Dec	5	" 1# Black	25
			4 25
Oct	13	by Acct	4 45
		Repairing hearse	18 00
			22 25

Paid

17 80

APR 10 1907

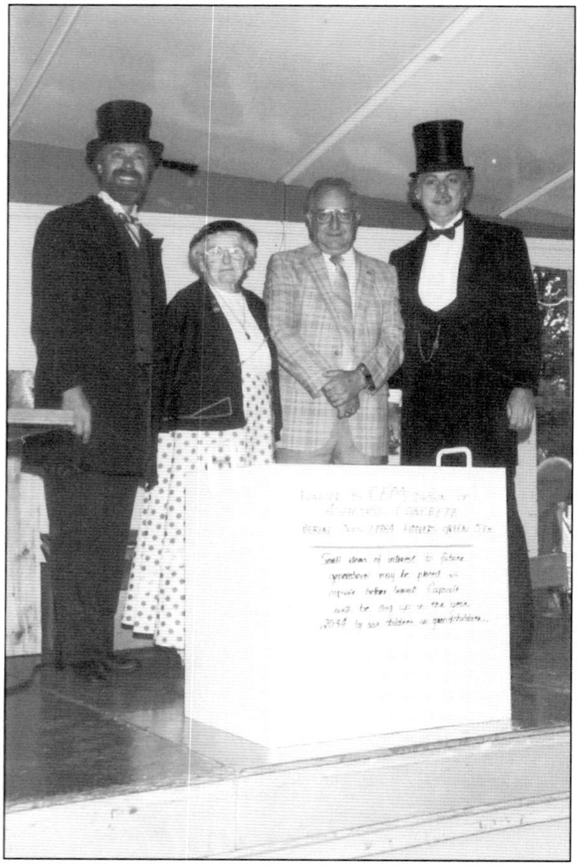

From left to right, Donald Orton, town historian Lillian Geiger, Mayor J. James Neff, and coauthor Alan V. Manchester pose on July 7, 1984, after presiding over the placement of the 1984 Village Sesquicentennial mementos. Interested citizens placed mementos in a steel-sealed container donated by Grover and Betty Riefler. They then turned it over to Boy Scout Troop 524, who lowered it into the ground between the Civil War Monument and the east side parking area of Fiddler's Green Park to be retrieved at some future date. A map showing its location is in the possession of Edwards and Moncreiff Engineers and the Concord Historical Society.

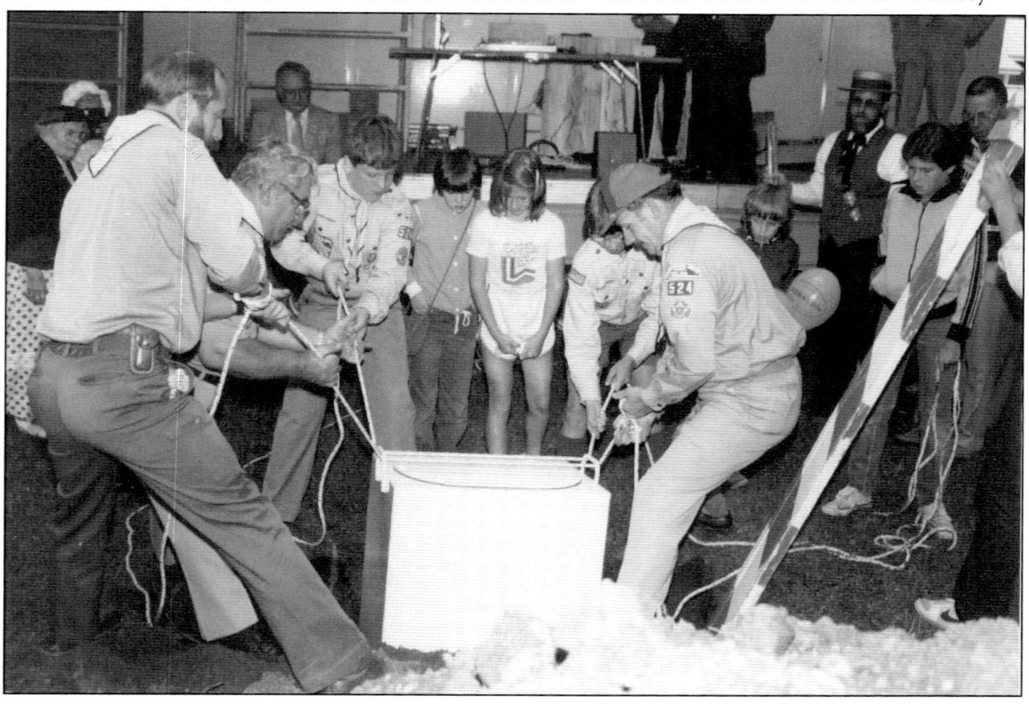

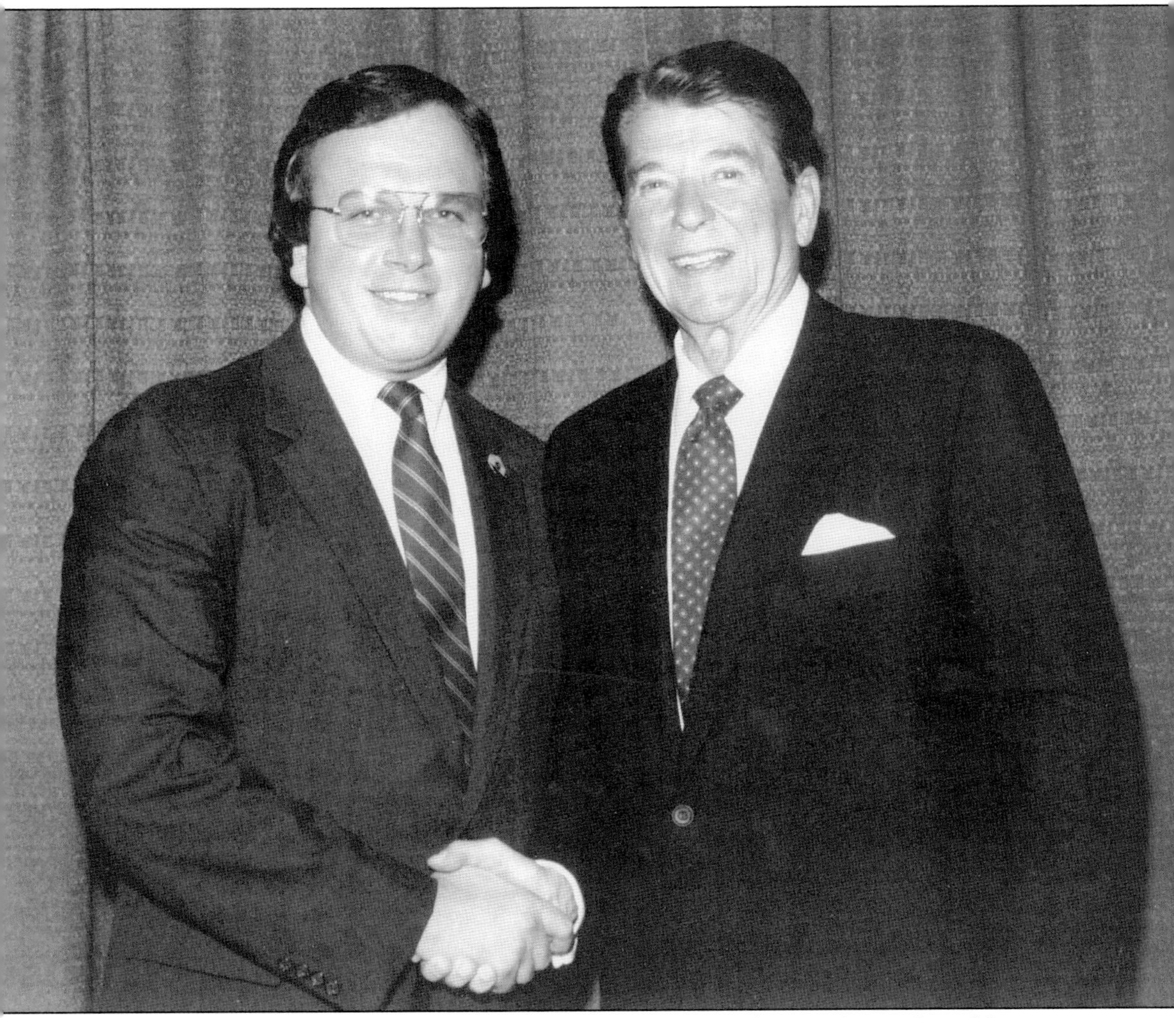

Congressman Thomas M. Reynolds, a 1968 Griffith Institute graduate and Kent State University alum, met Ronald Reagan in Buffalo. Reynolds was so impressed with Reagan that he remarked in supporting his election, "I would walk across America for that man." Reynolds entered the elected public service realm in 1974 when he became a member of the Concord town board. A *Buffalo News* feature called him "Mr. Clout" and "Western New York's most powerful politician." Following his election to the US House of Representatives in 1998, the *Washington Post* noted that "Reynolds has quietly become one of the most influential Republicans in the House." After 35 years of making legislation happen, being in the halls of Congress and in the presence of presidents, Representative Reynolds still regards himself as "just a kid from Springville."

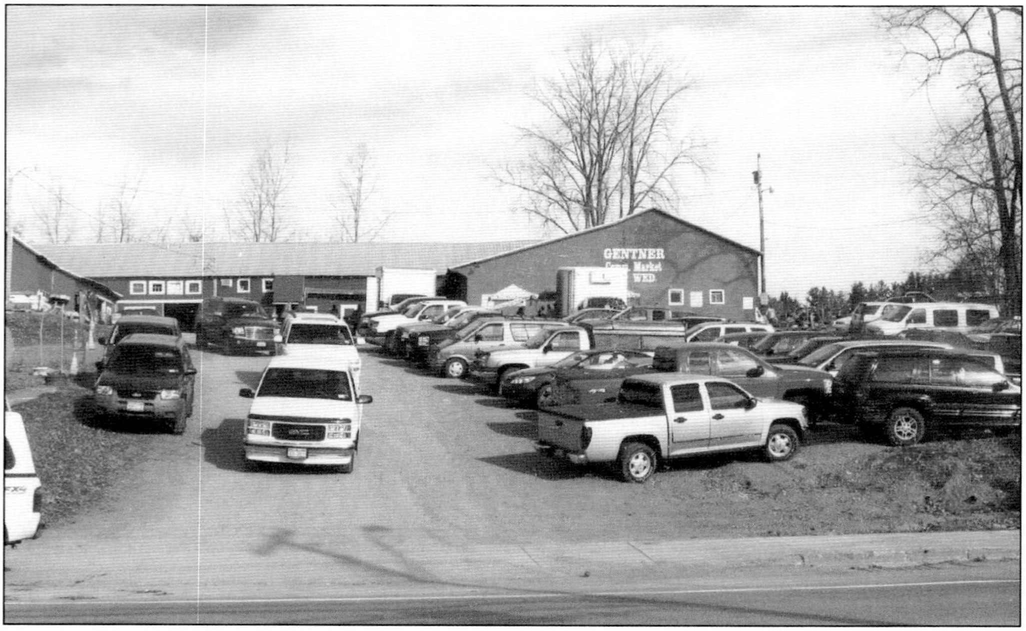

A mainstay on Wednesdays since 1939, Gentner's (originally Kessler and Gentner) Auction brings peak crowds of thousands to Springville for produce, cheese, flea market table offerings, and an item-by-item, row-after-row live auction on "the Hill." In "the Ring," the evening auction has, over the years, offered all manner of livestock and produce. Loyal buyers and lookers return to the Hill all winter.

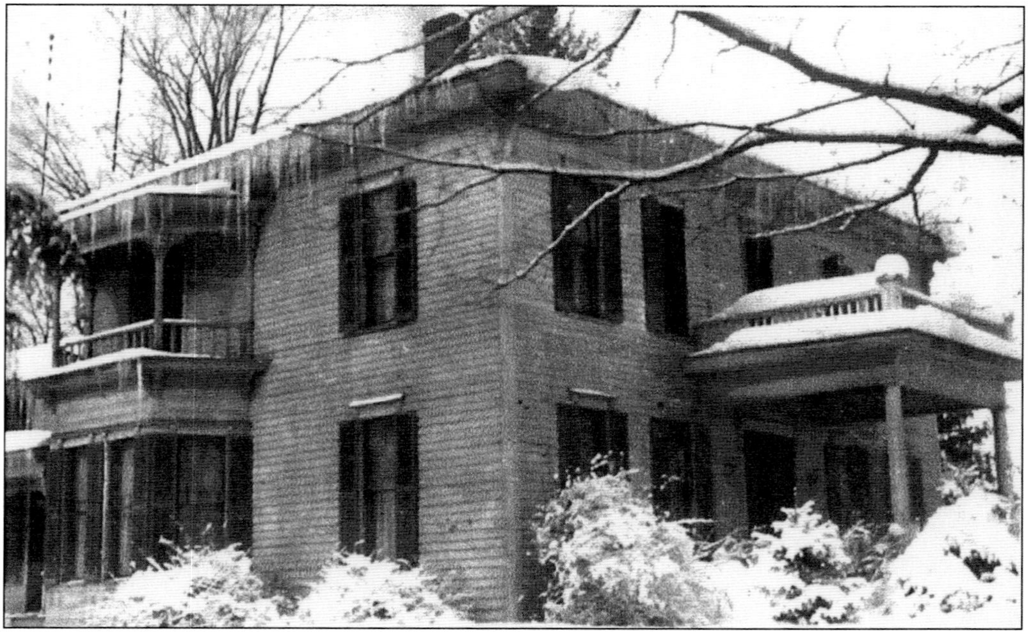

The Bates-Colby-Mitchell-Baker Home is on Buffalo Road. Research by Ruth Mitchell Fitch reveals that the structure predates 1892, as it is shown in the aerial-perspective lithograph on display at the Concord Historical Society's Lucy Bensley Center on North Buffalo Street. The image, containing all village structures of that year, shows Mr. and Mrs. (doctors) Bates, Electric Sanitarium, as proprietors.

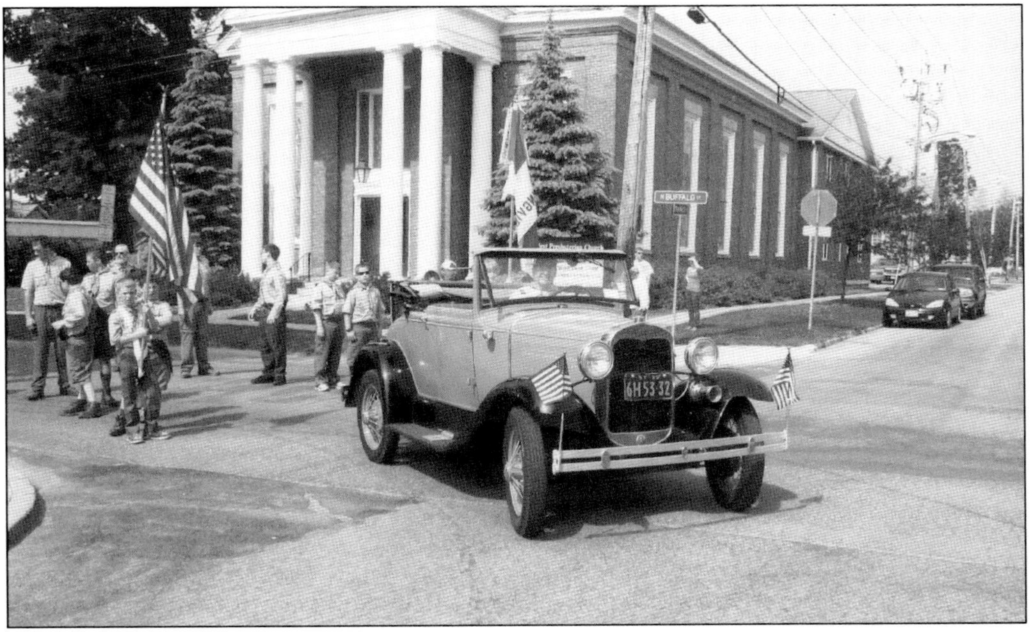

In his Ford Model A, Scout troop leader Joel Maul does the Memorial Day parade the easy way. Maul, Richard McDonald, John Allen, and A. Sanford Kenyon are among those regarded as life-long Scouts. McDonald and Maul, on one of their scouting trips into Canada, once had a royal encounter, marching their troop unwittingly into a camp occupied by Queen Elizabeth and the royal family.

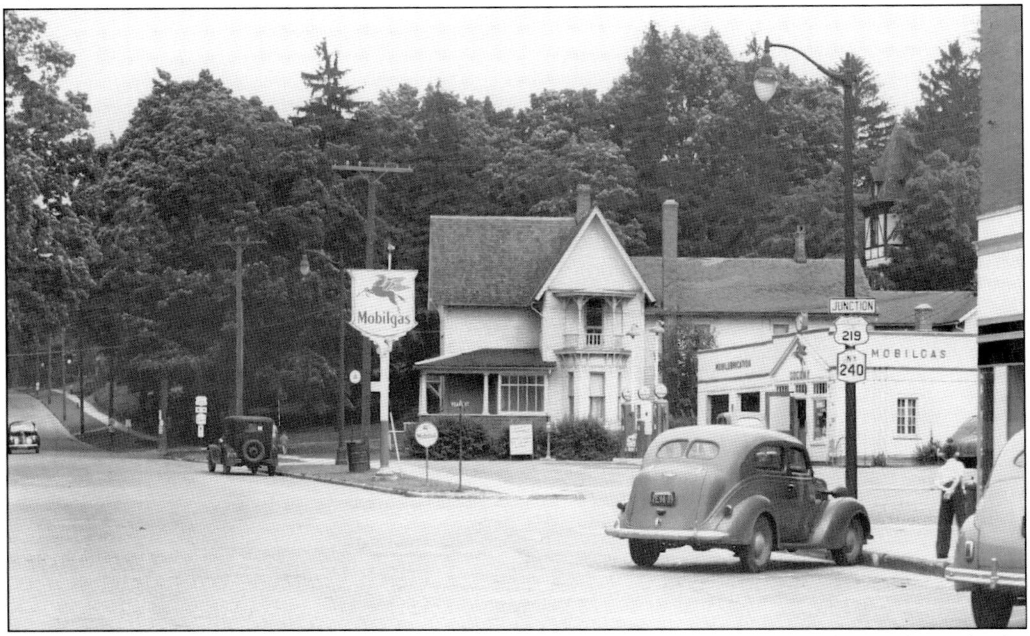

For decades, Route 219 began its southward journey at Hamburg, winding down through the Boston Valley, up Nunweiler Hill, down Buffalo Road, past the Trout Pond to North Buffalo Street, and on to Main Street before turning left and passing through the business district to Elk Street, turning right up the hill to Cattaraugus Street, then left down to the green/blue 1928 bridge, and up the hill to West Valley and on southward.

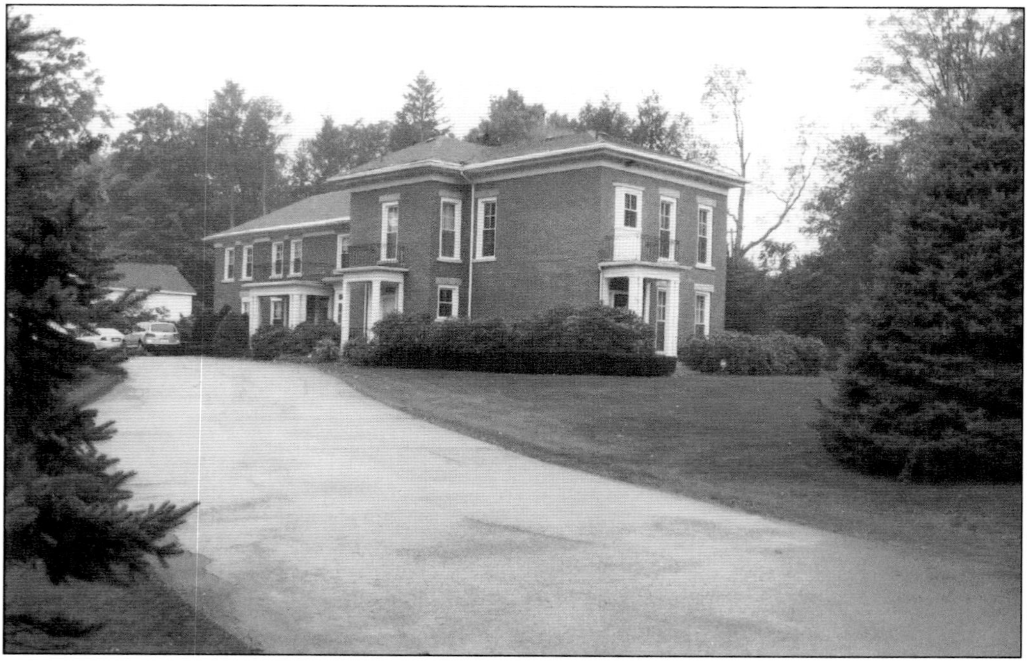

Now the home of Michael and Diane Beatty, 367 East Main Street was occupied by the Dr. Ralph Britton Waite family from 1920 to 1965. "R.B.," as he preferred to be called, did not, as is often claimed, invent Novocain. However, he was licensed to manufacture the German invention at his 25 Main Street Antidolor Manufacturing Company. He developed a local anesthetic for painless extractions containing one percent cocaine and two percent Novocain. His success led to worldwide distribution of products including toothpaste and mouthwash. At its peak, Antidolor employed a staff of 150. Dr. Waite also owned Springville's first automobile, a 1901 Winton.

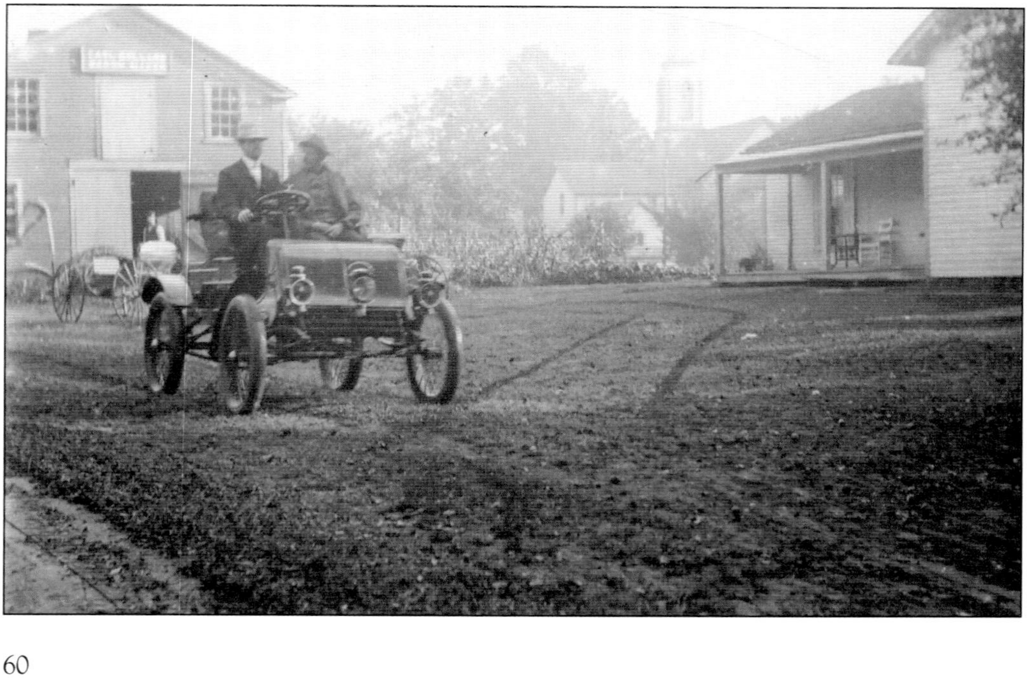

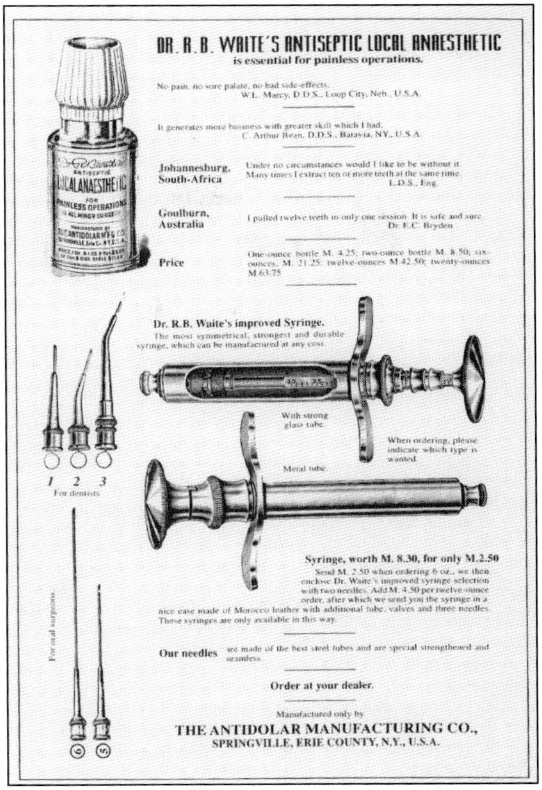

Dr. R.B. Waite's father, Dr. Carlos Waite (1840–1901), came to Springville to practice dentistry following the Civil War. Often accompanied by young Ralph, he went into the countryside to serve patients with his black bag, forceps, foot-powered drill, and whiskey for anesthesia. R.B.'s son Sheridan (1895–1992) was also a dentist, as well as an author and promoter of Antidolor Manufacturing Company products. (Right, courtesy Ralph A. Schmauss, DDS.)

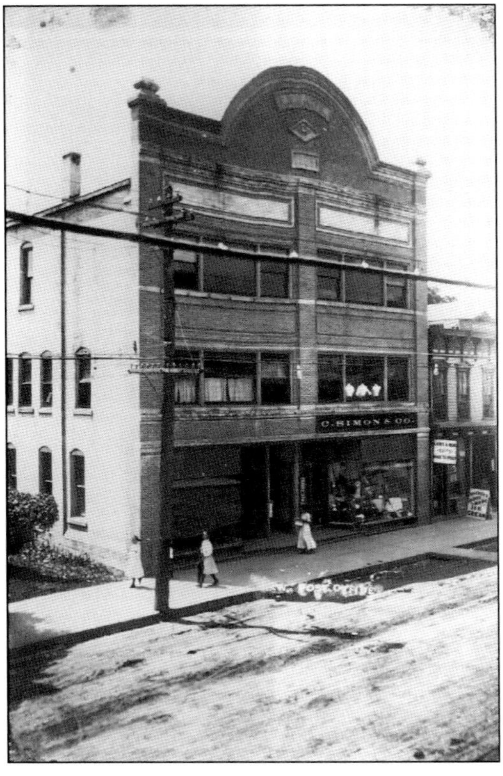

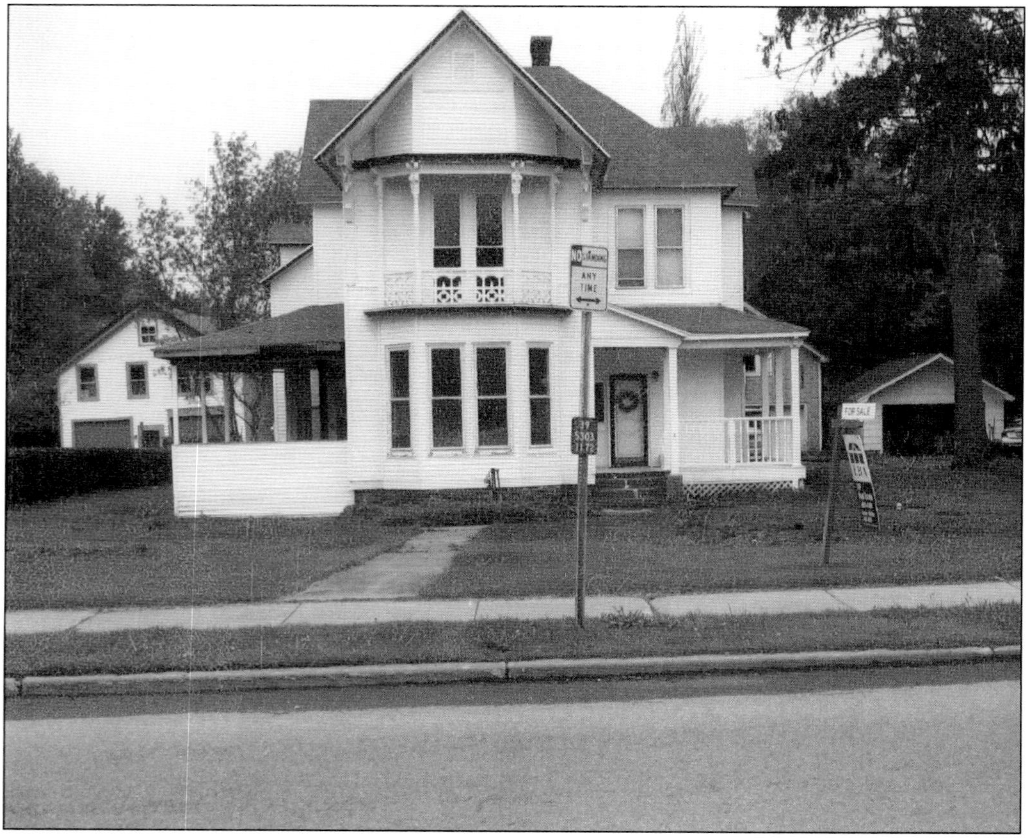

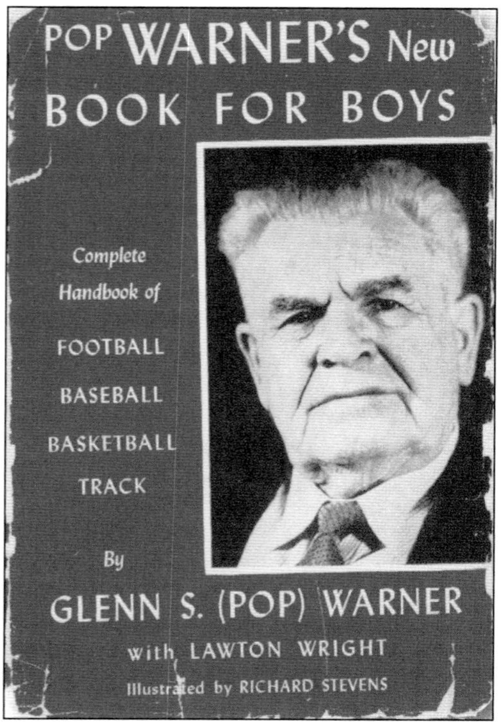

William and Adeline Scobey Warner came to live in this house at 253 East Main Street when they left the farm, Glenn "Pop" Warner's birthplace, on Springville-Boston and Genesee Roads. While there, Glenn likely attended the Sharp Street School—now a home on the southeast corner of Genesee Road and Sharp Street—before attending Griffith Institute and graduating in 1889. It was on this front lawn that Adeline Warner defended her active, lawn-destroying sons with the statement, "I'm raising boys, not grass." In 1970, tenant Emerson Havens, while playing toss football with his young son, damaged some of neighbor Mrs. Bury's flowers. He quickly apologized and was greeted with, "Don't worry young man, those flowers have been trampled by 'Pop' Warner and Jim Thorpe."

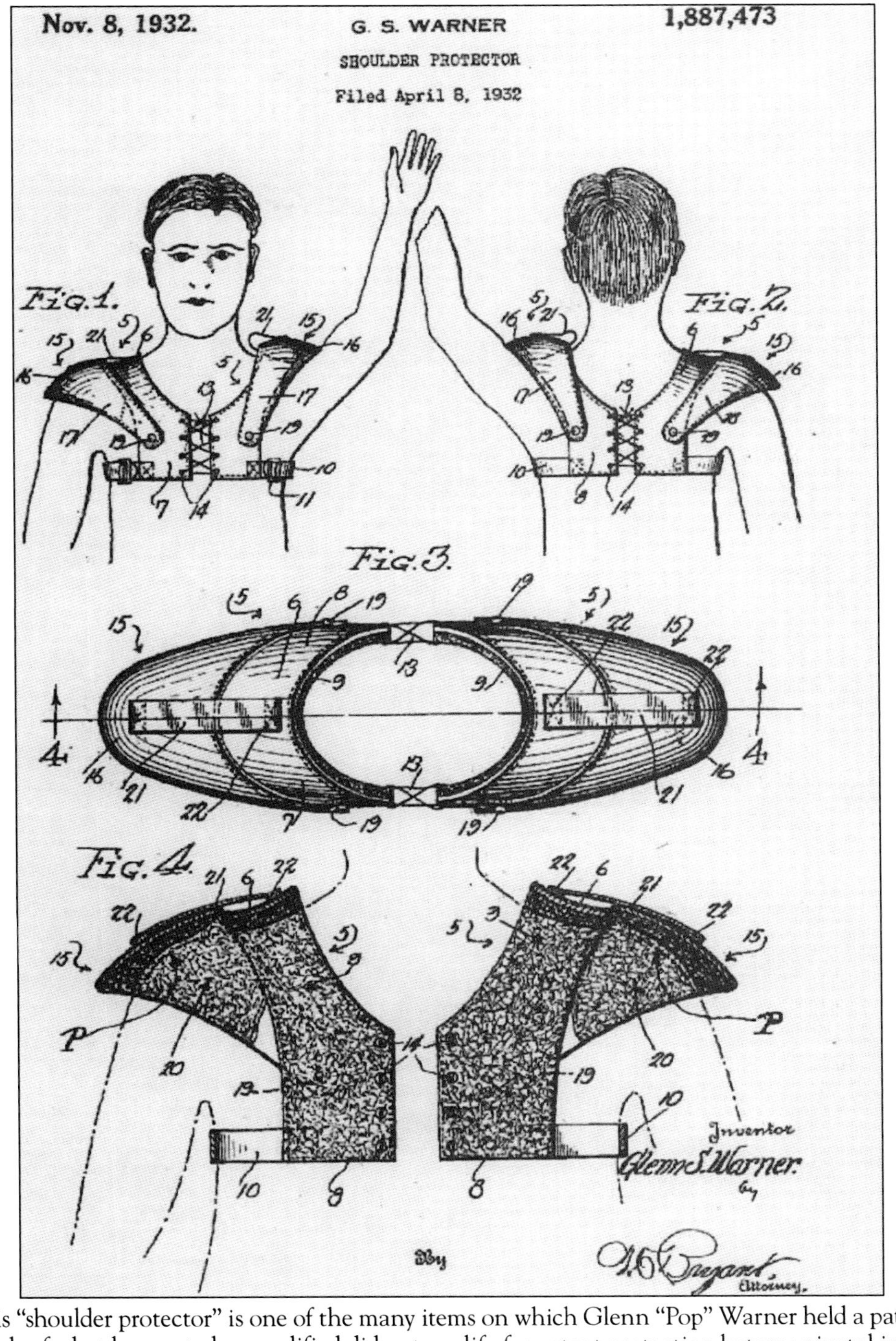

This "shoulder protector" is one of the many items on which Glenn "Pop" Warner held a patent. Much of what he created or modified did not qualify for patent protection but was pivotal in the early days of football. In the list that follows, Warner was in nearly every case the originator and an early advocate of a few: single-wing formation, double-wing formation, three-point stance, numbered plays, jersey numbers, knee guards, fiber padding, early head gear, spiral punt, center snap to ball carrier, bootleg, reverse, screen, mouse trap (misdirection), rolling body block, hidden ball, free forward passing, and more.

July 18, 1979 **CONGRESSIONAL RECORD — *Extensions of Remarks*** **E 3703**

A TRIBUTE TO "POP" WARNER

HON. JACK F. KEMP

OF NEW YORK

IN THE HOUSE OF REPRESENTATIVES

Wednesday, July 18, 1979

• Mr. KEMP. Mr. Speaker, I would like to pause in the business of the House to honor the memory of a great American. Glenn Scobey Warner was an incredible man who left an indelible imprint on the game of football.

Born at Springville, Erie County, N.Y., in 1871, he was an outstanding baseball player at Springville's Griffith Institute which he graduated from in 1889. He remains that school's most distinguished graduate as it prepares for its 150th anniversary in 1980.

Having enrolled in Cornell University in 1892, he soon became known as "Pop" to his younger team and classmates. His first encounter with a football was at Cornell, where he also participated in baseball, track, and boxing. His personal relationship with the game of football was to span a half a century; his influence will remain as long as the game is played. Football at that time was a brutal confrontation lacking rules and equipment to protect the player. Forward passing and end runs were yet to be developed.

"Pop" had intended to become a lawyer and practiced briefly. He was an exceptional artist. He also wrote practical coaching guides. In 44 years of coaching, he established himself as one of the architects of the game. Teams were fielded at Iowa State, University of Georgia, Cornell University, Carlisle Indian Industrial School, University of Pittsburgh, Stanford University, and Temple University. On two occasions he directed the fortunes of teams from two schools simultaneously, Iowa State and the University of Georgia during the 1895 and 1896 seasons, and the University of Pittsburgh and Stanford University during 1922 and 1923.

Carlisle teams used the crouching three-point start for backs as early as 1899. The 1907 team, with Frank Mt. Pleasant at quarterback, made significant strides in perfecting the spiral aerial attack. That team beat Amos Alonzo Stagg's Big Ten champion, University of Chicago's Maroons, 18 to 4.

At Carlisle he perfected his single- and double-wing formations as part of the "Warner system," copied and imitated throughout football.

Chuck Knox, former head coach of the Los Angeles Rams—now of the Buffalo Bills—states that in his opinion, "the fullback slant to the weakside is the one great play in football." This play was an integral part of the single-wing offense invented by Pop Warner over a half-century ago.

Pop guided the development of the legendary Jim Thorpe in football and track. At Stockholm, following the 1912 Olympic Games in which Jim had won both the pentathlon and decathlon, King Gustaf V of Sweden addressed Thorpe: "You sir, are the greatest athlete in the world." Jim Thorpe carried the "Warner system" to the professional teams and served in 1920 as the founding president of a predecessor to the National Football League. He and Ernie Nevers, whom Pop coached at Stanford University, were regarded as two of the three greatest football players before 1930. The third was Harold "Red' Grange.

In his tenure at the University of Pittsburgh, starting in 1915, he produced teams that, at the end of the 1918 season had won 29 successive games scoring 861 points while allowing the opposition a mere 71 points. Victims of that streak included John Heisman's Ramblin' Wreck of Georgia Tech, by a score of 32 to 0. Out of the Pittsburgh years which extended to 1923 came many all-Americans and disciples of the "Warner system," including nine who became coaches from the 1916 team alone. These men carried Warner strategy to teams in every part of America. The great Pittsburgh tradition of college and professional football was begun by Pop Warner.

An offer by Stanford University, and the necessity for a more moderate climate for reasons of health attracted Pop to California where he developed mighty Stanford teams that attracted other great coaches to rival schools and established big time football for the Pacific coast colleges. He coached Erne Nevers, who with Jim Thorpe, is enshrined in the NFL Football Hall of Fame, and many other Stanford all-Americans. He took his team to the Rose Bowl three times. In the 1925 game against Knute Rockne's Irish, the Four Horsemen were pitted against Ernie Nevers. The Indians out-rushed, out-gained, and out-passed the Irish, only to succumb 27 to 10.

Pop returned to the east to coach Temple University of Philadelphia in 1933, where he remained until 1938. At the end of his brilliant coaching career, he had established himself as one of the three "winningest" college and professional coaches of all time with 312 victories, 104 defeats and 32 ties. His teams scored 8,795 points to the oppositions' 2,810.

In addition to his single- and double-wing offenses, he had introduced or perfected: fiber padding, knee guards, shin guards, tackling dummy team, hidden ball, three point stance, screened pass, bootleg, and the spiral punt. He also advocated free forward passing, which was adopted by the NFL in 1933 and the NCAA in 1945.

The 6,000 Little League football teams which play under Pop Warner sanction in nearly every State are testimony to this great man. They represent 25 percent of all organized "kid football" teams in the Nation. Eleven-thousand high school teams, 600 college teams and the pros all use Warner equipment and strategy.

In 1954 the year of his death, the Associated Press rated him the "top coach of all time."

Mr. Walter Byers, executive director of the National Collegiate Athletic Association states:

> He was one of the principal contributors to the game's development.

Mr. Pete Elliott, director of the Pro-Football Hall of Fame, states:

> Pop Warner was not "just another athlete and coach." He is truly a legend in the history of the great game of football.

On behalf of the justifiably proud community and the millions of Americans who have thrilled to football as players and spectators, and with special thanks to Alan Manchester, Village of Springville trustee who has dedicated so much time and energy to Pop's memory, I ask my colleauges to join me in saluting this great American.•

Best wishes— Jack Kemp

To honor the memory of "Pop" Warner, a number of initiatives were undertaken to make people aware of his accomplishments, culminating in the issue of his own US postage stamp.

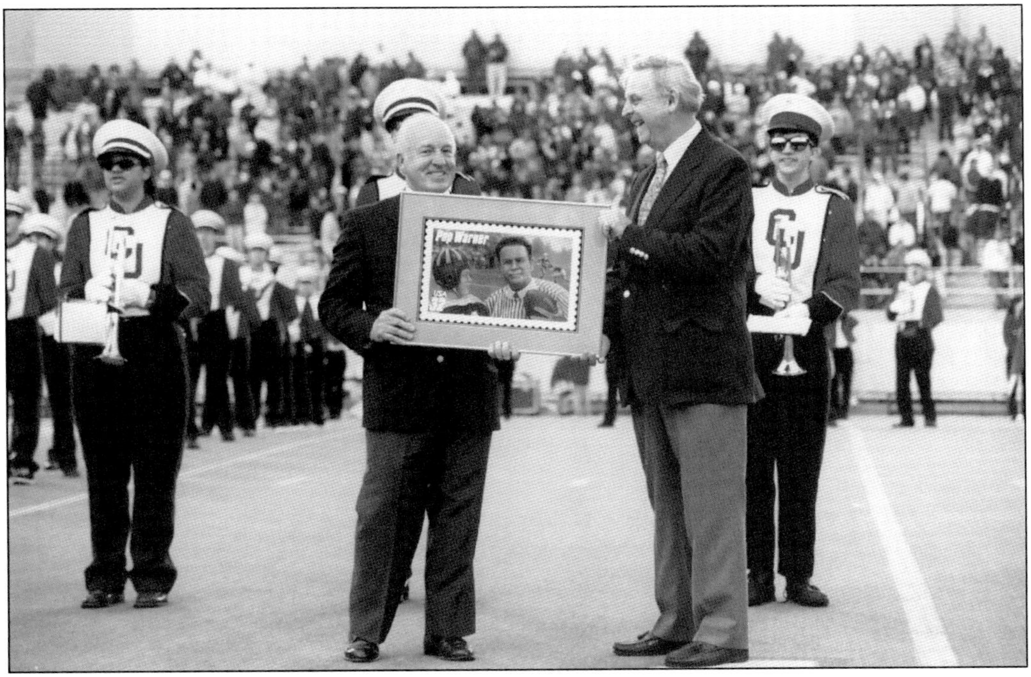

Coauthor Alan V. Manchester (right), Griffith Institute, 1956, Cornell University, 1960, receives a replica Warner stamp from Ithaca postmaster Edward Gatch on behalf of Cornell University at the Princeton game on September 20, 1997. (Courtesy of David Wohlhueter, Sports information director, Cornell University.).

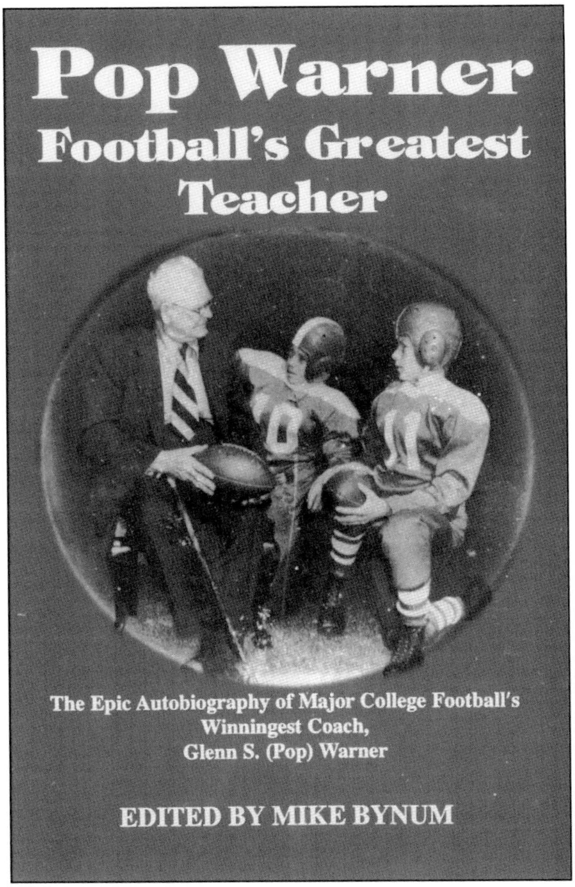

When he retired in 1938 after 44 years on the sidelines, Warner's win-loss-tie record was 312-104-32. This mark stood until 1946 and was broken by Amos Alonzo Stagg, Paul "Bear" Bryant, and a select group of others. Mike Bynum, in reviewing "Pop's" achievements, discovered that Warner dual-coached in the years 1895–1899, accumulating wins from two teams at the same time. Pop's updated totals are 341-118-33.

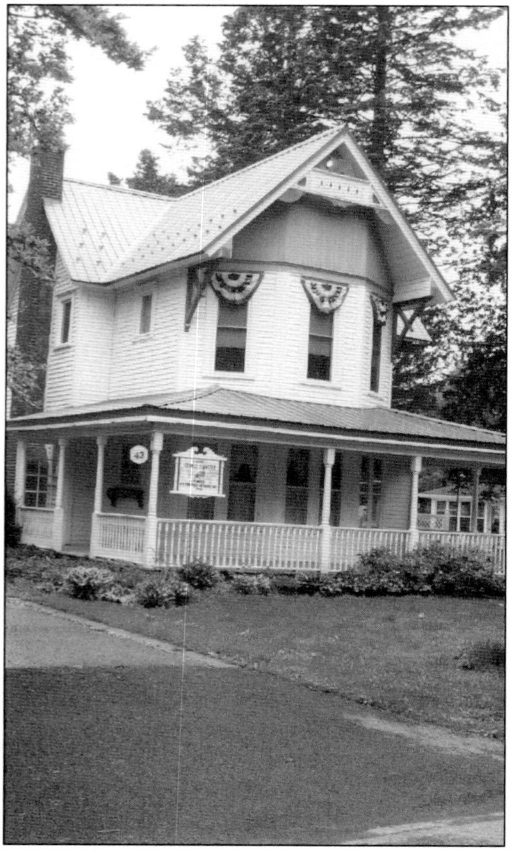

This is the East Avenue home where George N. Schuster (1873–1972) spent his final years and was seen clearing snow from his driveway in his 98th year. In 1908, he raced his Thomas Flyer automobile victoriously into Paris, winning the Around the World Auto Race, which spanned 22,000 miles from New York to Paris in 169 days. His remains, at Maplewood Cemetery, are marked by a memorial where several ceremonies honoring the great man have taken place. When driving in Russia in the 24-hour-a-day, nonstop race, the relief driver sleeping in the front passenger seat would often fall out of the car. The solution was to strap him in, thereby inventing the automobile seatbelt. Once, when stranded at Lake Baikal with a leaking transmission, Schuster purchased 40 pounds of Vaseline to replace the lubricant he had lost. During his time abroad, his wife Rose wrote him a letter, addressing it, "George Schuster, World," and it was delivered. In addition to winter challenges like snow and the lack of roads, hundreds of pounds of mud accumulated on his chassis, necessitating stops at fire stations to hose down the mud, resulting in what many contend was the first car wash.

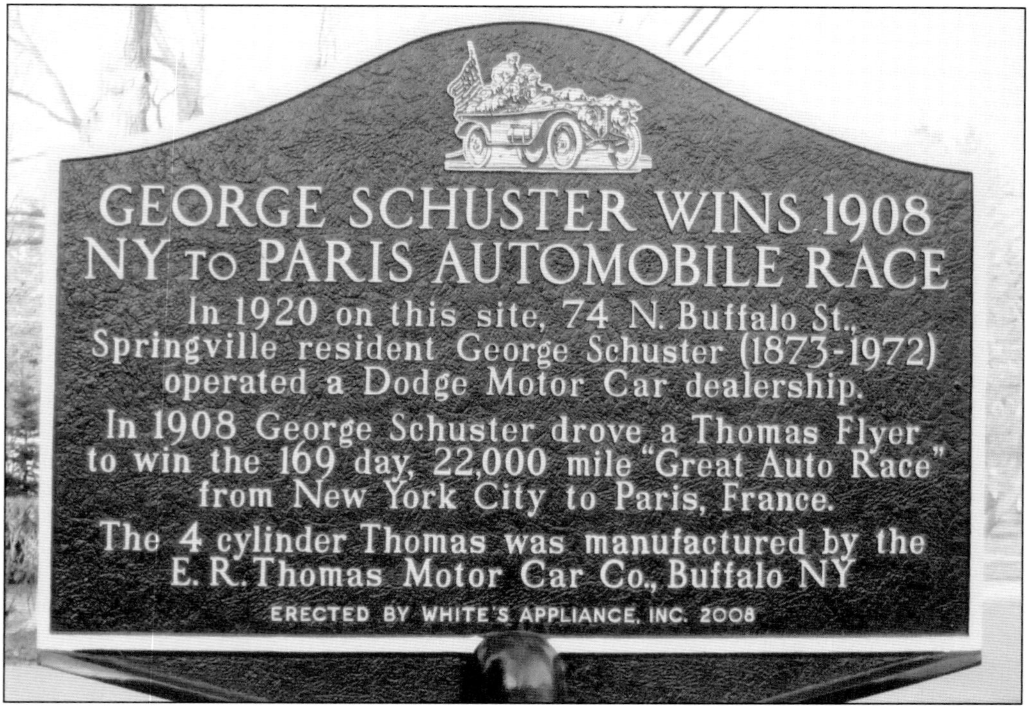

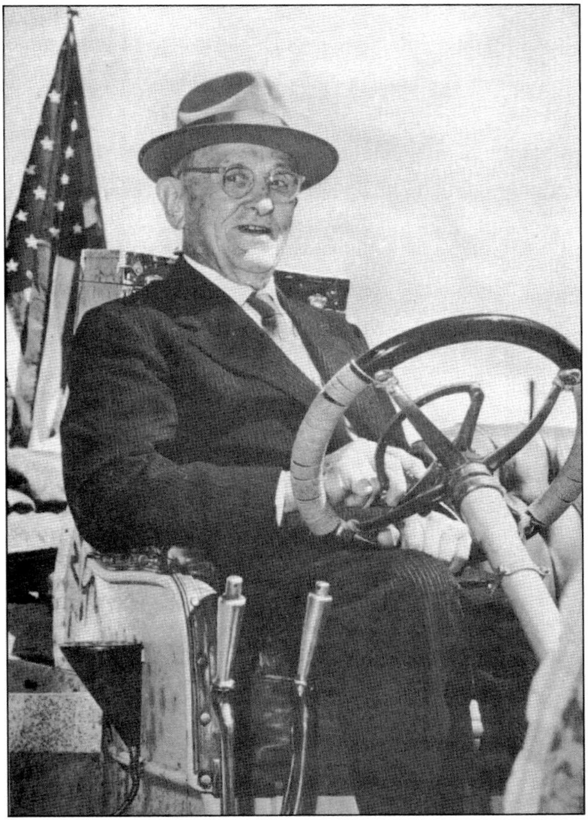

When he moved to Springville, Schuster operated a Dodge automobile dealership at the corner of North Buffalo and Church Streets. He is seen here at the wheel of the restored Thomas Flyer in 1964, fifty-six years after he drove it into Paris.

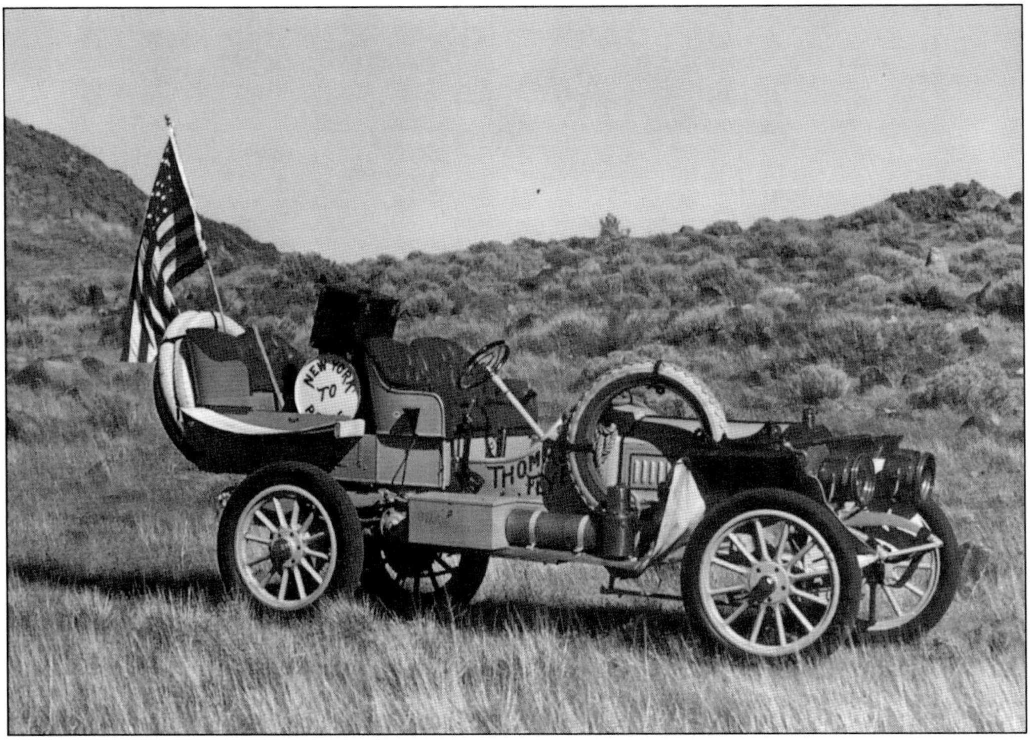

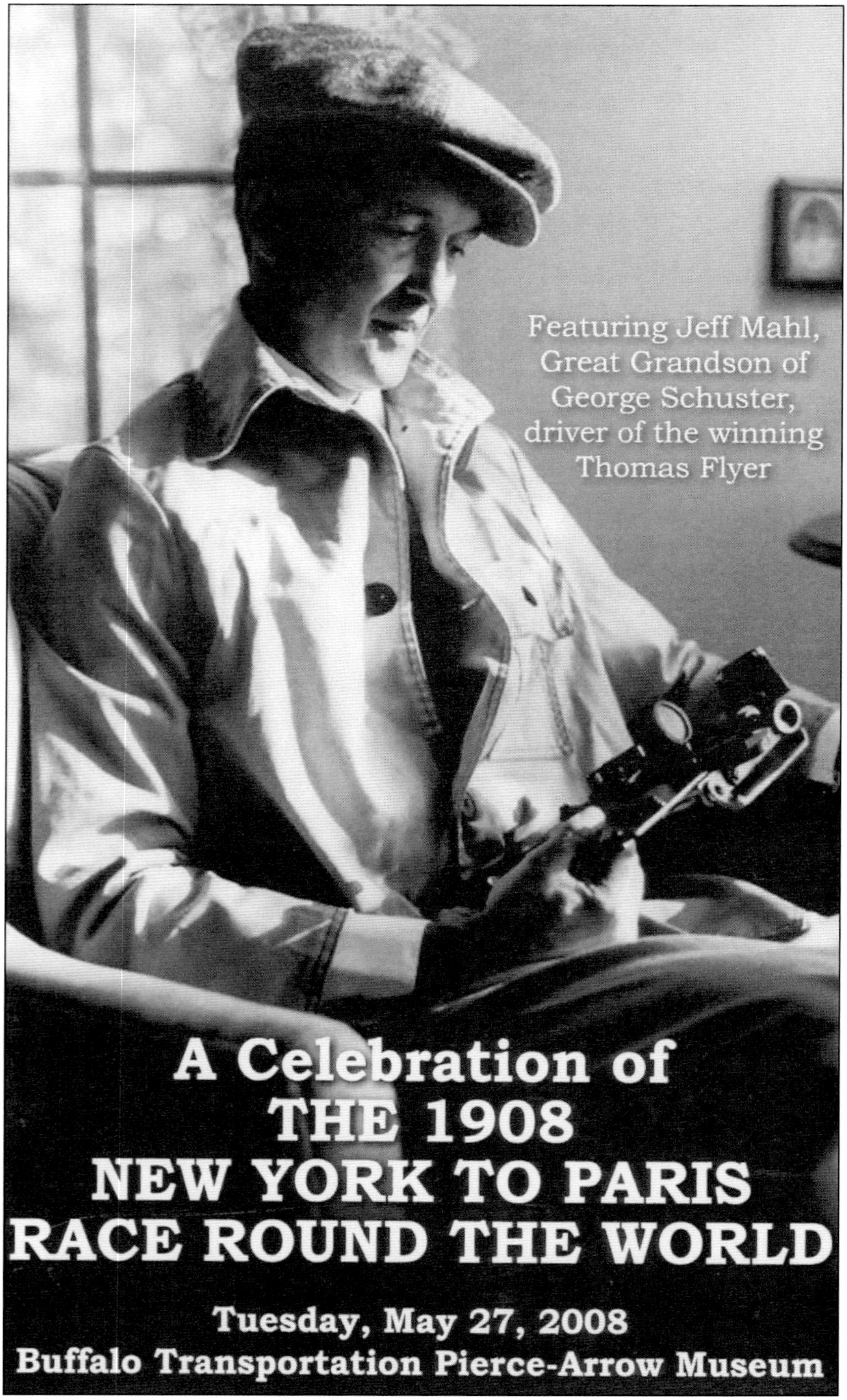

Jeff Mahl made first-person portrayal presentations of George Schuster, his great-grandfather, to audiences in several cities, including Springville; Buffalo; Hershey, Pennsylvania; and Reno, Nevada.

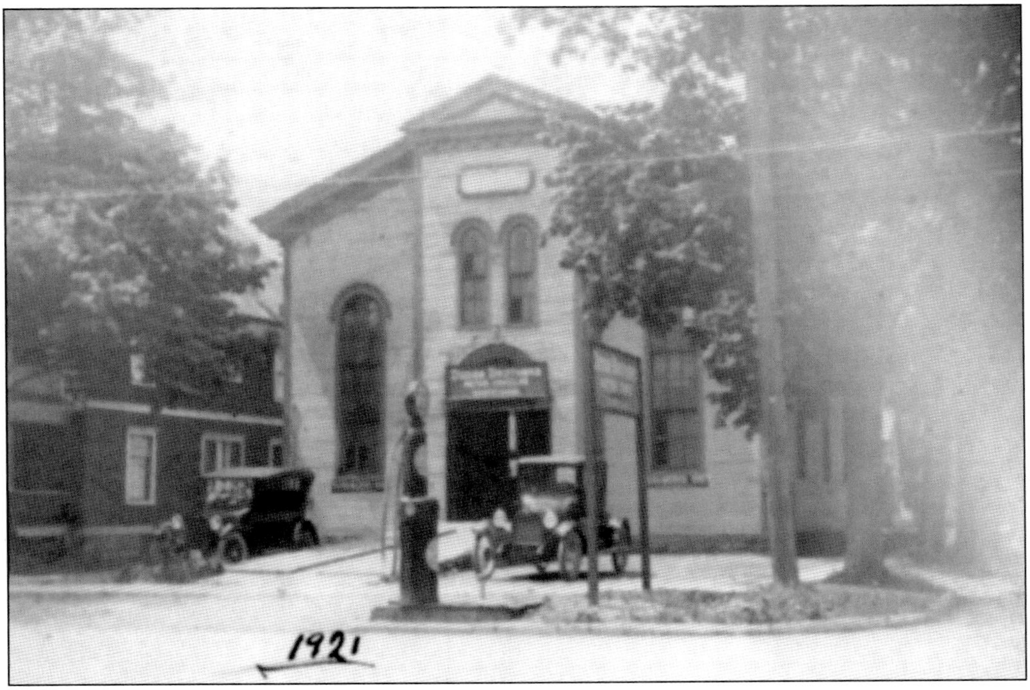

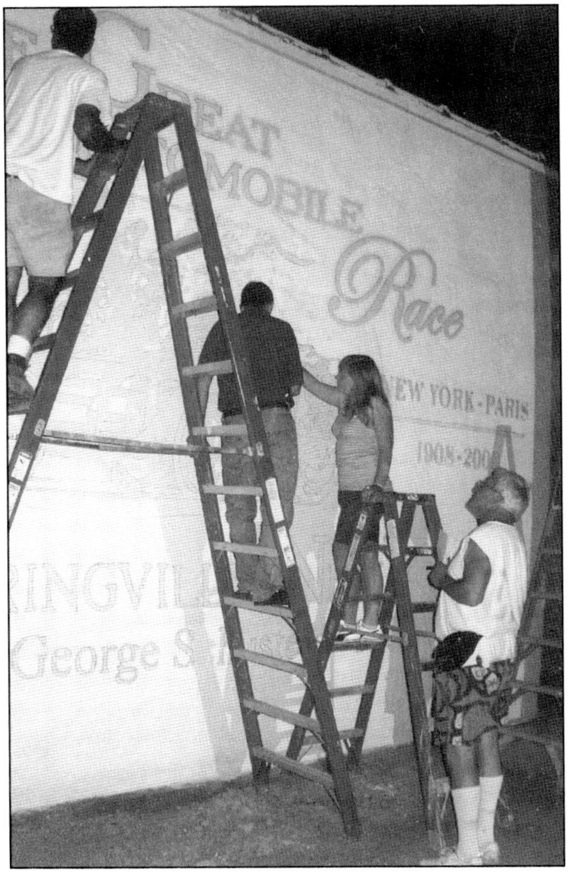

The Schuster Garage stood on North Buffalo and Church Streets, housed in the old First Baptist church from 1921 to 1936. It was later acquired by Richard Gentner and used as an automobile repair and equipment building shop named Dick's Service. The structure burned in 1941, and Gentner immediately offered the vacant lot to his neighbor, Dr. John Kerr, who responded, "No thank you!" Not giving up, Gentner contacted builder Raymond Schweikert and had him park a truckload of lumber at the site. When Kerr asked what was going on, Gentner replied, "We're building a new garage." Kerr exclaimed, "I'll buy the lot!" and then built the brick home found there today. From left to right, Joel Maul, Jeff Mahl, and Sarah Owen work on this commemorative banner under the watchful eye of Thomas Irish, the artist who, over several days, painted in the details.

WORLD RACE 2011
New York to Paris

http://worldrace2011.com

You are invited to a reception to welcome the drivers and crews of the
World Race 2011 - New York to Paris

Sponsored by the Concord Historical Society, this reception will be held 9:30 – 10:15 AM on Friday April 15, 2011 at the Concord Mercantile, 17 Franklin St. Springville, NY.

As these drivers begin their attempt to retrace the 1908 NY to Paris Race, they will be stopping in Springville to honor the 1908 race winner, George Schuster.

After the reception at the Mercantile, the cars and drivers will proceed to Maplewood Cemetery to place American Flags on Schuster's gravesite at 10:30 AM.

They will then leave Springville, continuing on their quest to arrive in Paris France on July 21.

Questions: Don Orton 592-4090
or Joel Maul 592-4766

An RSVP to the Concord Historical Society, by April 10, 2011 would be appreciated.

World Race 2011 was an offshoot of the plan to retrace the Around the World Auto Race 100 years later in 2008, which was cancelled because of destructive earthquakes in China and revocation of travel documents. The second day of the 2011 venture was celebrated in Springville with a reception for drivers and the public.

Following a visit to the former Schuster Home, the historical marker on North Buffalo Street, and Schuster's final resting place at Maplewood Cemetery, each driver signed this document identifying his vehicle. The document was then carried around the world by Jeff Mahl, who returned it to the Concord Historical Society for display.

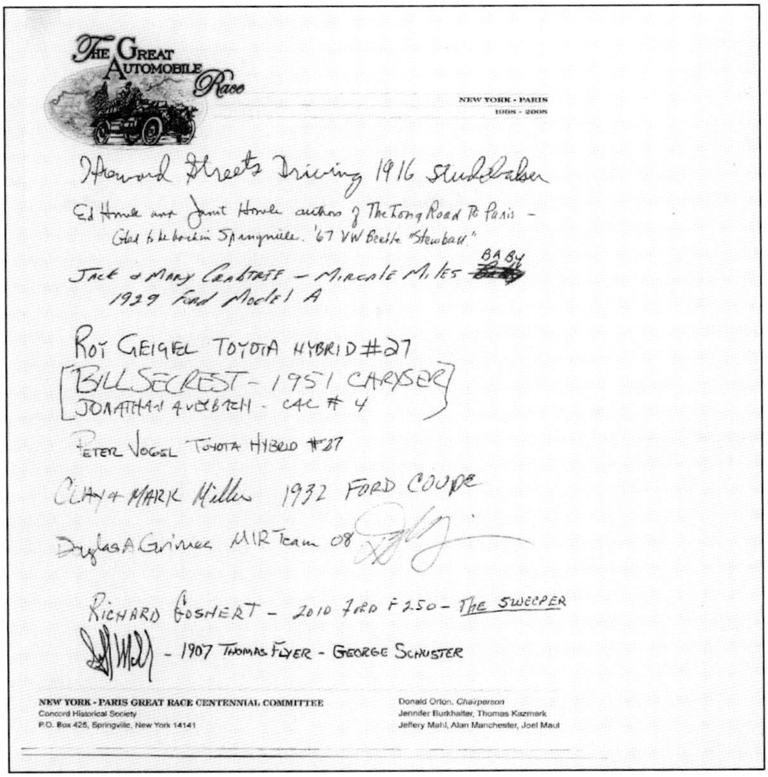
The Great Automobile Race
NEW YORK - PARIS
1908 - 2008

Howard Streets Driving 1916 Studebaker
Ed Howle and Janet Howle authors of The Long Road To Paris - Glad to be back in Springville. '67 VW Beetle "Stewball"
Jack & Mary Crabtree — Miracle Miles BABY
1929 Ford Model A
Roy Geigel Toyota Hybrid #27
[Bill Secrest - 1951 Chrysler
Jonathan Auerbach - Car # 4]
Peter Vogel Toyota Hybrid #27
Clay & Mark Miller 1932 Ford Coupe
Douglas A Grimes MIR Team 08
Richard Goshert - 2010 Ford F250 - The Sweeper
- 1907 Thomas Flyer - George Schuster

NEW YORK - PARIS GREAT RACE CENTENNIAL COMMITTEE
Concord Historical Society
P.O. Box 425, Springville, New York 14141

Donald Orton, *Chairperson*
Jennifer Burkhalter, Thomas Kazmark
Jeffery Mahl, Alan Manchester, Joel Maul

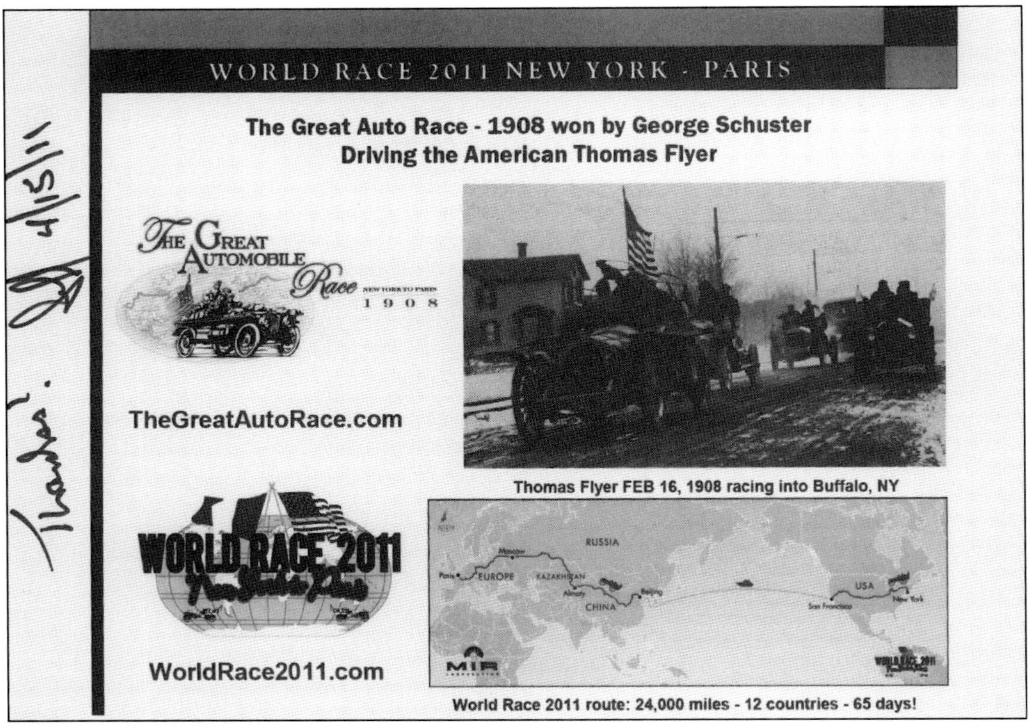

This courtesy-appreciation card was distributed by Jeff Mahl during his trip around the world during World Race 2011. The route was very similar to the one taken by George Schuster in 1908.

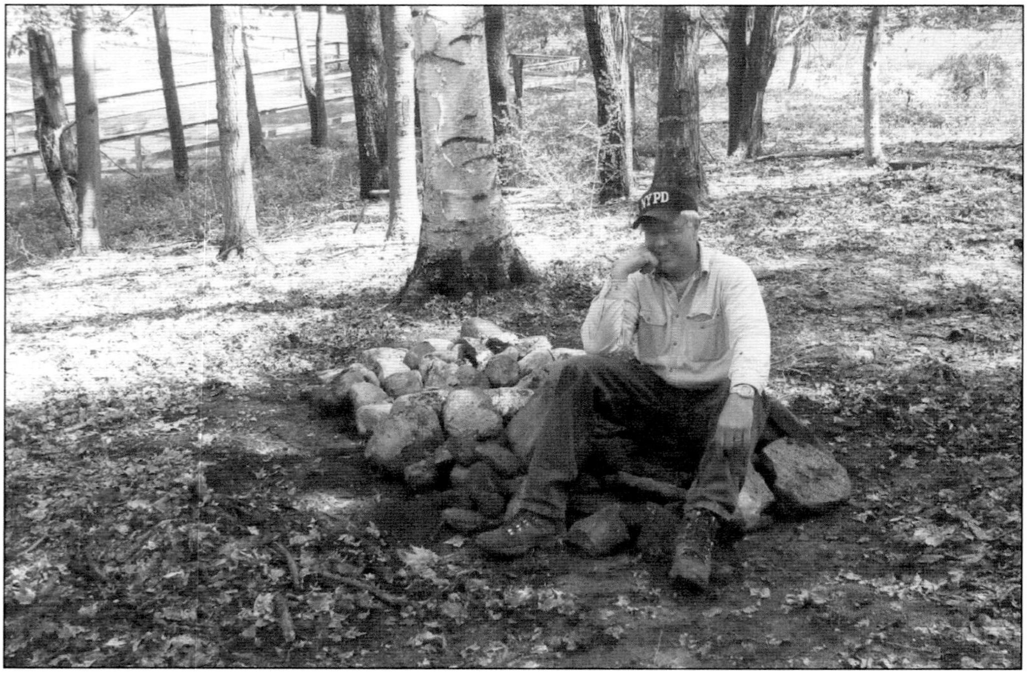

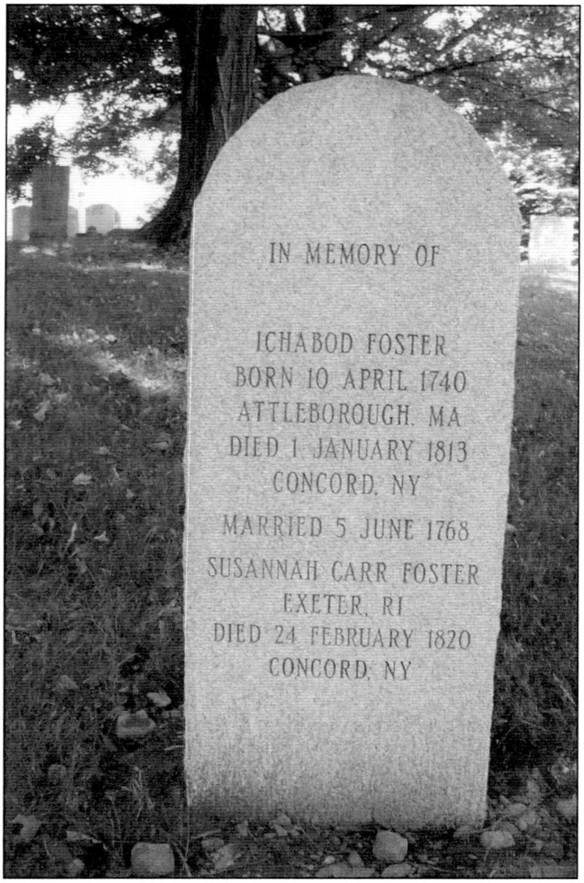

David C. Batterson, now the Village of Springville/Town of Concord historian (and coauthor of this book), took part in a five-hour exploratory dig crew in 2005. The dig was inspired by the historian at the time, Margaret Mayerat, and Julie Foster Van Camp, a descendant of Ichabod Foster (1740–1813). Joining in on the effort were John H. Conlin, editor of *Western New York Heritage Magazine*, and a number of volunteers. Van Camp had acquired her ancestor's diary covering the period from 1785 to his death on January 1, 1813. She had retraced his steps from Whiting, Vermont, to Willink (now Concord). Careful removal of the mounds near Springville-Boston and Genesee Roads and cautious excavation yielded no artifacts nearly two centuries later, and they were respectfully returned to the original positions. On September 10, 2005, Julie Foster Van Camp, schoolchildren, and society members dedicated a memorial to Foster in the pioneer section of Fairview Cemetery. (Left, courtesy of Kyle Manchester.)

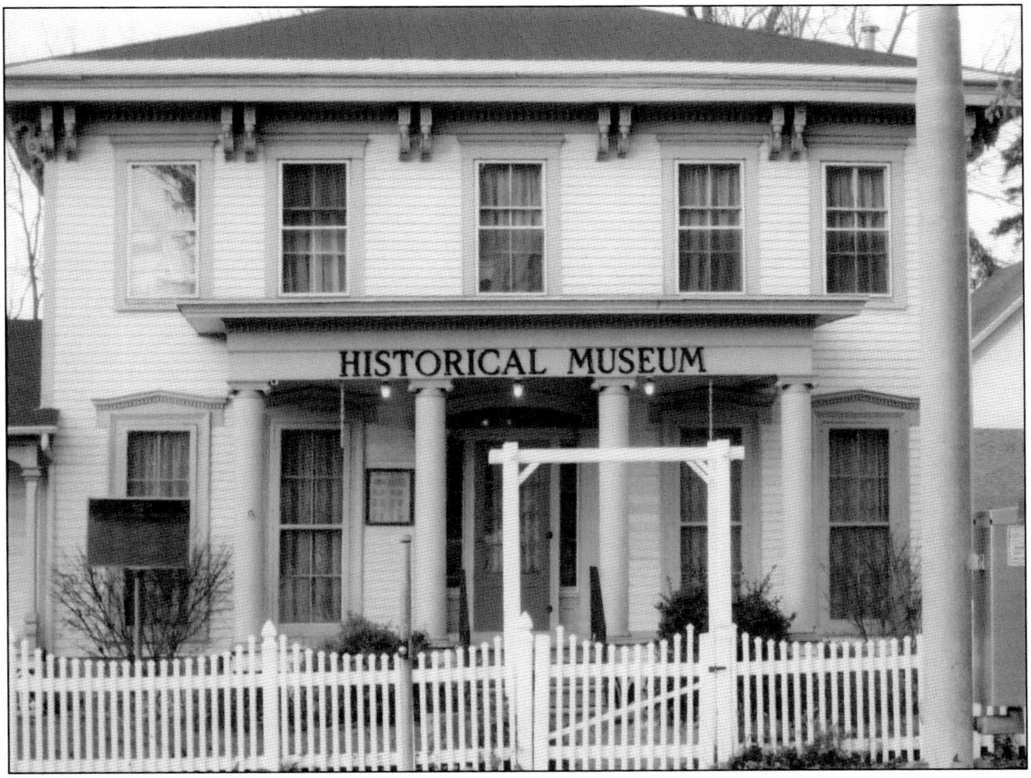

The historical museum, a gift from "Pop" Warner to house his Native American artifact collection and area history items, is located at the corner of Main and Franklin Streets. The first floor and carriage house have a variety of displays. The second-floor archival area will be moved to the second floor of the new mercantile building for better access by the curator. The Lucy Bensley Center at 23 North Buffalo Street, a former Universalist church given to the Town of Concord for public use, houses the Springville Area Chamber of Commerce and the Concord Historical Society's extensive historical and genealogical library. The space also holds public meetings, and plans are being made to open the great ceiling to once again expose the beautiful stained glass window.

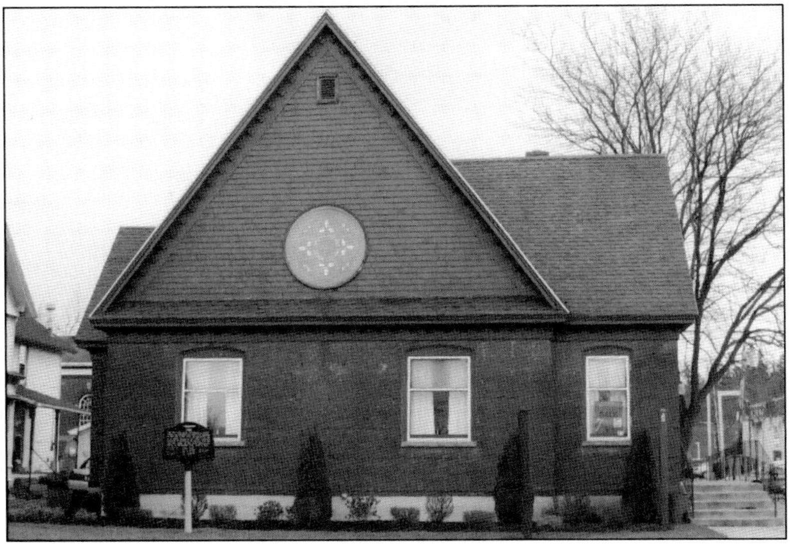

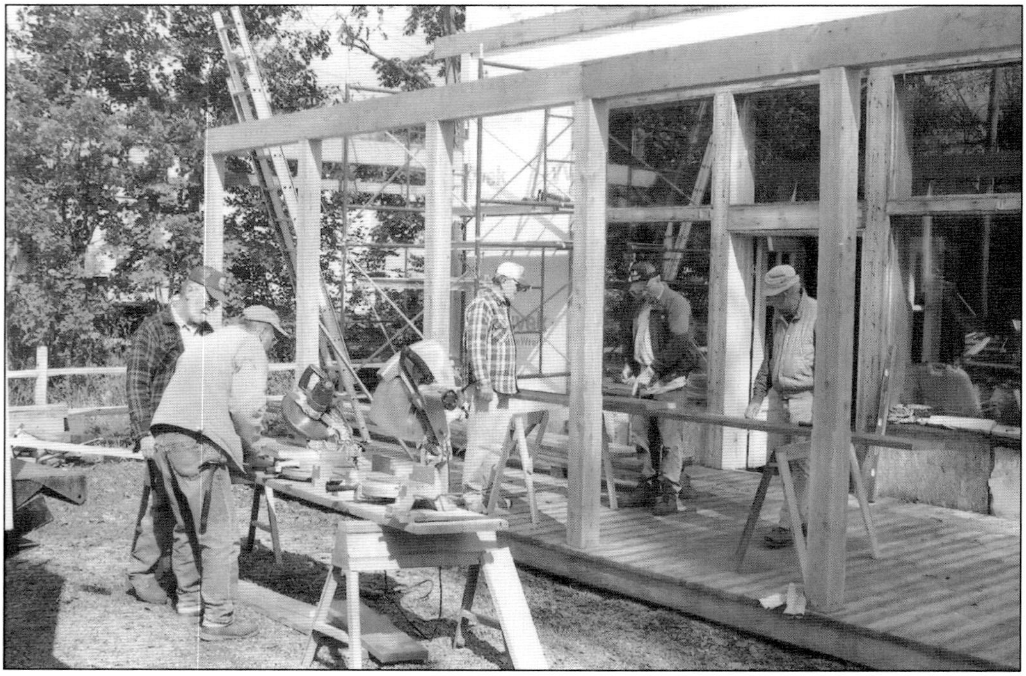

On the scaffolding, trustee Joel Maul frames the post office display unit. Several volunteers are seen building the great wraparound porch of the Mercantile.

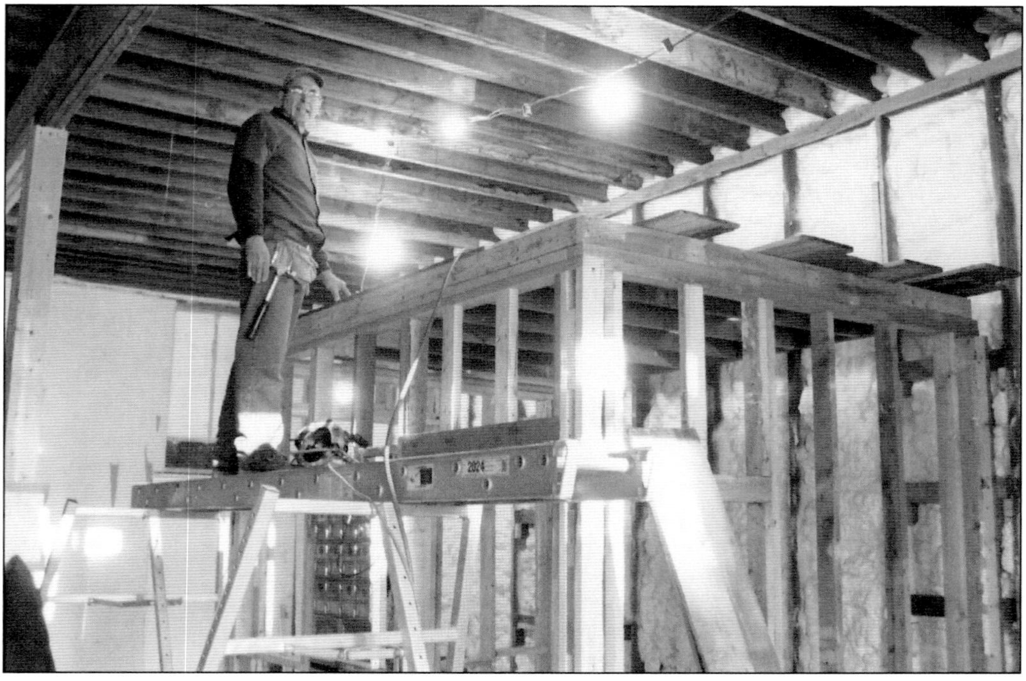

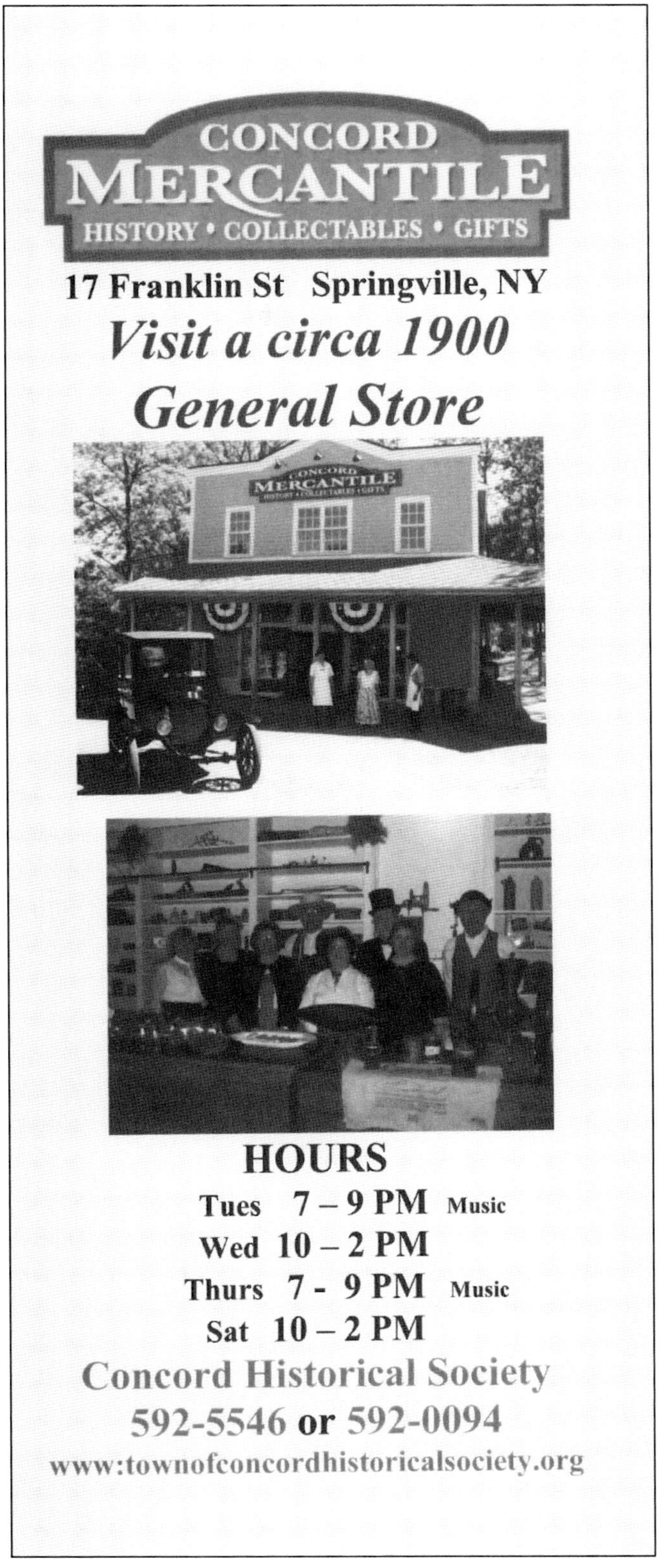

The Mercantile is stocked with authentic period merchandise for viewing and a variety of craft and historical items for sale. Regular hours and a warm reception greet all who pass through its doors. It also serves as a community meeting place and tour bus stop.

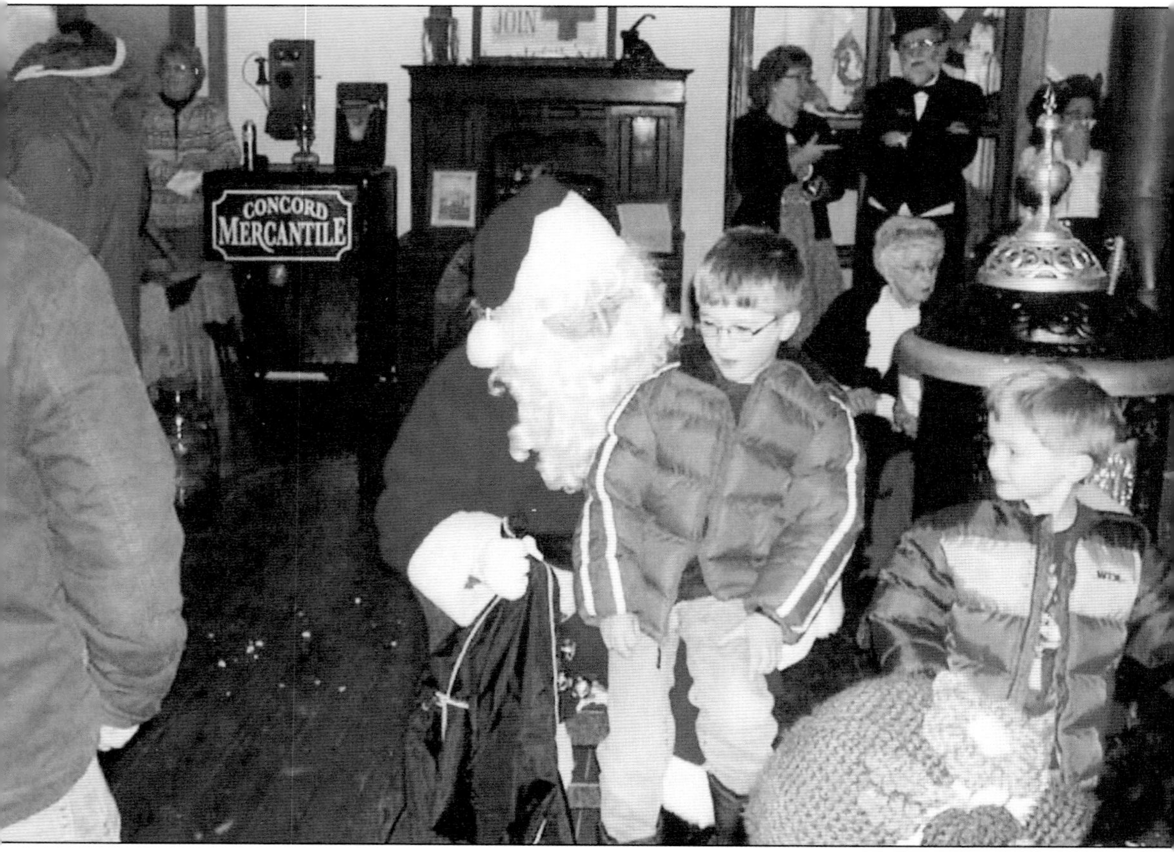

Concord Country Christmas was celebrated at the new Concord Mercantile with Santa, children, reindeer, and old-fashioned surroundings, like the potbelly stove to the right.

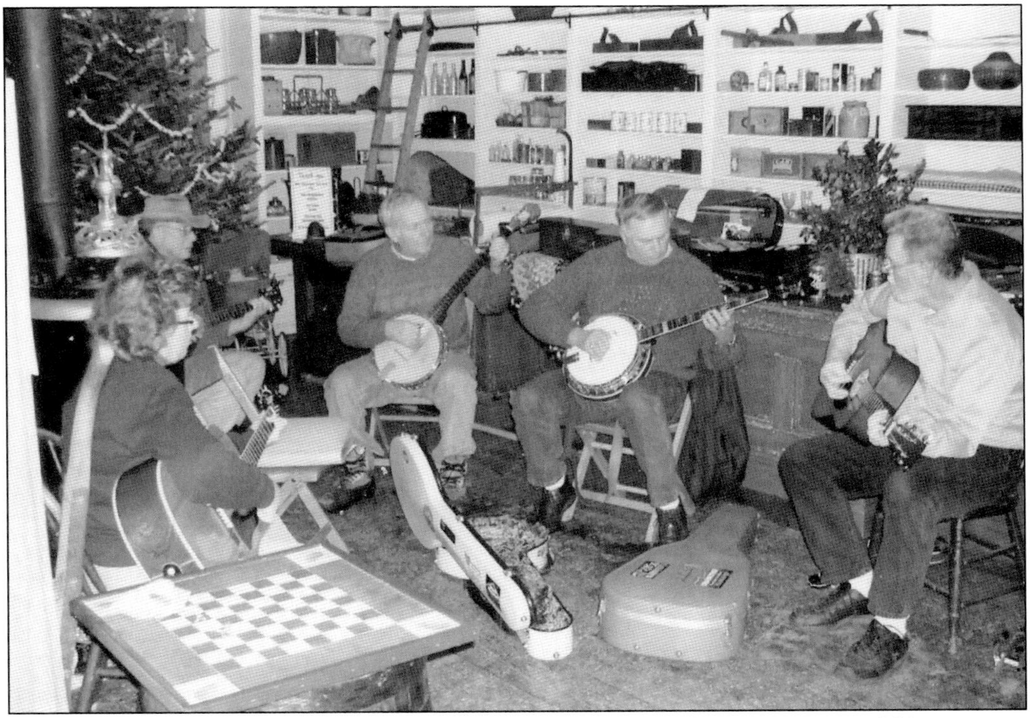

An informal group of musicians, the Middle Road Misfits, performs country and bluegrass on Tuesday evenings with 12 to 18 participants. Another group plays on Thursday nights; its specialty is gospel and country.

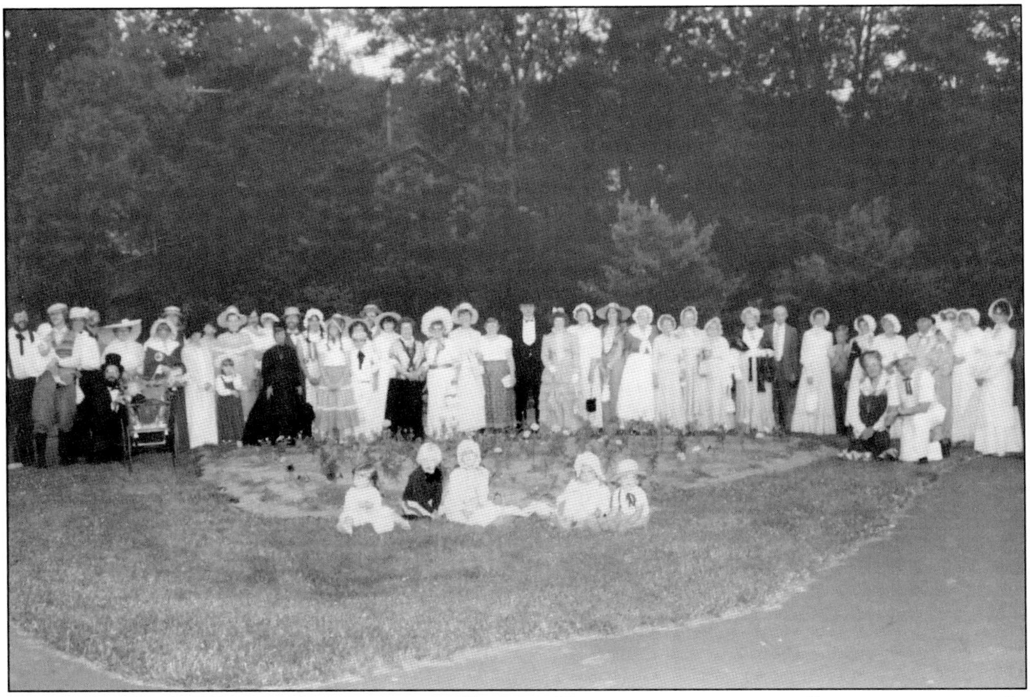

While this looks like a gathering from well over 100 years ago, it is actually just an extremely large group dressed for Springville's sesquicentennial celebration in 1984.

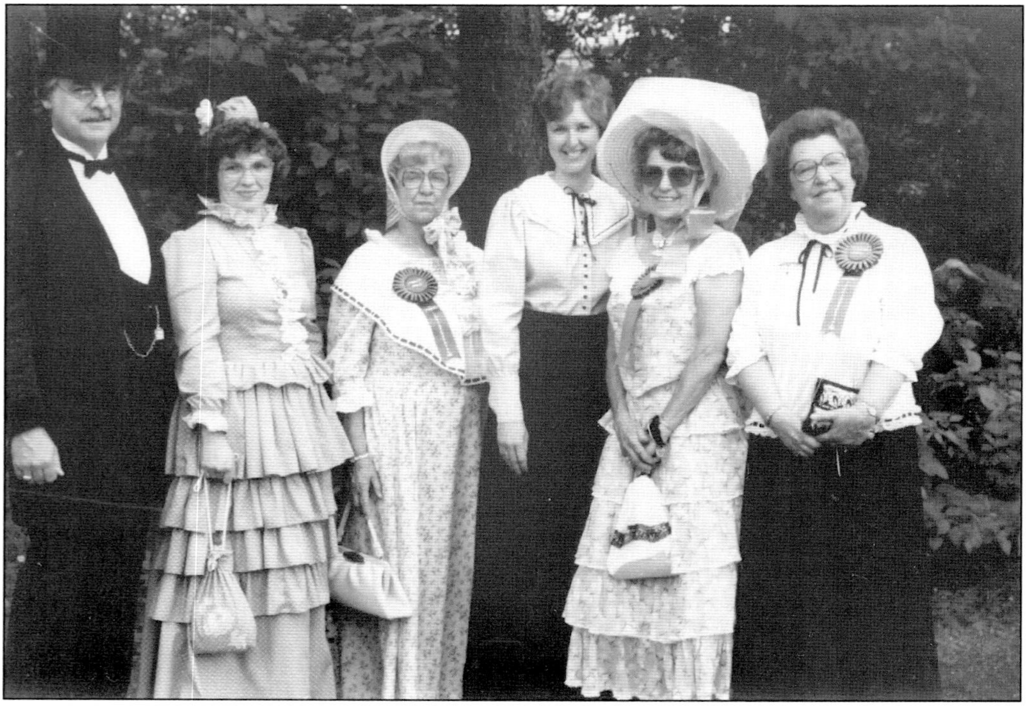

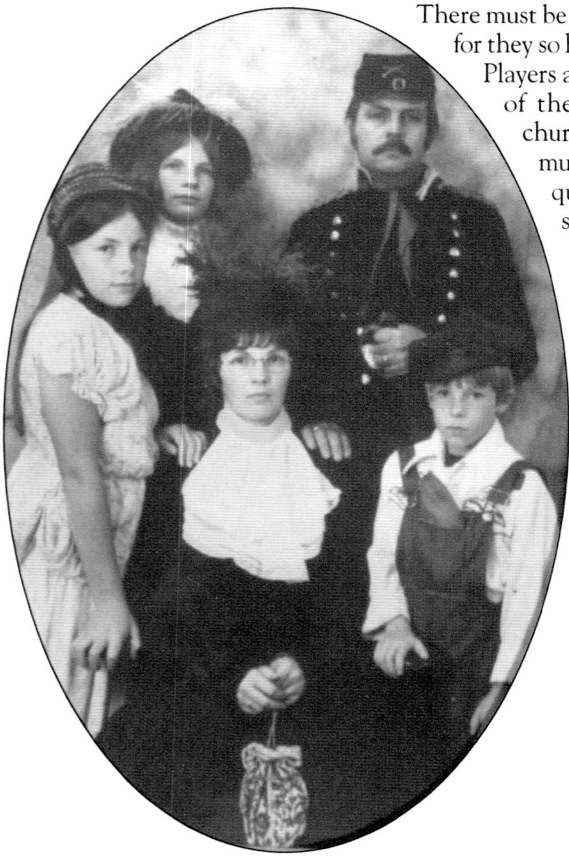

There must be thespian genes in the people of Springville, for they so heartily applaud and support the Springville Players and their frequent productions on the stage of their theater building, the former Baptist church. At the high school auditorium, student musicals and concerts are also of exceptional quality. Celebrations, often historic and sponsored by the Concord Historical Society, bring out spectators and participants in vintage costume.

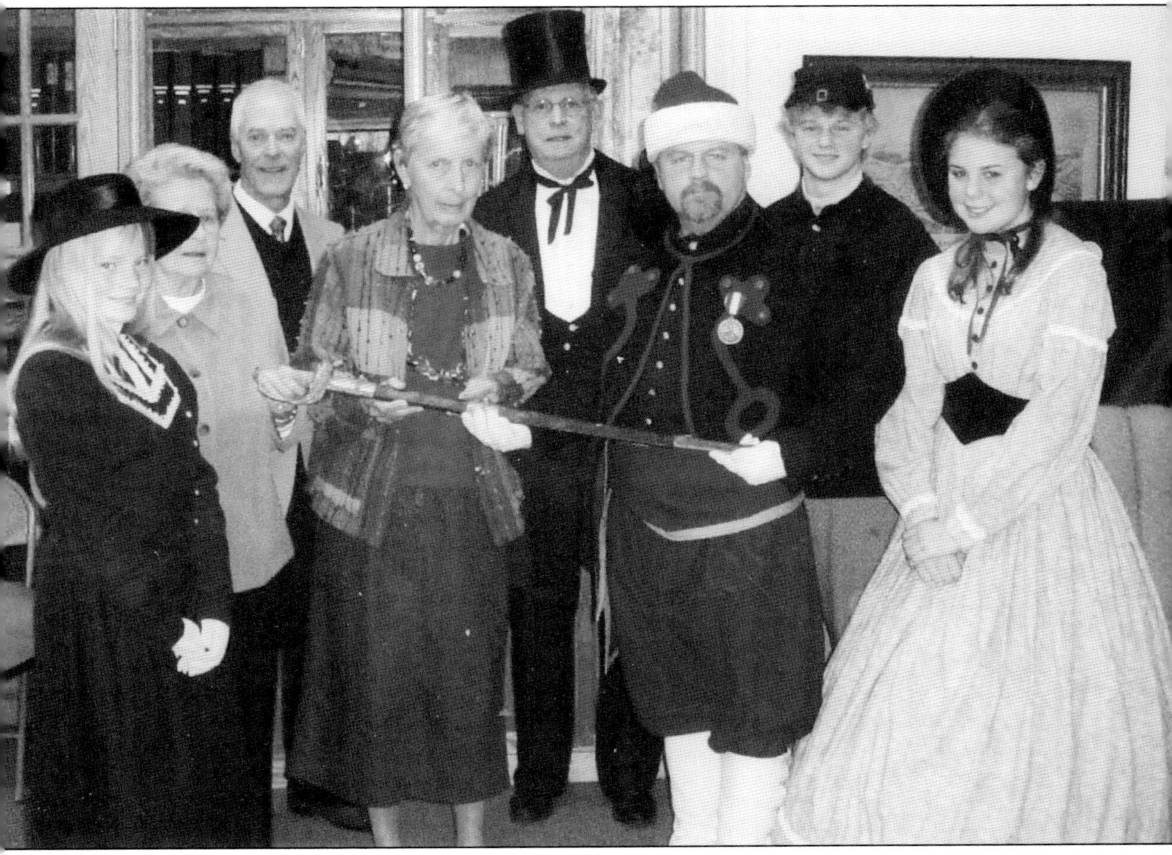

Carlos Richmond served in the Civil War and died in 1865 at the age of 26. In the 1890s, at the time of the death of Richmond's parents, Burt Chaffee built the Masonic hall on top of the building next to his Main Street mill. In 1955, Clarence Wohlhueter found Richmond's sword in a wall of that building and gave it to his daughter, Delores, who preserved it before presenting it to the Concord Historical Society. In October 2005, Civil War reenactor John Baronich led the society in a colorful and dignified ceremony of sword transfer. Participants are, from left to right: Sarah Owen, Gloria Neff, Donald Orton, Delores Wohlhueter-Pleuthner, Alan V. Manchester, John Baronich, Michael Baronich, and Emily Baronich.

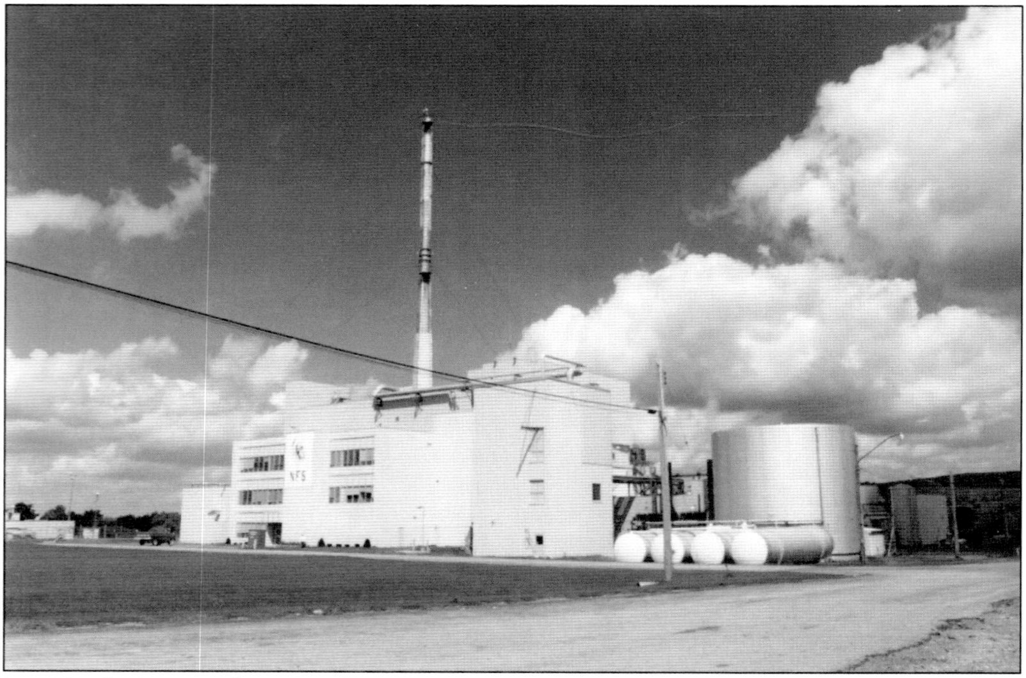

In 1961, the New York State Office of Atomic Development predicted that Western New York was standing on the threshold of leadership in the atomic age. Ashford's nuclear fuel reprocessing and atomic waste storage facility (eventually privately owned by W.R. Grace & Co. and American Machine and Foundry Co.) spawned the Route 219 expressway and $50 million in satellite industry at the 220-acre compound on the 3,331-acre preserve. Two thousand two hundred pounds of uranium would be recovered daily and 19,000 barrels of waste buried per year. Government and business applauded, but skeptics objected, as did the 28 families and landowners who had to move out and watch their buildings for the most part be burned. After six years of operation, control of the facility returned to state and federal jurisdiction, and hundreds of millions of dollars have since been spent in cleanup and technology.

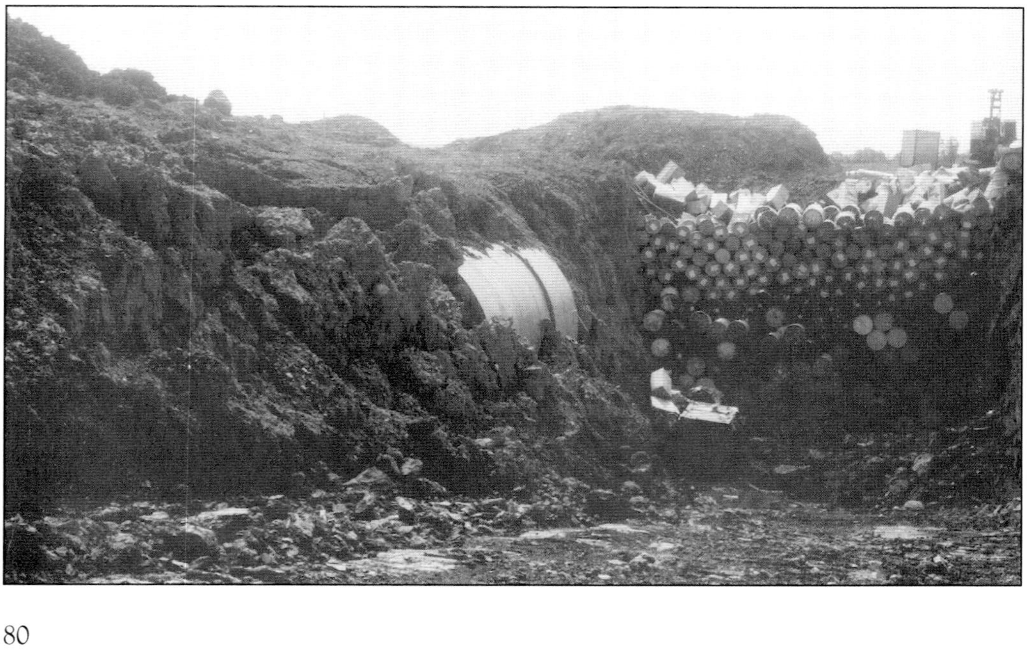

Drifted snow was 14 feet deep on Transit Line Road in 1977, and conventional plows were of no use on most roads in the "Blizzard of '77." The storm was the result of high winds blowing loose snow off frozen Lake Erie over a four-day period beginning on January 28. Photographs and accounts suggest that it was not any more severe than the "Storm of '47," referred to on page 33, in which a train stalled just a few yards north of the Springville station.

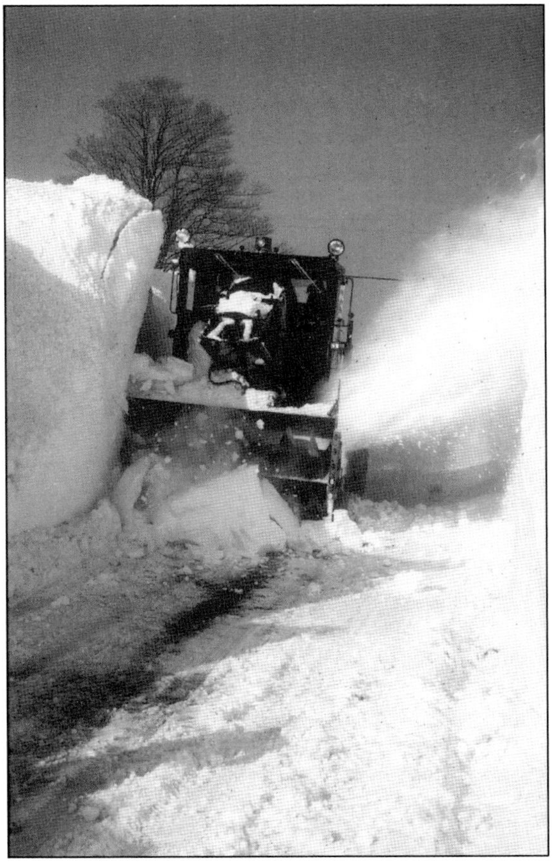

Years of work by the Route 219 Association, under the leadership of Arthur Benson and Robert Westfall, gained north–south designation over Route 16 interests for an expressway to connect Canada and Buffalo to southern markets. This improved the economy of the areas through which it passed. Ground-breaking ceremonies took place on October 21, 1978, when Benson and Westfall were joined by Gov. Hugh Carey, Supervisor Kenneth Barie, Mayor Paul Frank, and others. Three phases are now completed reaching to Peters Road in Cattaraugus County.

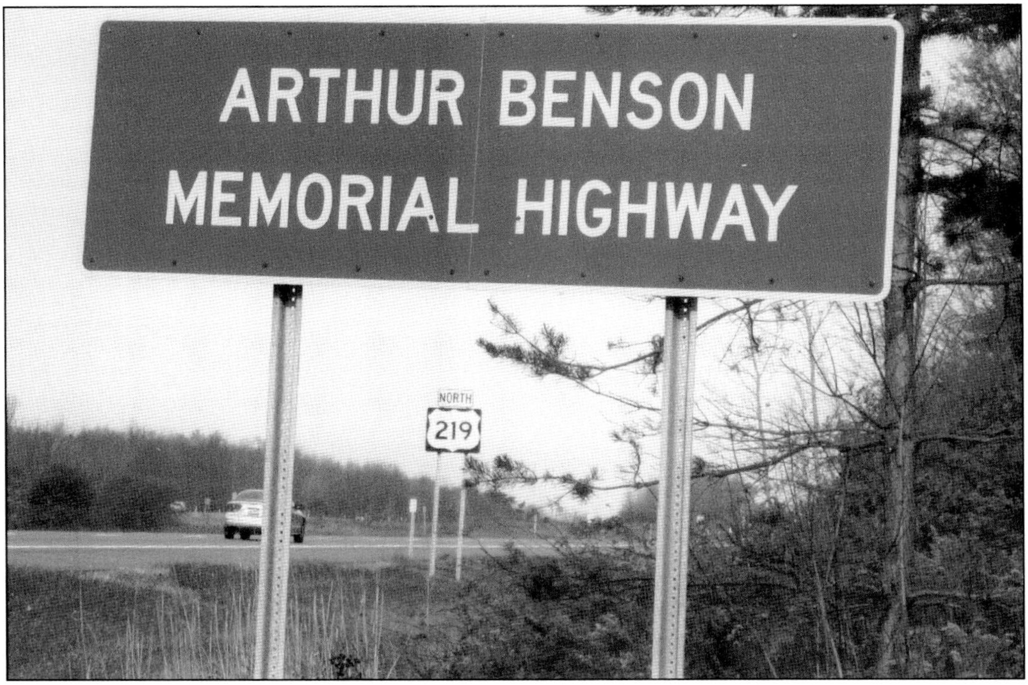

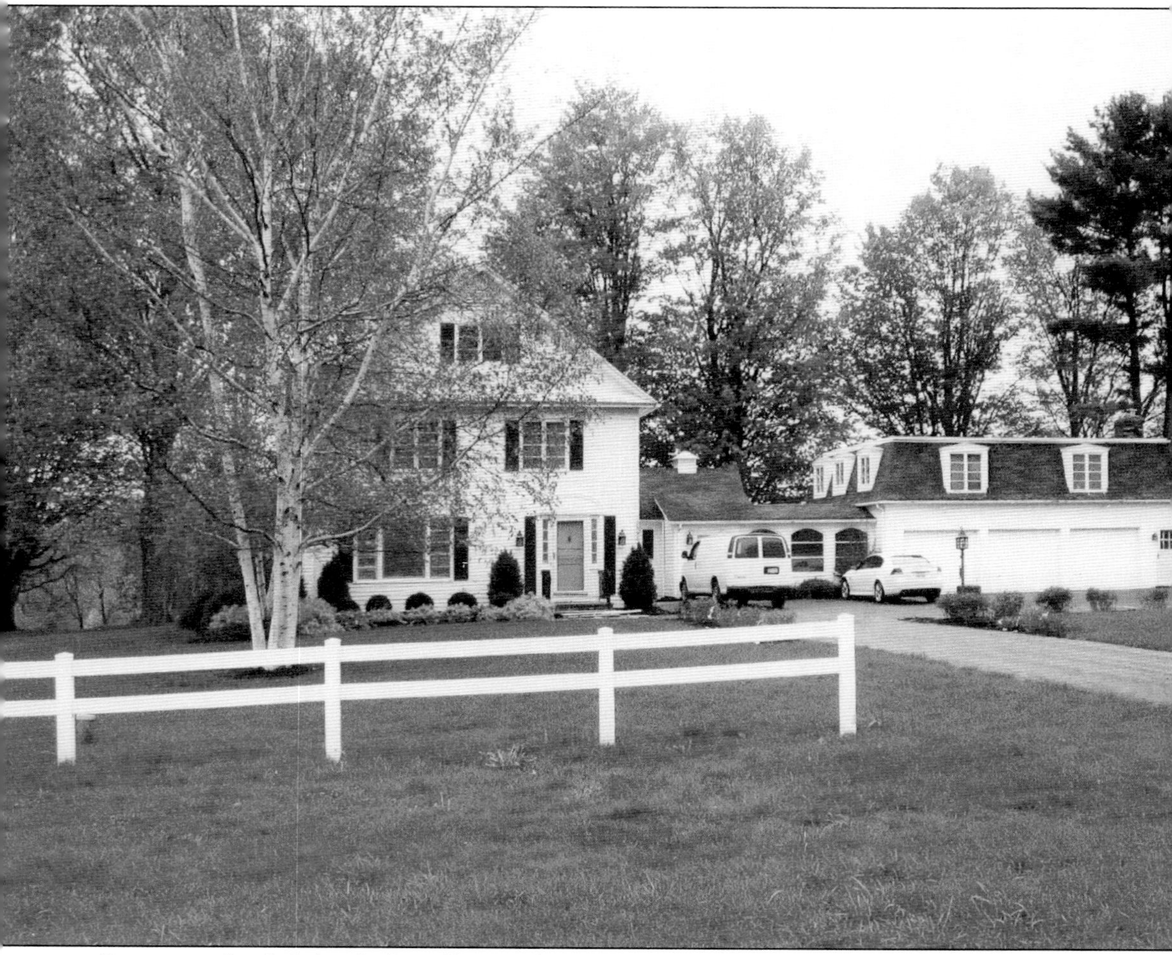

Songwriter Jacob Selig "Jack" Yellen was born in Poland in 1892 and lived with his wife, Lucille Hodgeman Yellen, on Mortons Corners Road from 1944 until his death in 1991. Yellen is remembered for writing "Happy Days Are Here Again," "Ain't She Sweet," "Hard Hearted Hannah," and hundreds of other titles including scores for Broadway productions and Hollywood films. Lucille Yellen, known as Lucille Day on stage, was a dancer and choreographer's assistant in musicals in the 1930s and 1940s, including *The Wizard of Oz*. Their show dogs attracted at least one prominent buyer, comedian Jack Benny, to their home. Lucille said that Paul McCartney visited her home to secure the rights to "Ain't She Sweet." Frederick Hofmann remembers when, as a youth, he would listen in on party-line telephone calls to celebrities like Sophie Tucker. A former employee remembers being called to the telephone to listen in as Frank Sinatra sang "Happy Birthday" to Lucille. She was still in their home at the time of her death at 95 in 2010.

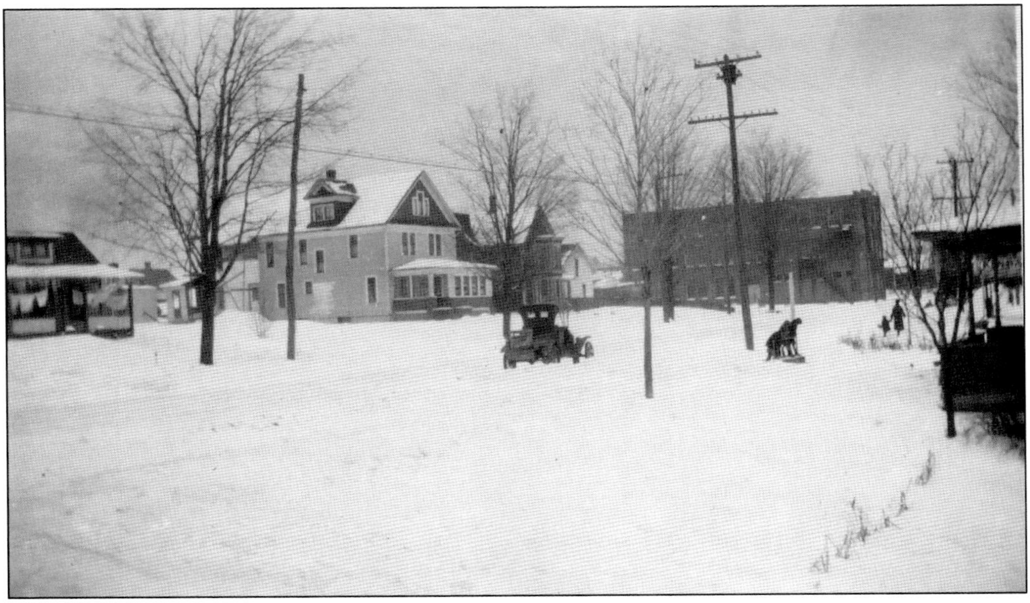

What looks like a late-1910s or early-1920s automobile is likely a Ford Model T. The block-like structure at center-right is the "Knife Works" building. The large building at center-left is now an apartment rental unit, and the empty lot to the left is now Root 39 Salon.

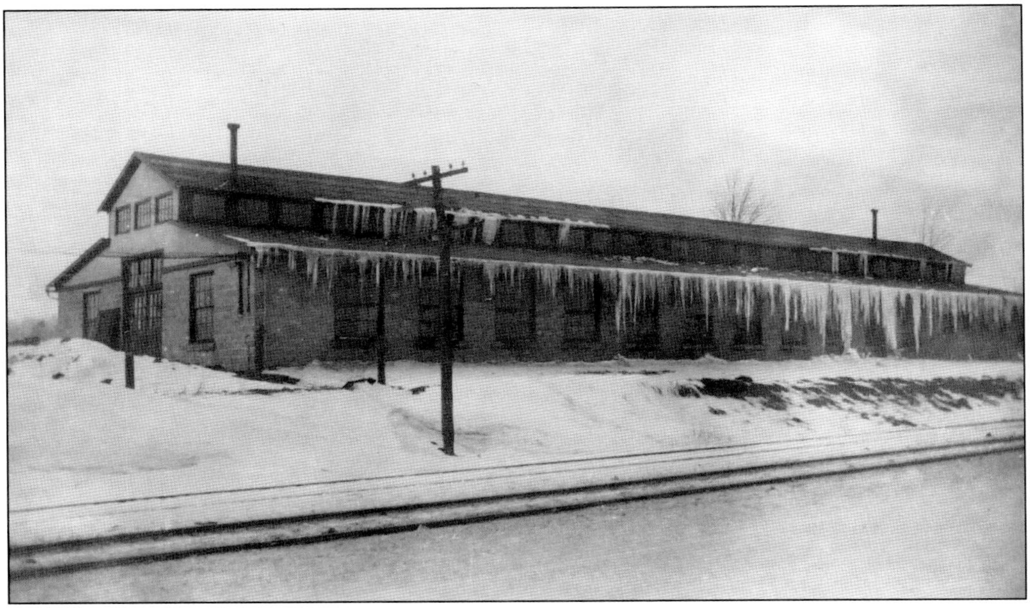

Peerless Winsmith, Inc., once called the "Pulley Works" Winsmith, has long had a product line of speed reducers, essentially a gearbox with a high-speed input shaft and a low speed output shaft. Among the thousands of applications for such a device are solar panel orientation drives and the bucking bronco at Gilley's Night Club in the movie *Urban Cowboy*.

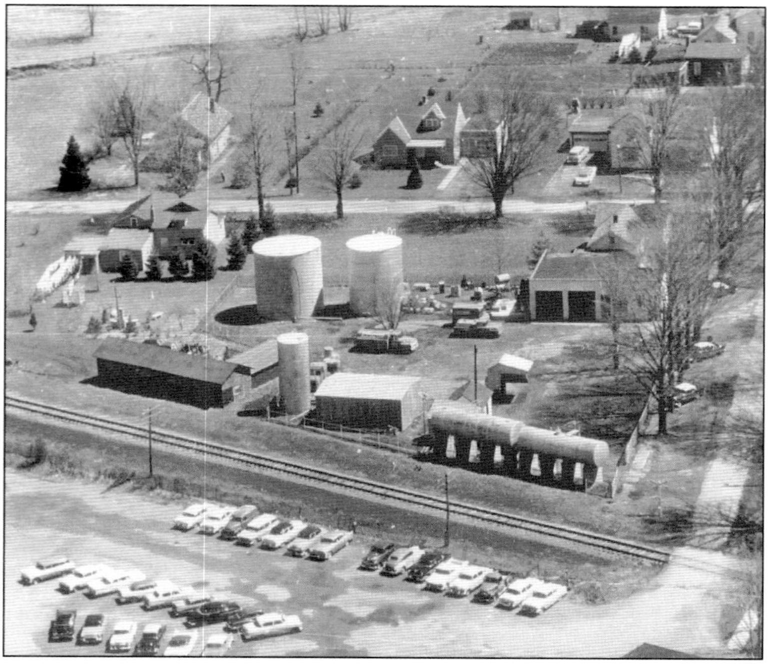

This view from about 1960 was taken looking east past the Peerless Winsmith parking lot, at the end of Eaton Street near Central Avenue, and Mahl Brothers Oil Company's fuel tank farm. Mahl's and Graff Motors on Mechanic Street were among the first to venture out to Cascade Drive, the temporary Route 219, which had less restricted space and more potential business traffic.

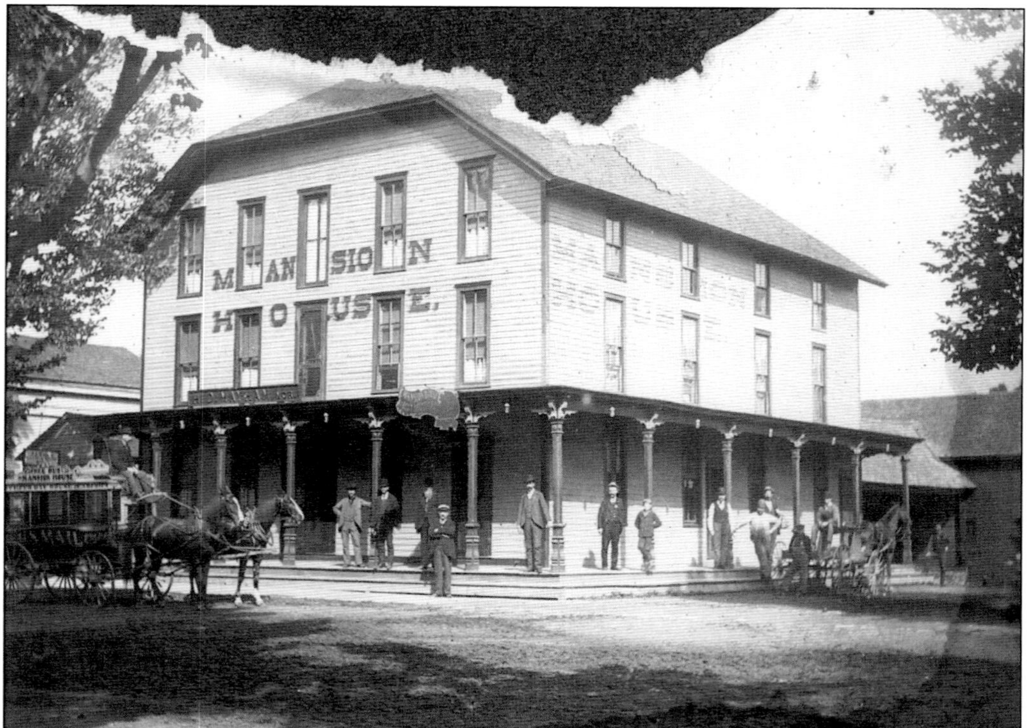

Those who know Springville will recognize the roof design and three-story construction of this building. Most recently the Springville Hotel, it was called Mansion House when this photograph was taken around 1885. Notice the mail-carrying stagecoach and free bus to the new BR&P Depot. After its Mansion House days, it was called the International Hotel in the early 1900s.

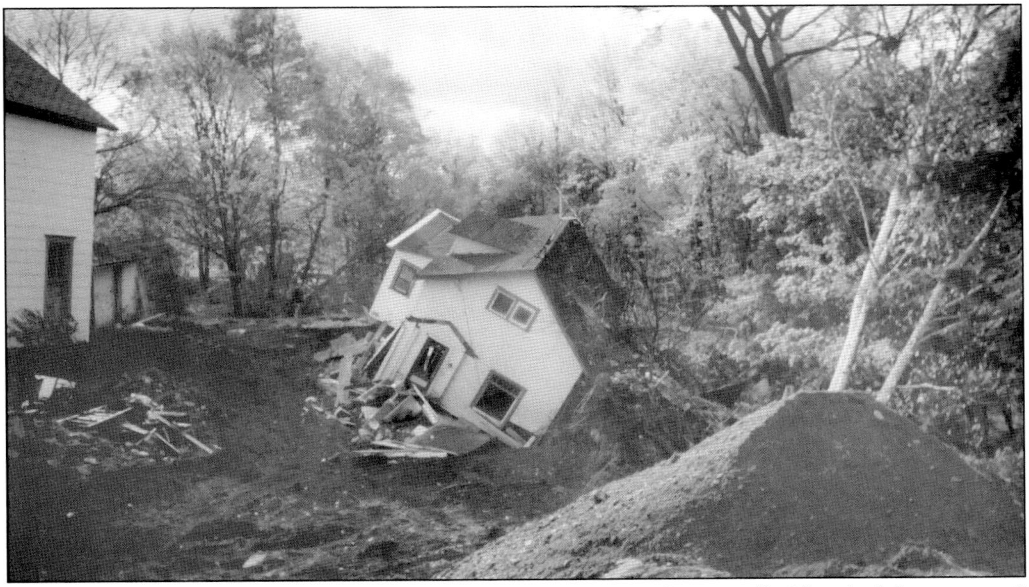

This was a Woodward Avenue casualty of the June 26, 1998, Springville "flood of the century," when unusual atmospheric conditions that only a meteorologist would understand dropped about five inches of rain in about an hour that Friday morning. Flash flooding took place, and the Trout Pond filled until it overflowed the railroad tracks at its edge. The roadbed below was damaged, a major factor in the abandonment of the line. The far greater danger was a roadbed blowout that would allow millions of gallons of water to race down Spring Brook, already being held back behind Leisure Laundry, where a garbage dumpster washed in and lodged under a Main Street building. Basements flooded, culverts washed out, blacktop was tossed aside, and high-water mud marks were left four feet above the deck of the South Vaughn Street/Route 240 Bridge.

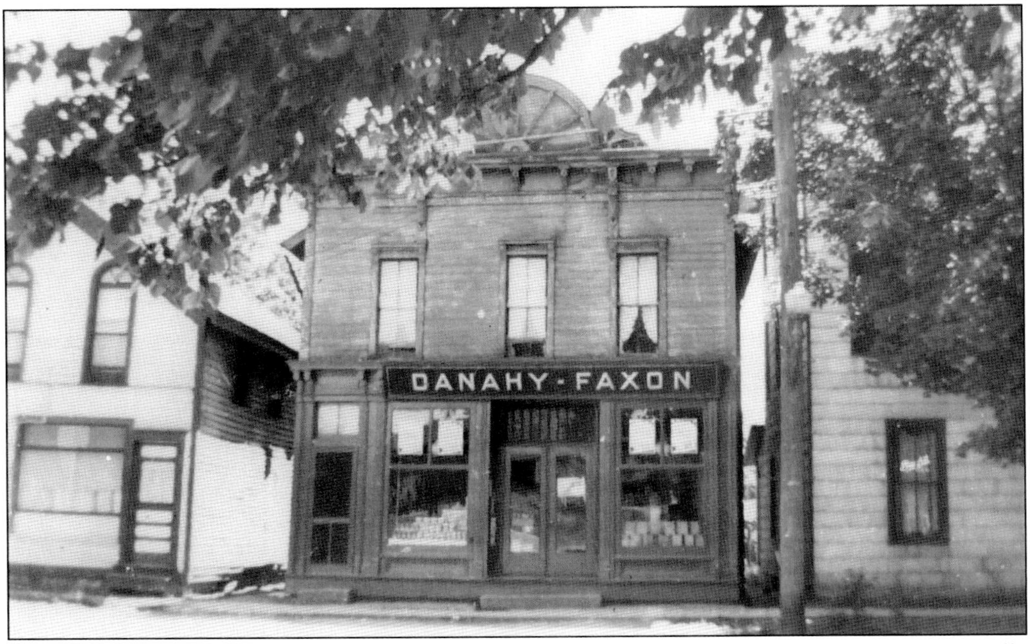

This is the same west-end neighborhood in 1939. Next to the Western House, which is partially shown at right, is a little grocery store once operated by Catherine Clarke.

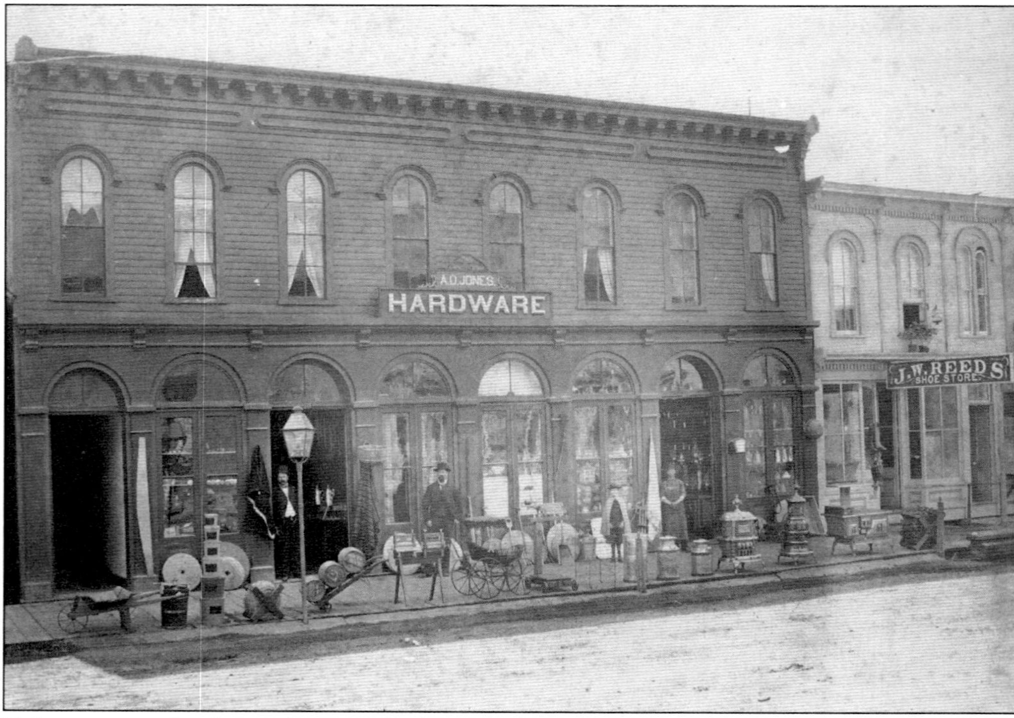

If the streets are brick in a photograph of Springville, it was taken after 1912. Pre-1912 photographs have a dirt street and wooden crosswalks. Very early images may have gaslights or no lights at all. The presence of wires is also an indicator of the times. The A.D. Jones sidewalk sale view is the earlier of these two photographs, while the view from the Leland House roof has a wooden crosswalk and wire clutter but no automobiles, placing it around 1900.

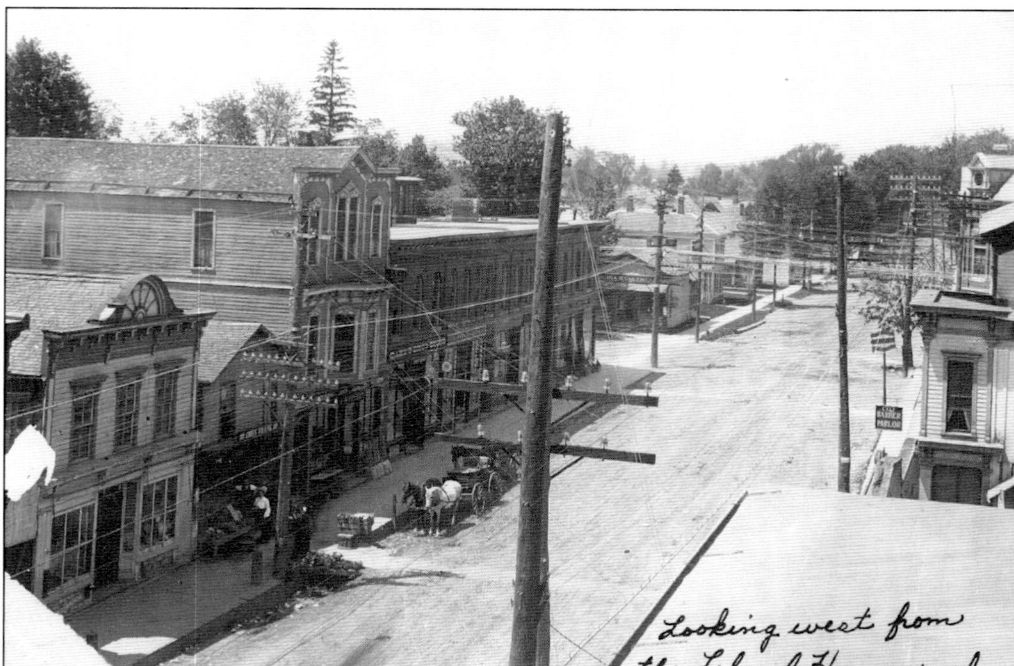

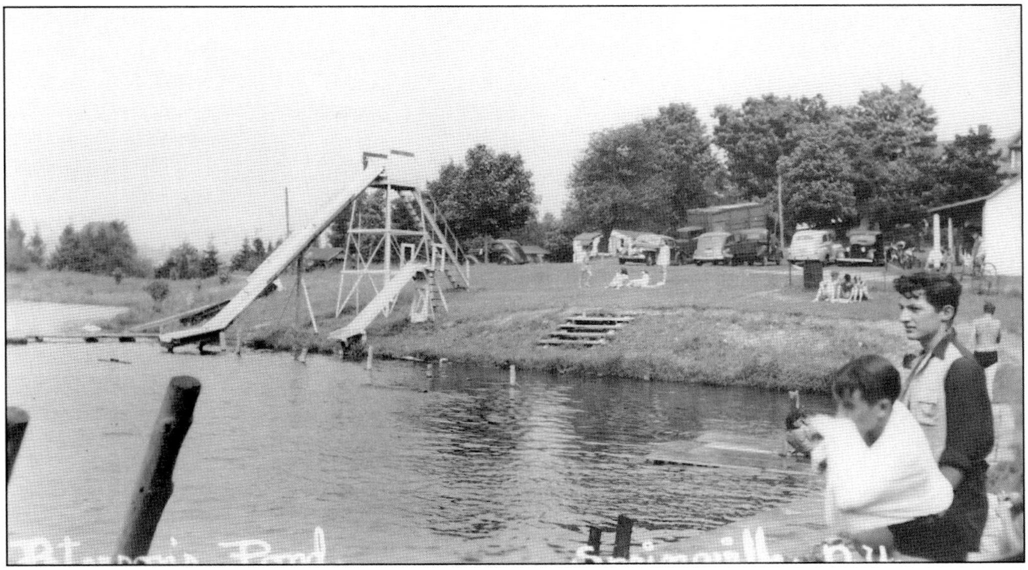

In 1948, Paul W. Fornes's parents acquired Pete's Pond, and he managed the concessions. Paul taught his friend Jud Strunk how to play the ukulele. Strunk went on to the banjo and eventually played it and performed stand-up comedy across America as the opening act for Glen Campbell. He appeared on national television and released two albums, including *A Daisy A Day*, which included local favorite "Who Cut the Maples on Nunweiler Hill." In this 1973 photograph, Strunk is shown with Fornes's daughter Kimberly. But the pond's brushes with fame do not stop there. Before Fornes's day, another young man spent summer days there while visiting his grandfather, a pastor at Springville Lutheran Church. His name was Robert Emil Schmidt, and he was better known as "Buffalo Bob" Smith, creator of Howdy Doody. (Both, courtesy of Paul W. Fornes.)

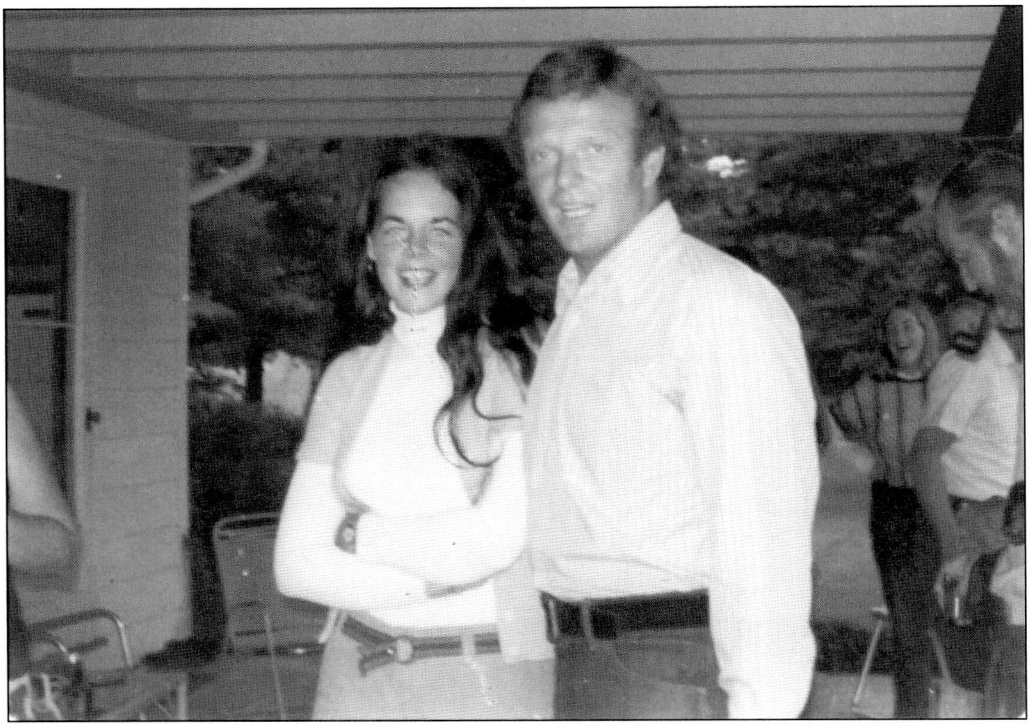

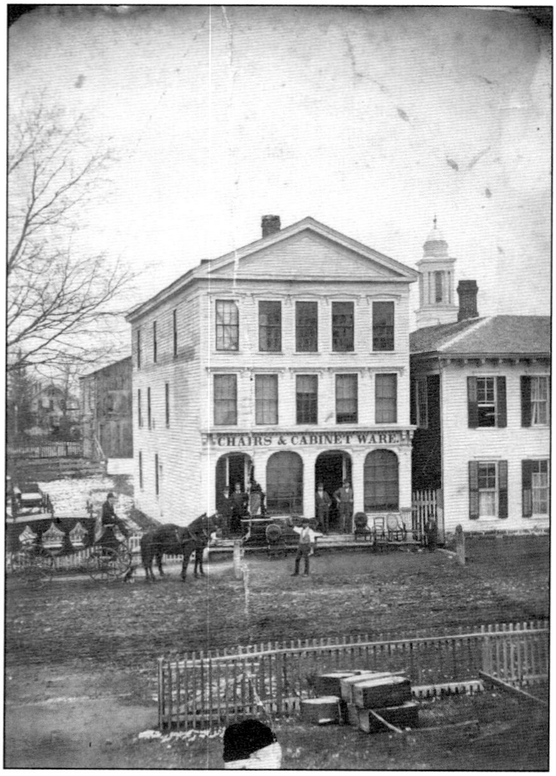

This photograph was taken before 1875, when the Presbyterian church clock tower (center background) was replaced with a 90-foot steeple. The building on Main Street near Academy Street with the horse-pulled hearse out front is likely the Empire Chair Company. A.L. Pingrey acquired the company about 1907 and had five salesmen on the road in New York, Pennsylvania, and Ohio, selling cane and wood seat chairs and rockers.

The Child's Opera House was located east of Fiddler's Green Park. The 1847 structure formerly owned by the Universalist Church of Springville was purchased by I.B. Childs and Morris Hall and remodeled to replace the opera house lost in the 1879 fire.

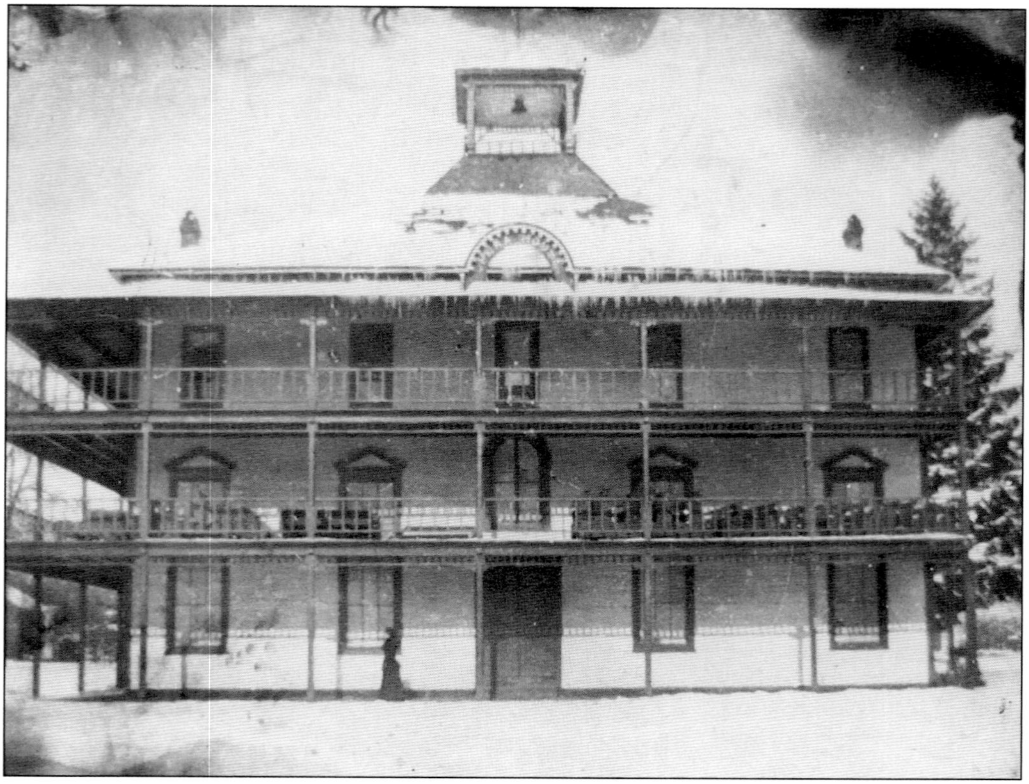

Six

Around Town

In its final years of service, Scobey Dam served to shave down peak-demand electrical charges. The New York Power Authority billed on the basis of a brief peak, often in March, and charged that high rate all year, even if demand was low. It was important that the generators operated when demand was high to lower the peak and reduce the overall yearly cost. The facilities are no longer in service and are part of the Erie County Parks Department.

The distinction of being the first person to have the courage to drive an automobile down into Spooner's Gulf and up the hill fast enough to climb the other side without downshifting from high gear belongs to Glenn Scobey "Pop" Warner. On occasions when early automobiles got stuck in Spooner's Gulf, pre-pavement mud drivers walked east to the top of the hill and Frank Gentner's farm (now the Route 219–Route 39 interchange) to persuade Gentner to pull their vehicle from the mire. Taking advantage of 1920s automobile design, the teamster hooked his horses to the front bumper, assumed the passenger seat, passed the driving reins through the opened windshield, and proceeded up the hill, emerging after suitable payment had been made.

The concept of building a university in Springville was floated in the area around 1960. It was going to be located on the rim of beautiful Zoar Valley, and students would be trained to be diplomats and leaders. Literature was released, and Gov. Nelson Rockefeller's administration was in favor, but then the movement stopped. It was rumored that the administration at the University of Buffalo saw it as a competitive entity with which they did not wish to deal.

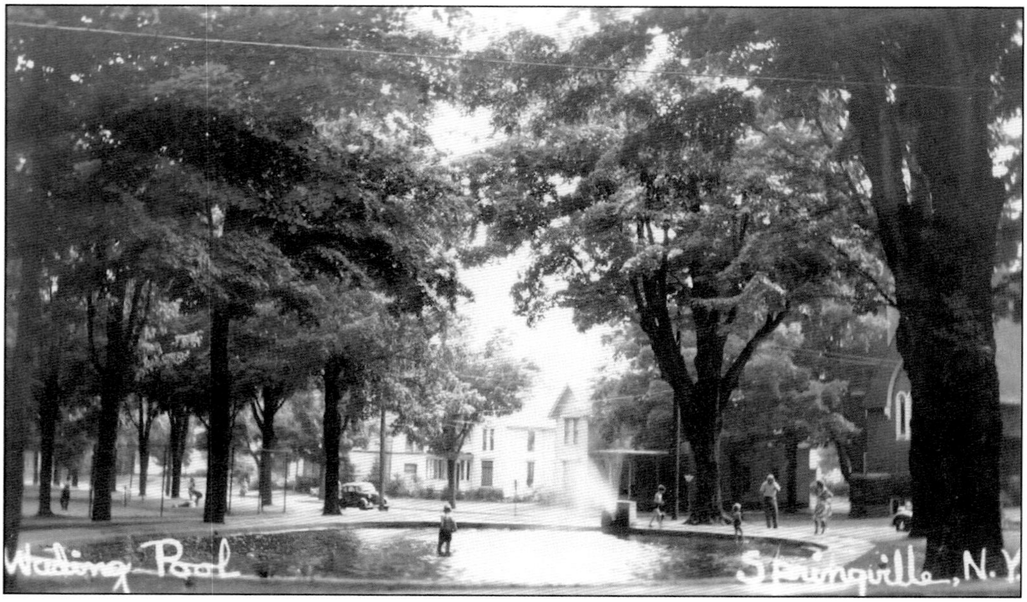

The Little Tots Wading Pool was made possible with funds provided by service organizations utilizing Springville's pure water for children's recreation. Private springs and wells served residents until 1887. In that year, C.J. Shuttleworth started a water company by collecting spring water at Spring Street and Elk Street and directing it via wooden pipe under Shuttleworth Pond to a South Buffalo Street reservoir. The springs could not meet the increasing demands for water, and, in 1931, Well No. 1 was drilled next to the village baseball field—now the high school baseball field. That pump building is still in use. The dark structure is the Laban Smith Farm barn, which became the bus barn garage, and the house to the right was used for classrooms and district offices. Demand made it necessary to add Well No. 2 on North Central Avenue to the system in 1941.

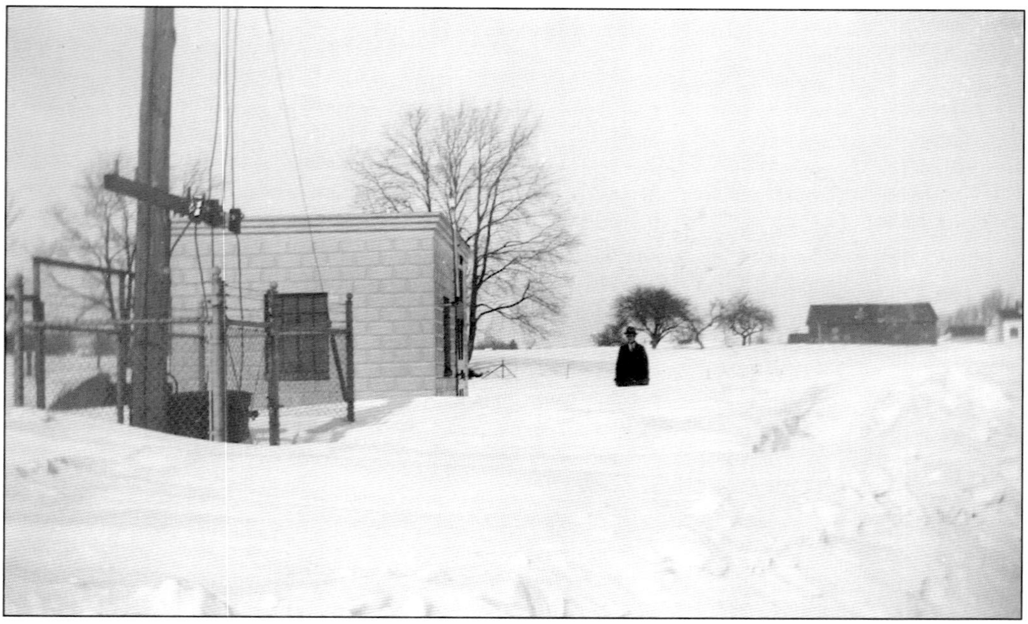

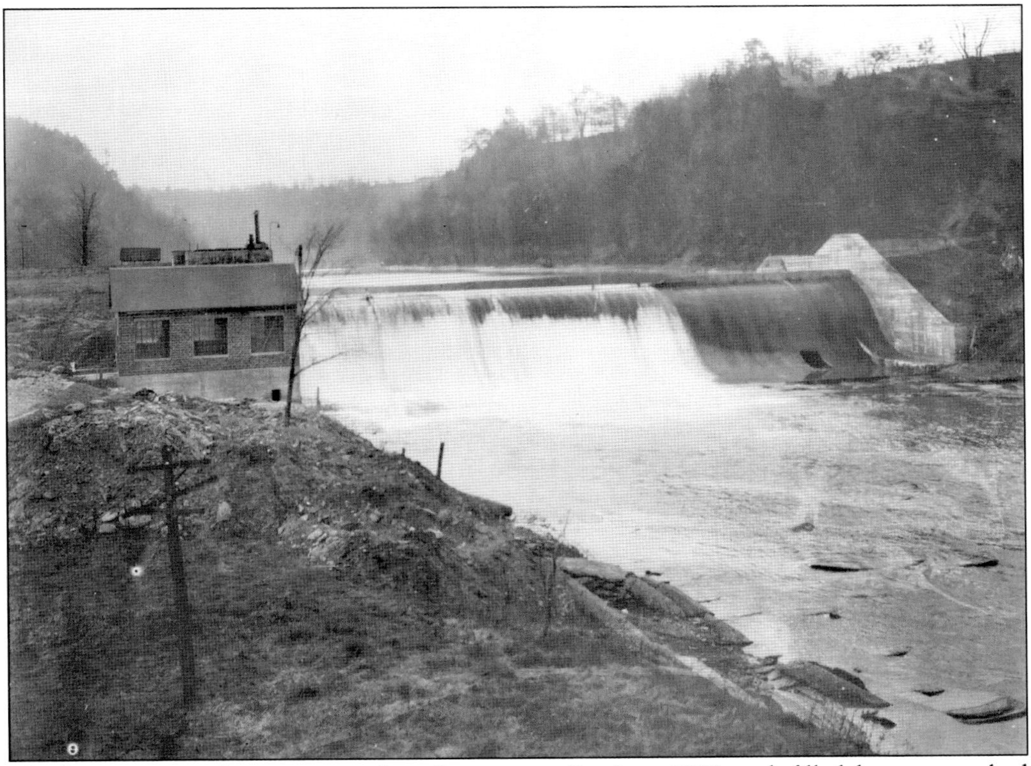

The first attempt to harness power from Cattaraugus Creek, an 1896 earth-filled dam, was washed out by spring rains. These facilities were completed in 1924 and modified in the 1980s, and they produced 500 kilowatts of power, briefly meeting Springville's needs. The concrete dam is 30 feet high and 130 feet long and, when operational, had three-foot flashboards to increase the volume of the up-creek reservoir. Manned 24 hours a day, it proved a convenient emergency dispatch control center. The facilities are no longer in service and are part of the Erie County Parks Department.

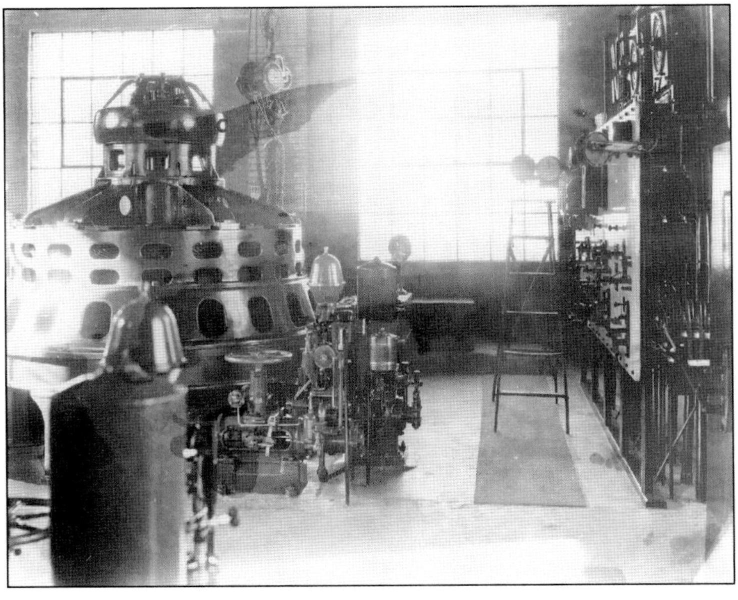

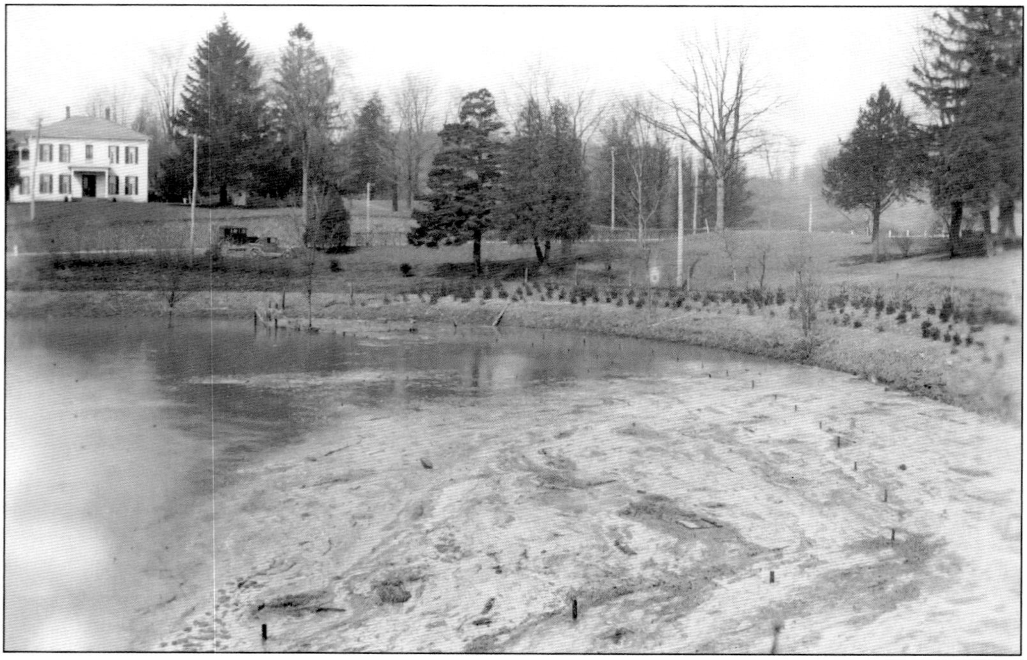

Shown here in 1929, Eaton Spring (now the Trout Pond) was located across from the Bates-Colby-Mitchell-Baker House on Buffalo Road. It supplemented the Spring Street and Elk Street springs until flooding contaminated it, prompting the village to seek a well-water source. Over the years, it has had a railroad locomotive derail into it, and it experienced overflow from the 1998 flood.

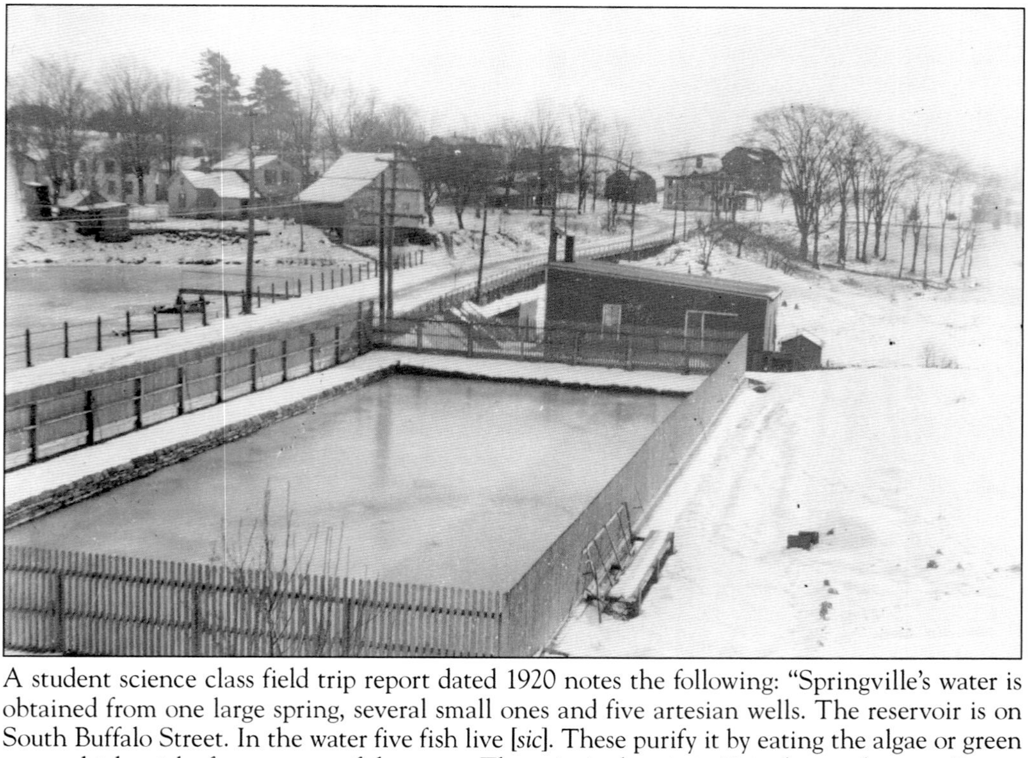

A student science class field trip report dated 1920 notes the following: "Springville's water is obtained from one large spring, several small ones and five artesian wells. The reservoir is on South Buffalo Street. In the water five fish live [*sic*]. These purify it by eating the algae or green scum which might form on top of the water. The principal main is 10 inches in diameter."

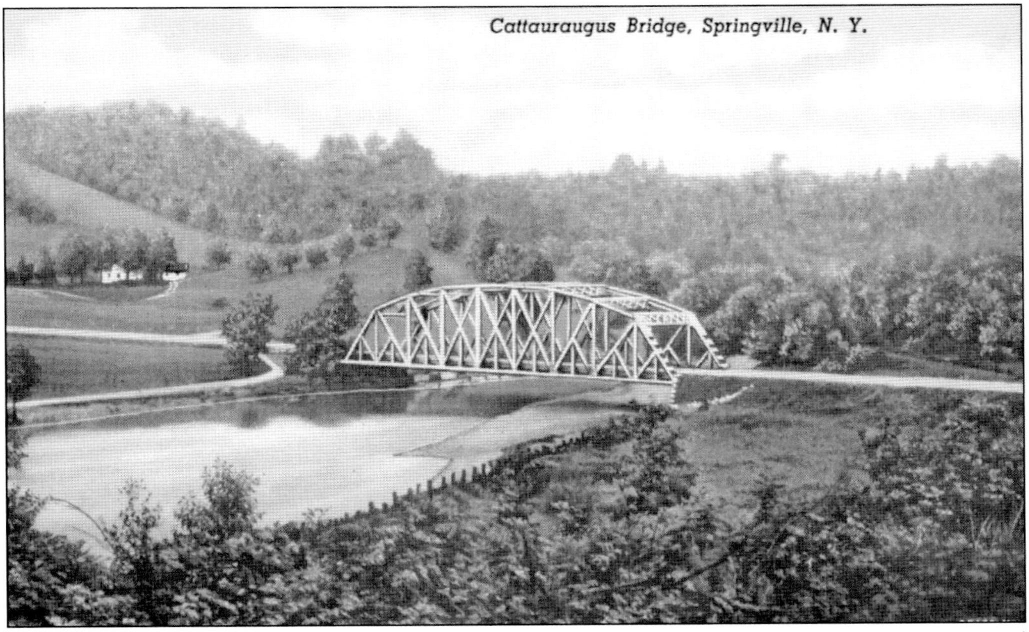

This is the 1928 South Vaughn Street Bridge over Cattaraugus Creek. The road once designated Route 219, which carried all north-south traffic, is now a fishing deck, having been replaced by a new structure. The freshwater springs that supply Pete's Pond also feed a creek that was dammed behind the home. At the edge of that pond was a water wheel—an electric generator complex serving the needs of the Joseph F. Benz family from the 1930s through the 1950s. Joseph R. Benz remembers being sent out to close the spillway, which shut down the waterwheel, and then racing back to the house and getting into bed just as the lights dimmed and went out.

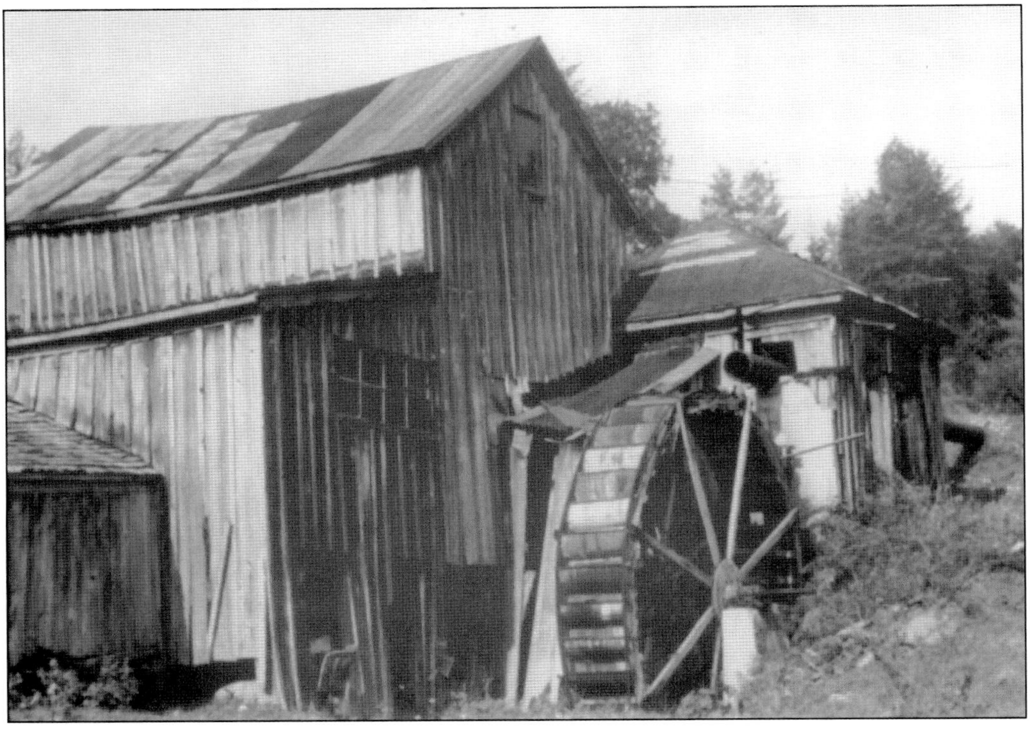

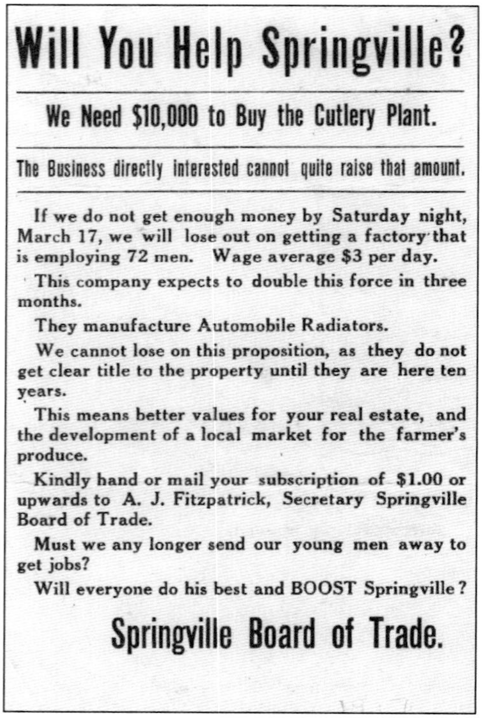

Will You Help Springville?

We Need $10,000 to Buy the Cutlery Plant.

The Business directly interested cannot quite raise that amount.

If we do not get enough money by Saturday night, March 17, we will lose out on getting a factory that is employing 72 men. Wage average $3 per day.

This company expects to double this force in three months.

They manufacture Automobile Radiators.

We cannot lose on this proposition, as they do not get clear title to the property until they are here ten years.

This means better values for your real estate, and the development of a local market for the farmer's produce.

Kindly hand or mail your subscription of $1.00 or upwards to A. J. Fitzpatrick, Secretary Springville Board of Trade.

Must we any longer send our young men away to get jobs?

Will everyone do his best and BOOST Springville?

Springville Board of Trade.

Around 1912, Case XX Knife Company produced razors, scissors, and a variety of knives in the "Knife Works" building. Knives marked "Case Springville" are now sought by collectors. By 1917, the Springville Board of Trade was seeking financial support to acquire the building for the Youngsville Radiator Company. Robinson Knife Company, the company that used the building for several decades, eventually fell victim to foreign competition and ceased its Springville operations. This 1960s aerial view shows, counterclockwise from the depot, the railroad freight house, Cleveland Metal Abrasives Company, Robinson Knife Company, residences, and (across Main Street) Salzler Brothers Lumber Company and Agway cooperative feed mill.

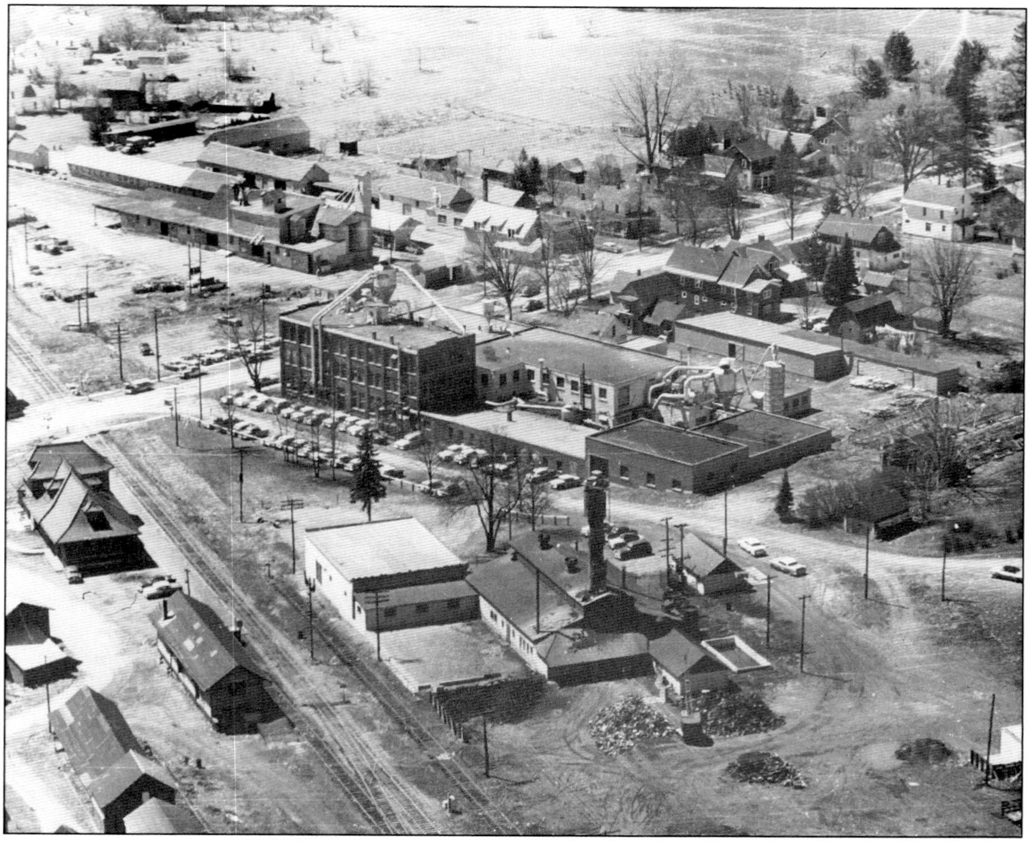

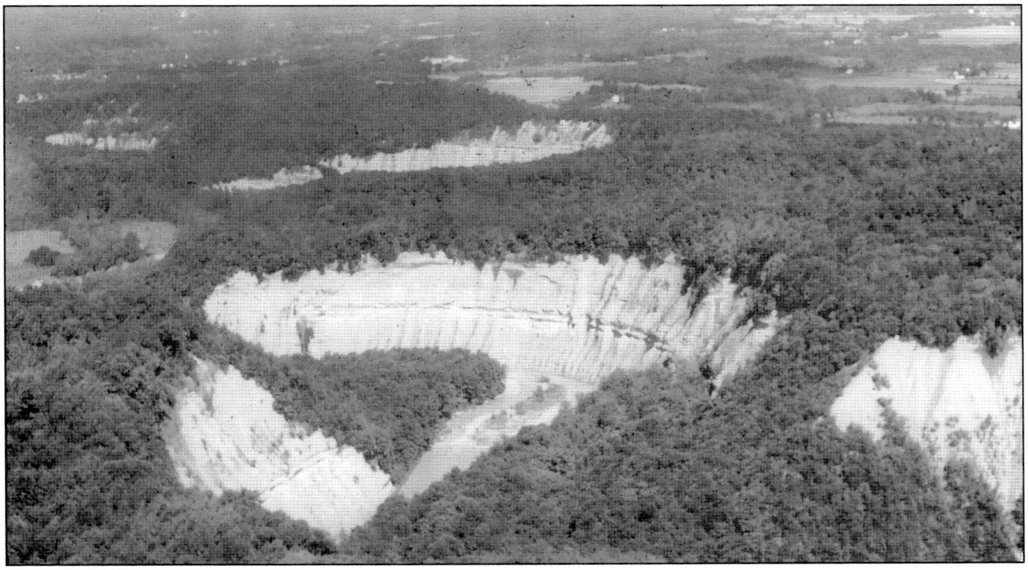

Zoar Valley is a 20-mile-long canyon; 180 feet deep near the Springville end and over 400 feet deep near Gowanda. In many places, the canyon's walls have old-growth trees up to 500 years old. There are waterfalls, rapids, spectacular vistas, trees with diameters of four feet or more, and the world's longest wild grapevine, approaching a quarter-mile in length.

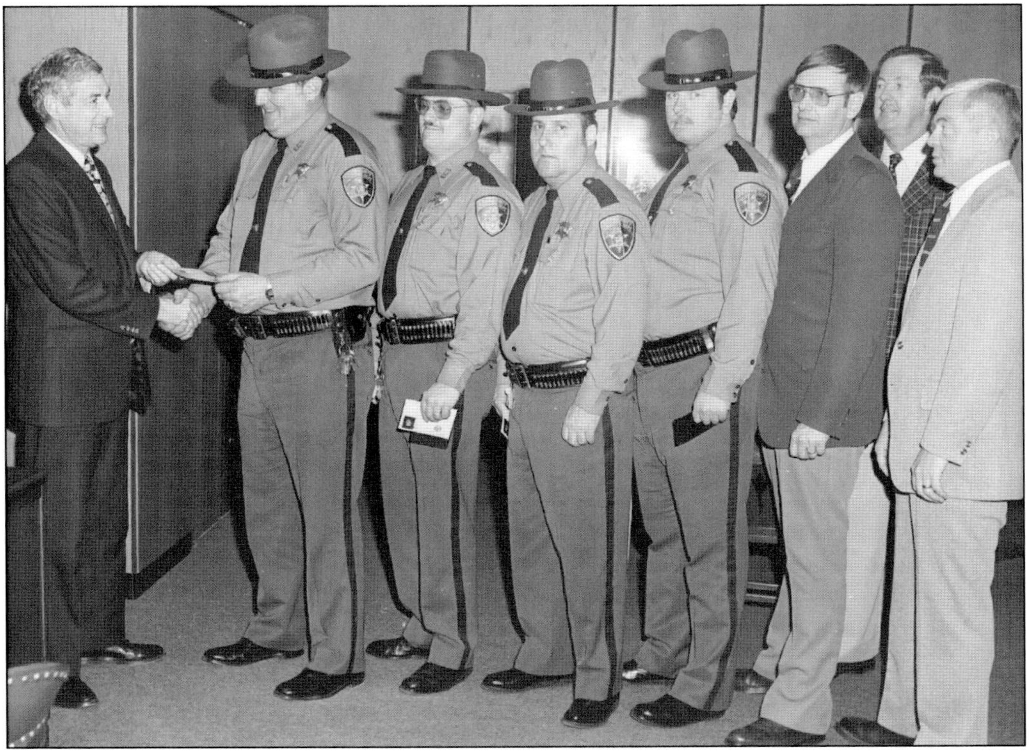

In this change of command, former Springville Police Department officers become part of the Erie County Sheriff's Department in 1981. Pictured from left to right are Edward Tutuska, James Hannon, Charles Reeves, William Cannon, Vincent Bolt, Robert Connors, Thomas Higgins, and Anthony Tolan.

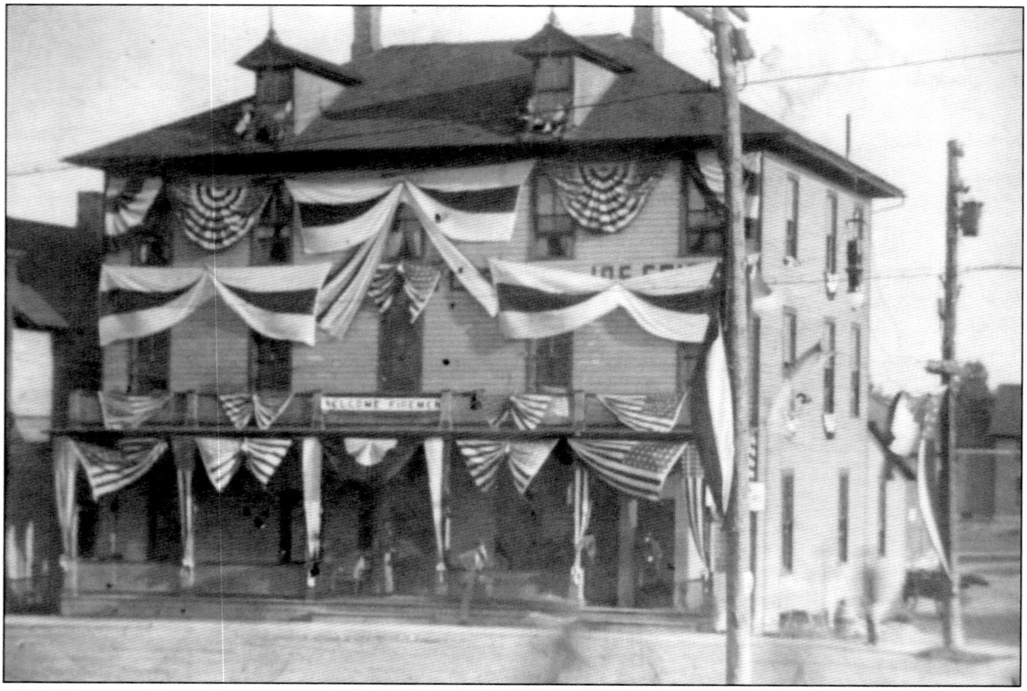

The Western House has witnessed much in its long history. At one time, farm machinery unloaded from the railroad was offered. Nearby, toward the feed mill and closer to Waverly Street, sits a fuel distribution center, the former J.C. Seider Oil Company. In later years, Mark Steffan, owner of the Western House, tore down the barn behind the hotel and discovered a secret storage facility below it, presumably a remnant of Prohibition.

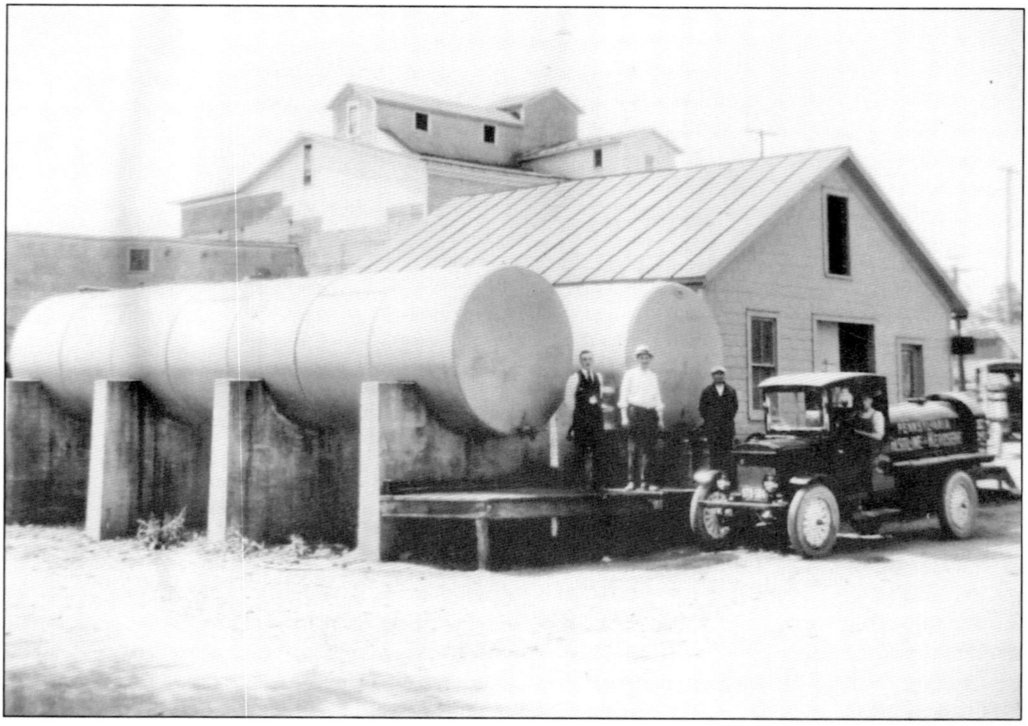

Seven

MISCELLANY

There are several historical anecdotes that do not necessarily fit into neat categories but are intriguing nonetheless. There are even a few without images to go along with them.

A Concord Historical Society memo states that "Grover Cleveland came to Springville to fish with Burt Chaffee in Spring Brook [Creek]." It is presumed that this was during the time that Cleveland was Erie County sheriff and Chaffee was politically active, around the 1870s.

As a youth, E. Richard Lowe (1899–1986), longtime owner and editor of the *Springville Journal*, would gather with friends at the top of the hill near the intersection of Prospect Avenue and Elk Street. They would "belly flop" onto their sleds and take a trip down the hill across Main Street to Franklin Street and, on a good run, almost to Mechanic Street. One day, a friend speeding downhill on a sled met a team of horses pulling a heavy sleigh at Main Street. Incredibly, the lad passed under the pair of horses and emerged on the Franklin Street side unhurt. Needless to say, lookouts were posted from that day forward.

When the village fathers contemplated creating new brick streets in 1912, they were concerned with the prospect of "road apples," or horse droppings, fouling their surface. After they were built, a man named Cooper was issued a cart, broom, and shovel. At the end of his first day, he exclaimed, "Don't tell me that this is a one horse town!"

Erastus Webster came to Springville in 1850 and established the *Springville Herald* (now the *Springville Journal*). After leaving, he supported William H. Seward for president in 1860. Lincoln won the election and named Seward his secretary of state. Seward, in turn, named Webster his personal secretary. During the Trent Affair in 1861, the Union boarded a British ship on the high seas in an "act of war." Had England entered the war, the North may well have lost. Lincoln and Seward sent Webster to Cape Cod to return the prisoners to a British ship, defusing the situation and potentially saving the North from defeat.

Springville also had a connection to the Brooklyn Bridge. It was guarded by Heary Brothers Lightning Protection Company, established in 1895. They also protected the scaffolding during Lee Iacocca's $500-million renovation of the Statue of Liberty and Howard Hughes's *Spruce Goose* in Long Beach, California. Sports facilities across the nation use Heary Bros. lightning protection, including Buffalo's First Niagara Center.

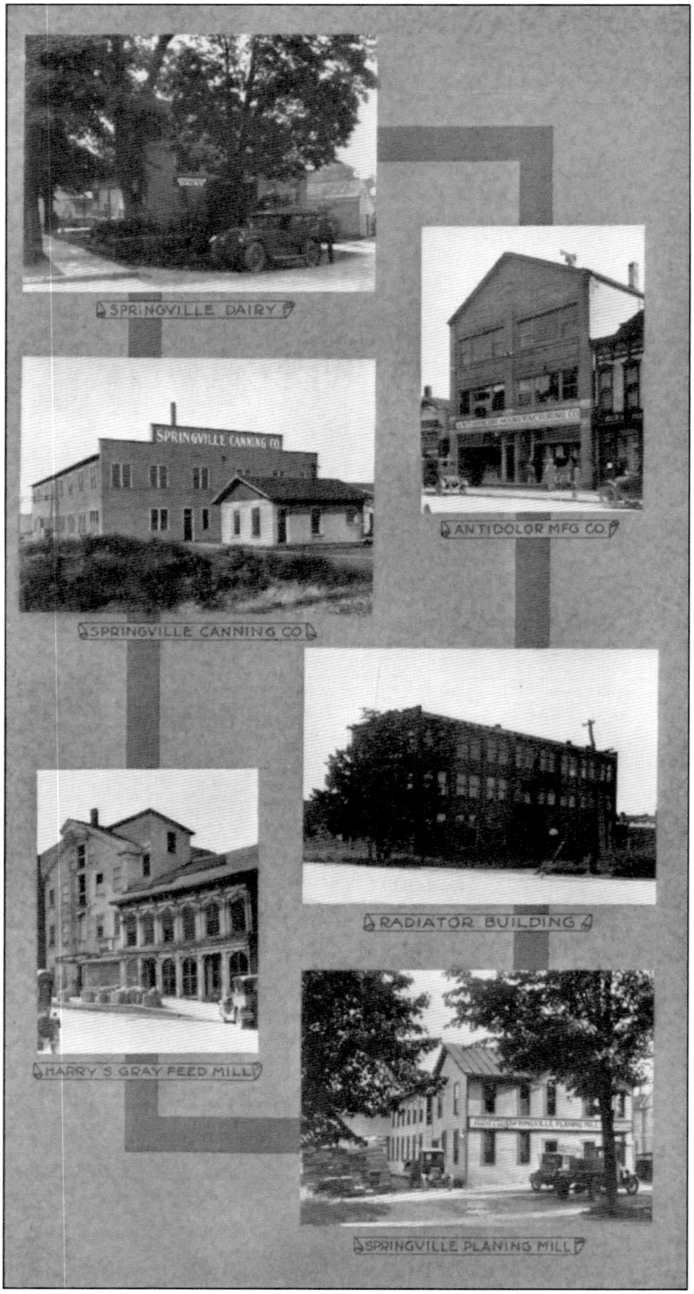

The Citizens National Bank, founded in 1902, celebrated a quarter-century of growth, producing pamphlet that contained, among other information, a collage of 1927 structures, some of which are still recognizable today. Springville Dairy was in the basement of the brick home at the northwest corner on Main and Franklin Streets, and the R.B. Waite building is still there, while Springville Canning Company's only remnant is the Boys and Girls Club on Maple Avenue. The Radiator Building was Case XX Knives and later Robinson Knife Company, and now it is a mixed-use building. The Main Street Harry S. Gray Feed Mill burned in 1946. The Springville Planing Mill was mid-block on the south side of Woodward Avenue, between South Buffalo Street and South Central Avenue.

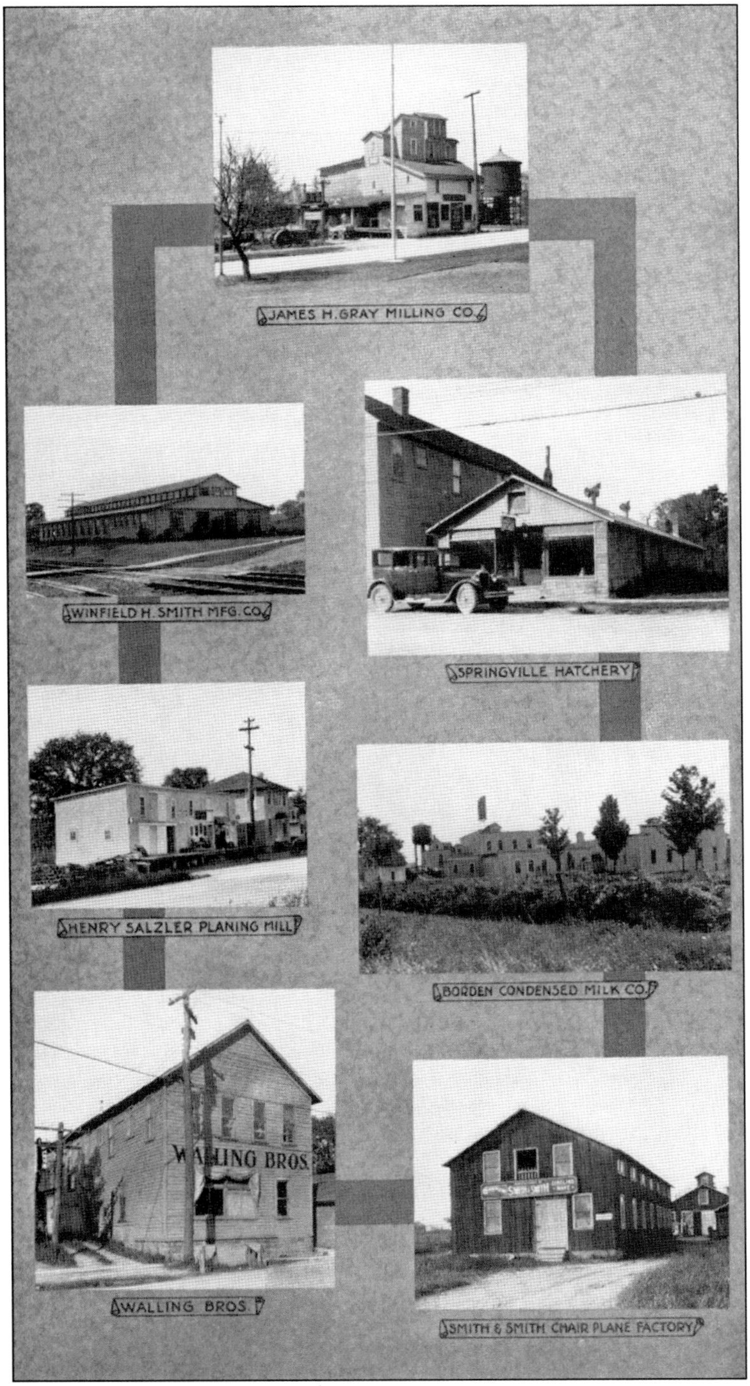

On West Main Street opposite the depot is the James H. Gray Milling Company, which was later abandoned and burned. The Winfield H. Smith Manufacturing Company has new ownership and has been enlarged, and Springville Hatchery near the creek on the north side of Franklin Street is now Spring Creek Plaza. Henry Salzler Planing Mill was on Mill Street near the entrance to the waste water facility, Walling Brothers was on the west side of the hatchery, and Smith and Smith Chair Plane Factory was across the tracks from Peerless Winsmith.

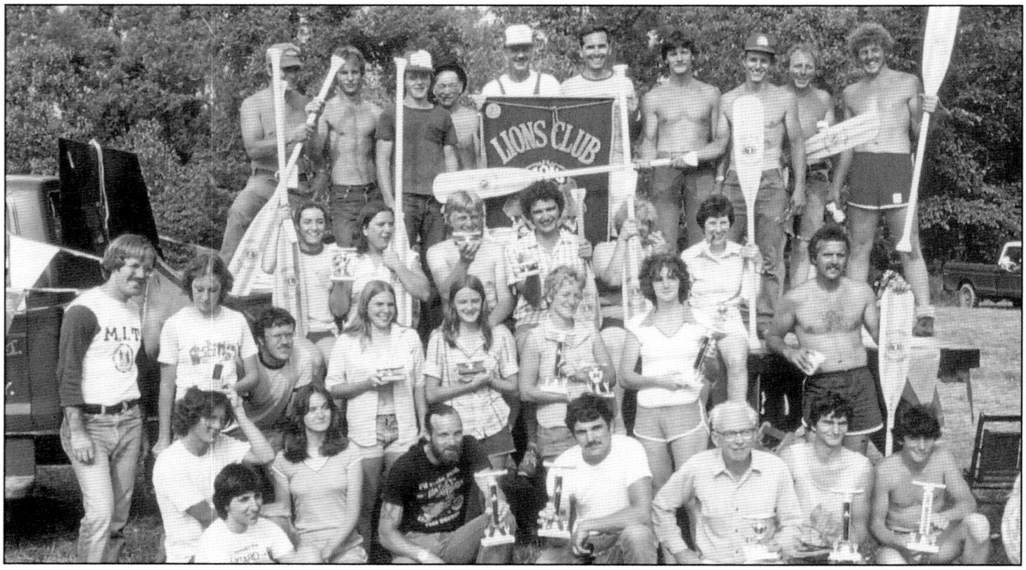

The Springville Lions Club Regatta (1979–1986) was the brainchild of Joel and Jean Maul and featured anything that would float on the Cattaraugus Creek over a 7.5-mile course between Hakes and Felton Bridges. In 1984, three thousand participants rode 1,250 craft in it. In both 1984 and 1985, over $10,000 was raised for the Lions Blind and Charity Fund, while 5,000 barbecued chickens were served.

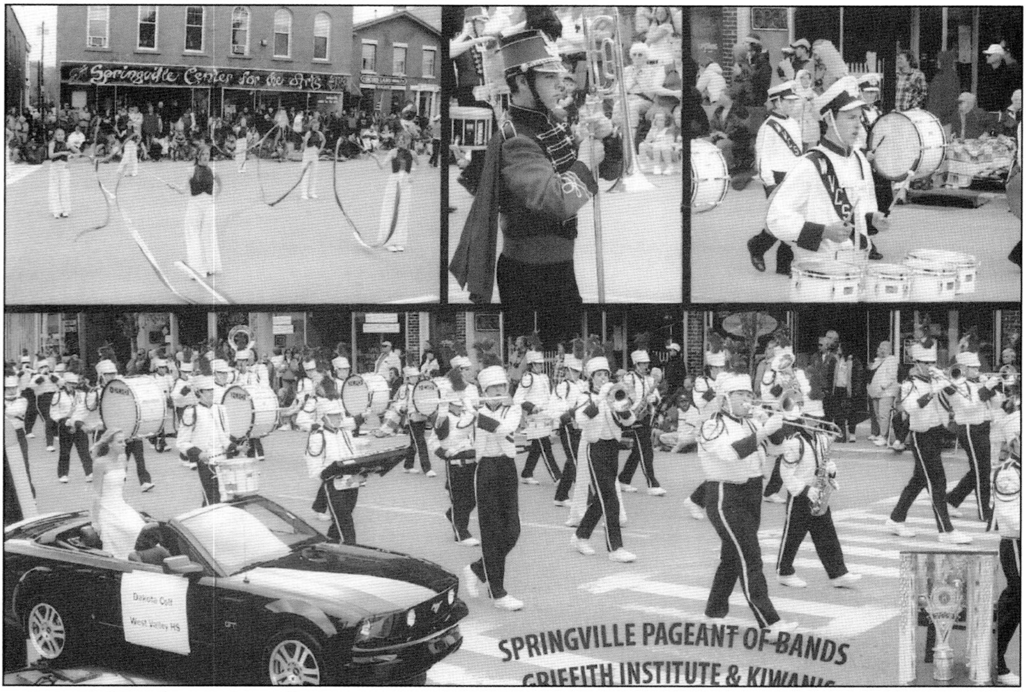

Sponsored by the Springville Kiwanis and Griffith Institute, the Pageant of Bands is New York's longest-running pageant. Springville Kiwanis, founded in 1961, established the pageant in 1962 as the largest of its many youth projects. Up to 20 marching bands have participated in the parade division of the many competitions held each year at the high school. Concert competitions are held the evening before the parade.

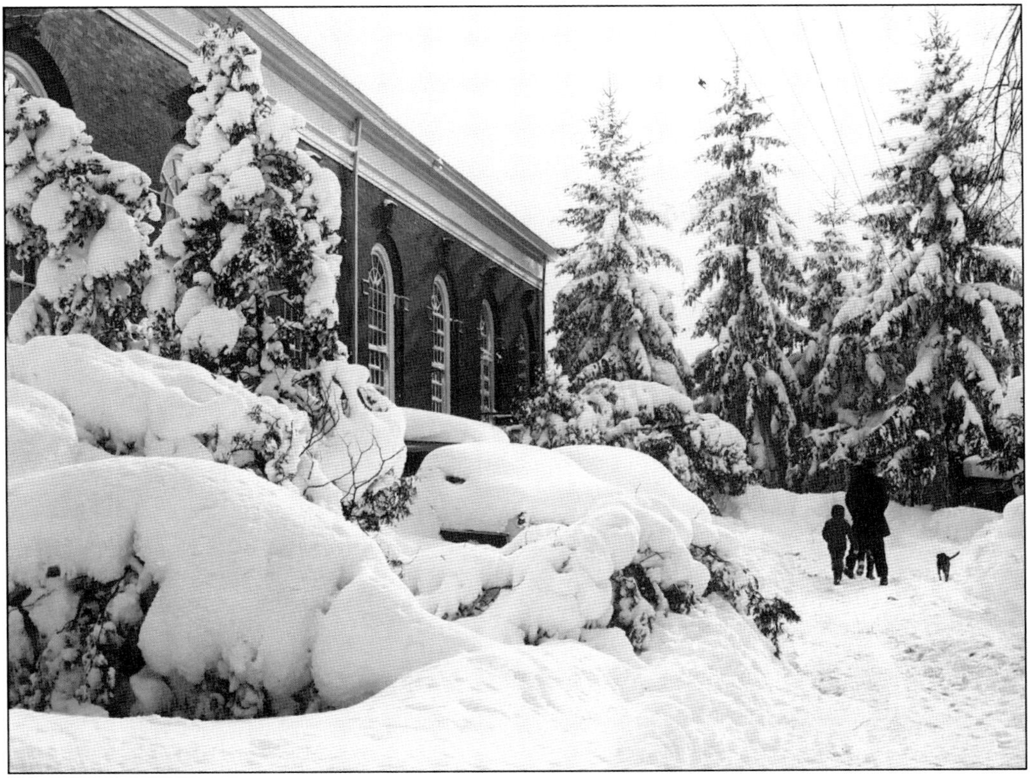

An automobile lies under a mountain of snow outside of Concord Town Hall in the 1950s. On a much earlier date, on the other side of town hall on Mechanic Street, an unsightly mass of snow-covered wires obscures a Spearmint Gum sign on the peak of the what is now the Carolsel Shop building. On the small building, a sign for the Big Little Valley Fair, along with the horses, dates this photograph to the early 1900s.

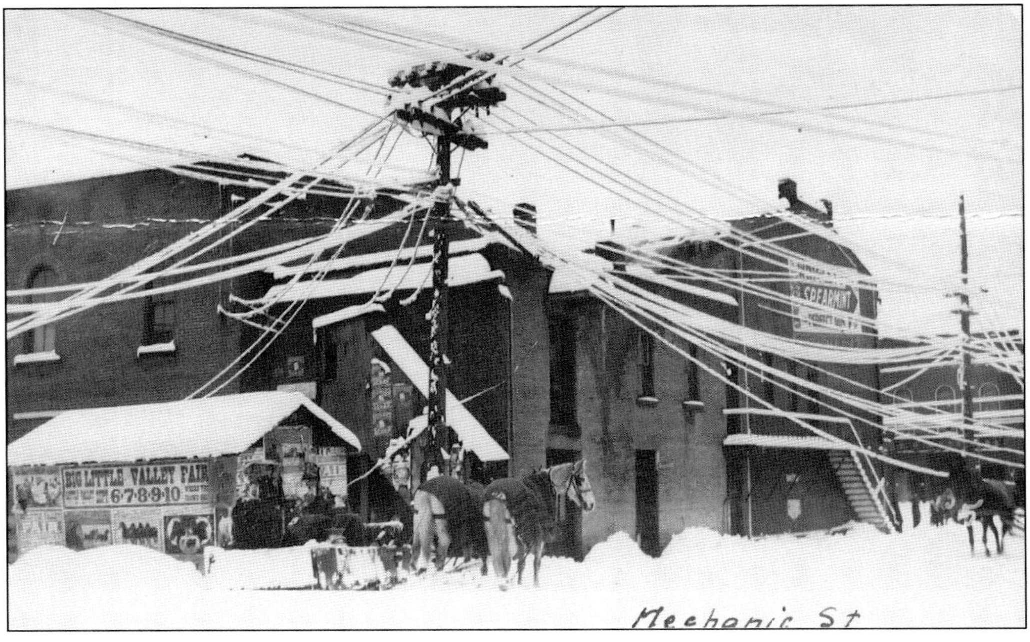

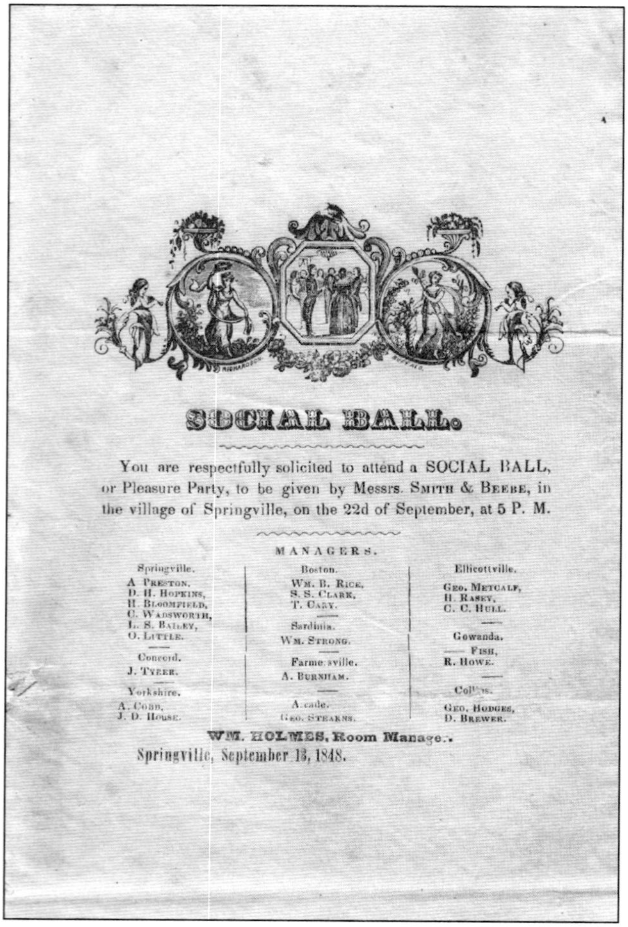

SOCIAL BALL.

You are respectfully solicited to attend a SOCIAL BALL, or Pleasure Party, to be given by Messrs. SMITH & BEEBE, in the village of Springville, on the 22d of September, at 5 P. M.

MANAGERS.

Springville.
A PRESTON,
D. H. HOPKINS,
H. BLOOMFIELD,
C. WADSWORTH,
L. S. BAILEY,
O. LITTLE.

Concord.
J. TYRER.

Yorkshire.
A. COBB,
J. D. HOUSE.

Boston.
WM. B. RICE,
S. S. CLARK,
T. CARY.

Sardinia.
WM. STRONG.

Farmersville.
A. BURNHAM.

Arcade.
GEO. STEARNS.

Ellicottville.
GEO. METCALF,
H. RASEY,
C. C. HULL.

Gowanda.
—— FISH,
R. HOWE.

Collins.
GEO. HODGES,
D. BREWER.

WM. HOLMES, Room Manager.

Springville, September 13, 1848.

This invitation does not suggest what facility could accommodate guests from Concord, Yorkshire, Boston, Sardinia, Farmersville, Arcade, Ellicottville, Gowanda, and Collins. They must have traveled by carriage or stagecoach, since 1848 predates Springville's first railroad by 30 years. This is one of only a few early paper items to have survived numerous destructive fires.

Springville airport operated briefly after World War II. The landing strip that paralleled North Street is now wooded, with houses. The hangar became the S-GI bus storage and service center.

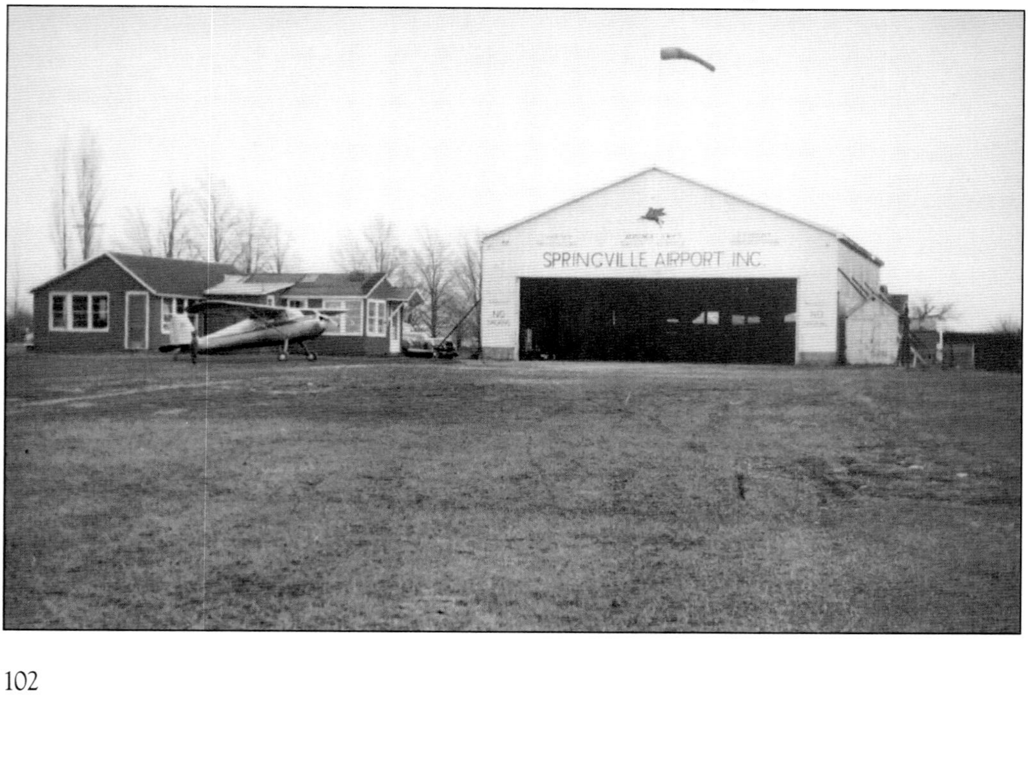

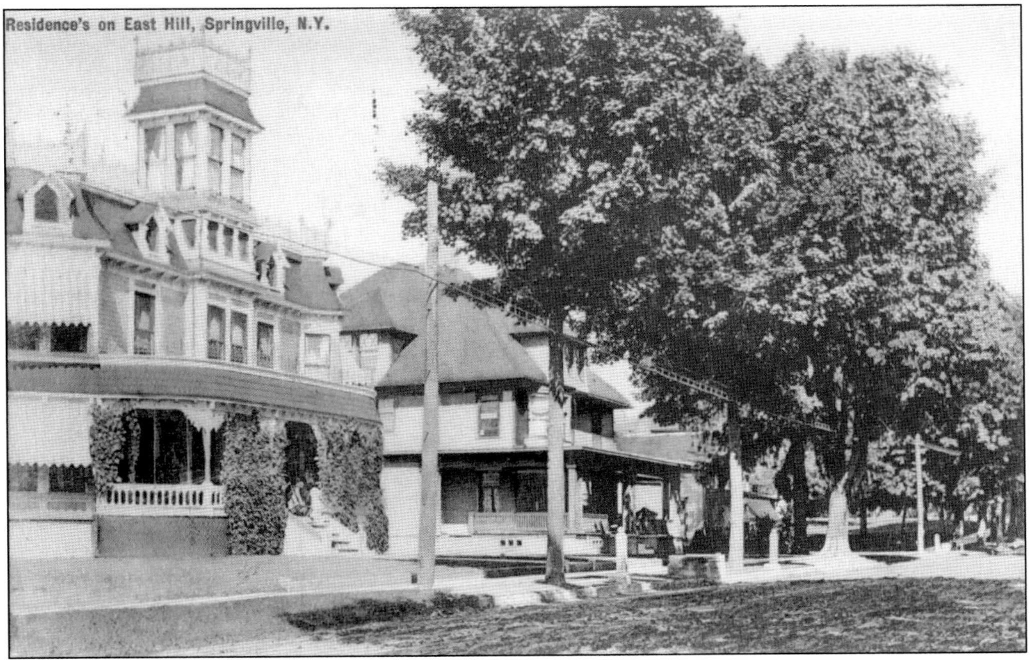

The A.D. Jones House, located at 192 East Main Street, is seen here before the ornate trim, awnings, porches, and turret were removed, likely because of excessive maintenance costs. The middle structure in both photographs was razed to make room for the next phase of the Concord Medical Group complex, shown in its infancy below.

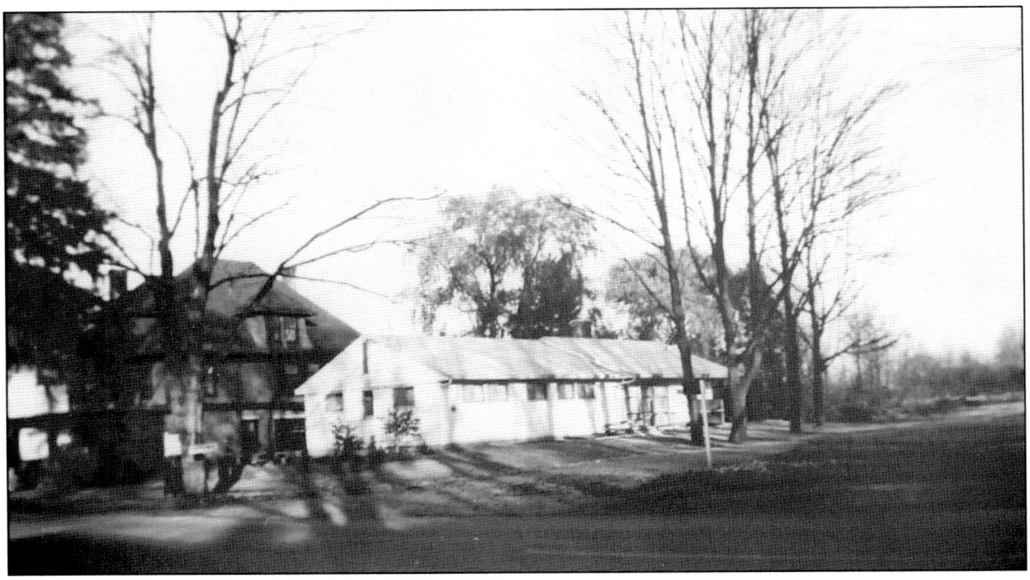

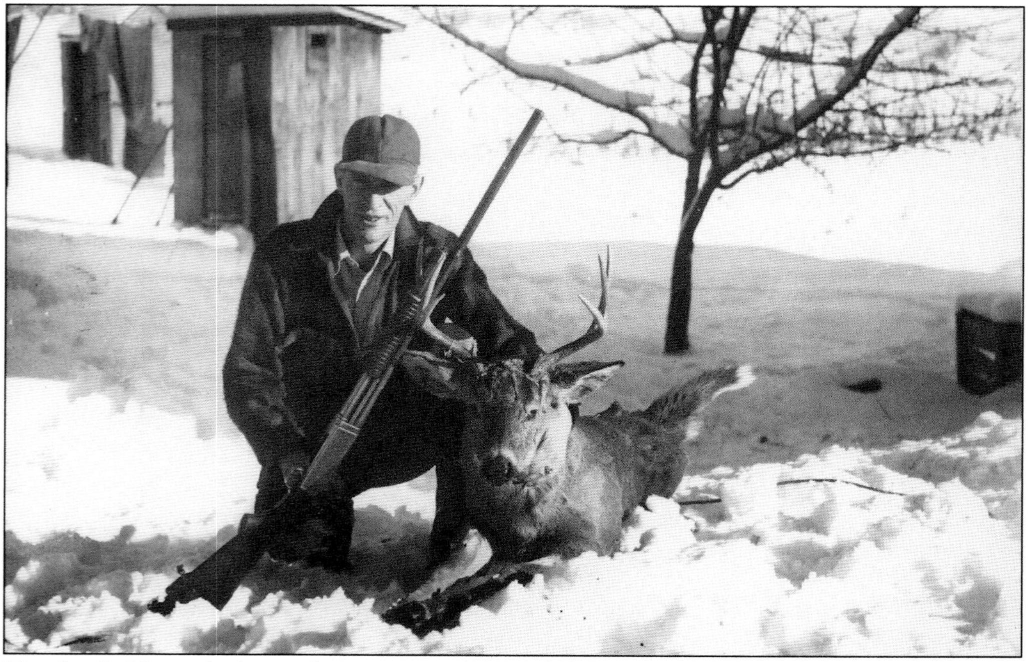

Nice buck, Howard! An avid sportsman who resided at 202 Waverly Street, Howard Hoffman and his wife, Louise, were foster parents to numerous children, including Lawrence Balog and Richard McDonald, who shared the gift of this photograph. It was the mid-1940s, and although the Hoffmans had indoor plumbing, the next five homes east on Waverly Street had privies, two of which are visible behind Hoffman.

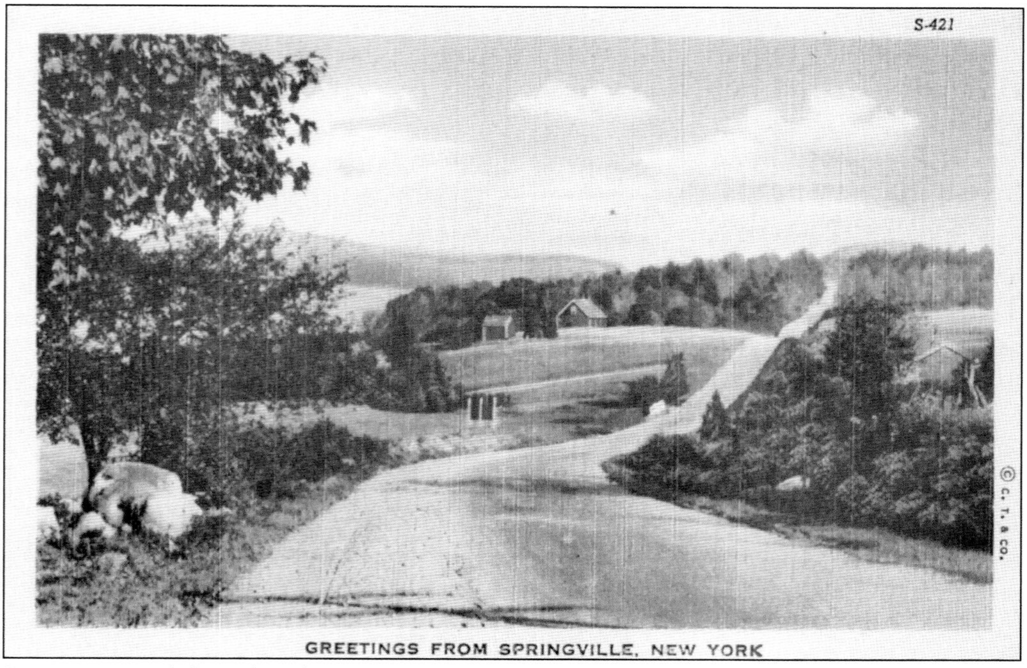

Picture postcards have long been a valuable source of early-20th-century insight. Look closely to see if a road, hill, or building can be recognized. In reality, these images were sold to thousands of communities with just a name change, and this is not a Springville scene.

The date of this commercial venture is unknown, although there were artesian wells here. Great Bear Springs Water Company obtained at least some of its water here. Every day, 18-wheel tanker trucks still haul thousands of gallons of local water to an urban center for bottling.

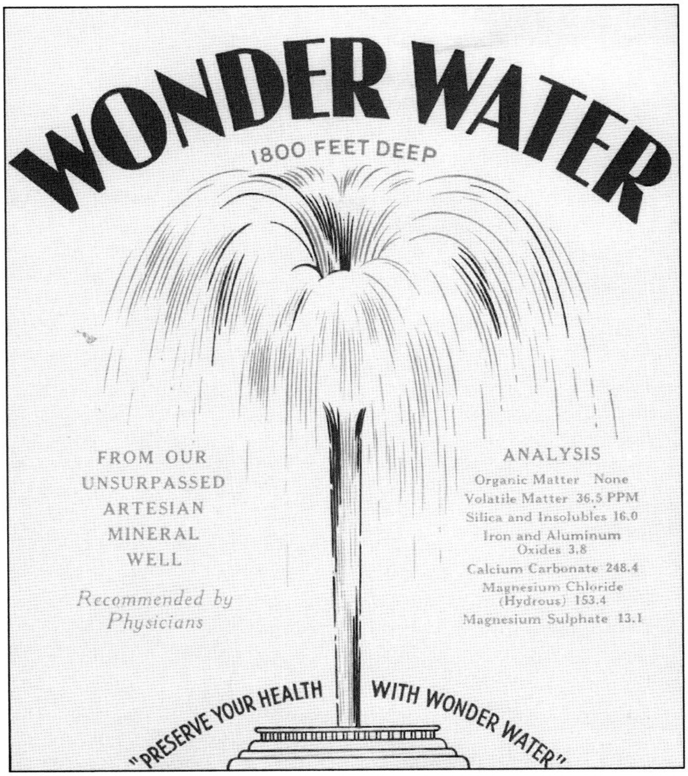

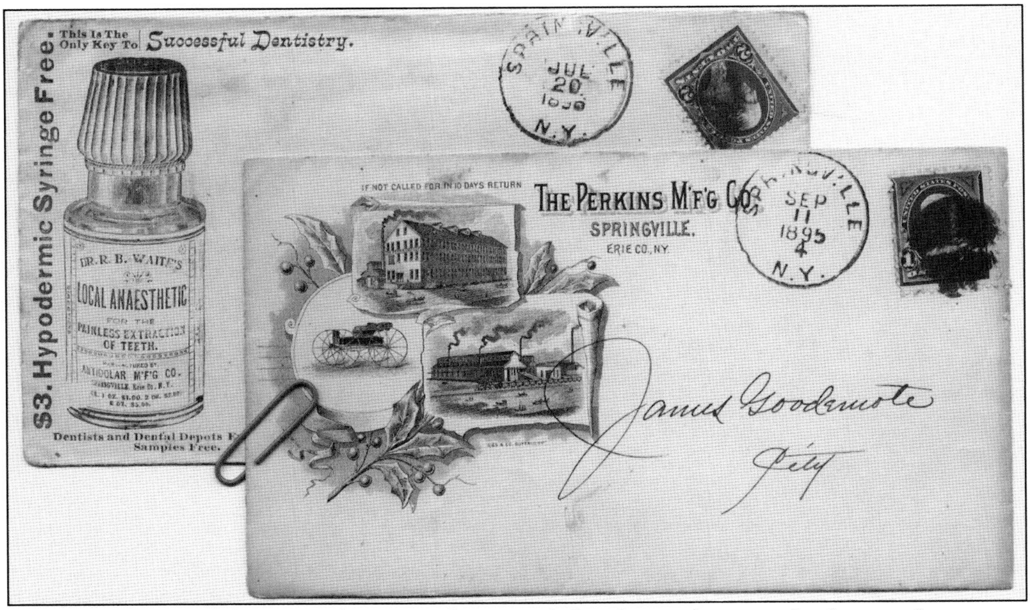

R.B. Waite's Antidolor Manufacturing Company's local anesthetic and other products were marketed worldwide due partly to their effectiveness and partly to the 50,000 pieces of mail Waite sent out each month through the post office located on the first floor of his Main Street building (now Harry's Barber Shop). The Perkins Manufacturing Company was of short duration, and the facilities shown were not in Springville. In those days, local mail could merely be marked "City" and reach its destination.

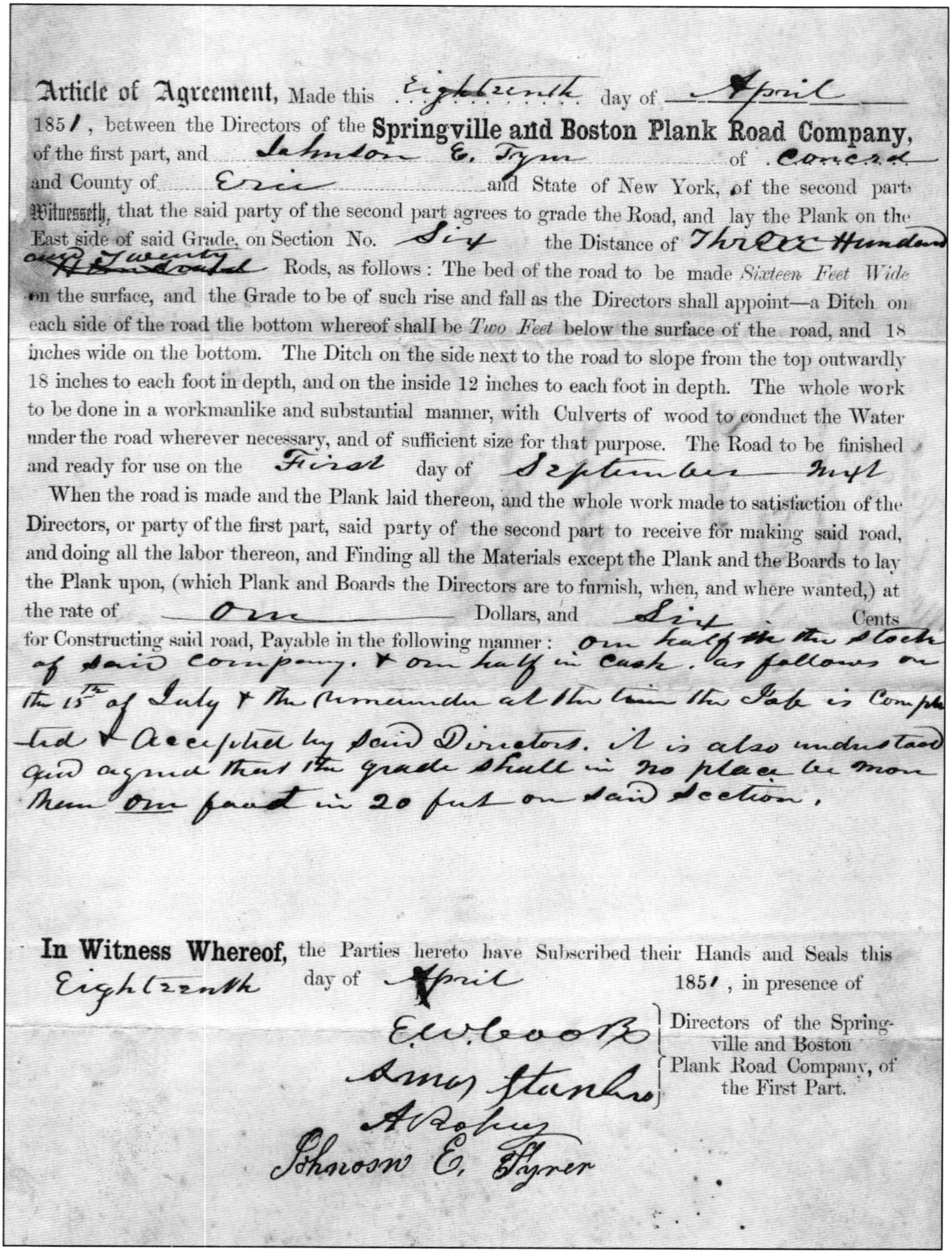

Article of Agreement, Made this Eighteenth day of April 1851, between the Directors of the **Springville and Boston Plank Road Company,** of the first part, and Johnson E. Tyrer of Concord and County of Erie and State of New York, of the second part: **Witnesseth,** that the said party of the second part agrees to grade the Road, and lay the Plank on the East side of said Grade, on Section No. Six the Distance of Three Hundred and Twenty Rods, as follows: The bed of the road to be made *Sixteen Feet Wide* on the surface, and the Grade to be of such rise and fall as the Directors shall appoint—a Ditch on each side of the road the bottom whereof shall be *Two Feet* below the surface of the road, and 18 inches wide on the bottom. The Ditch on the side next to the road to slope from the top outwardly 18 inches to each foot in depth, and on the inside 12 inches to each foot in depth. The whole work to be done in a workmanlike and substantial manner, with Culverts of wood to conduct the Water under the road wherever necessary, and of sufficient size for that purpose. The Road to be finished and ready for use on the First day of September next.

When the road is made and the Plank laid thereon, and the whole work made to satisfaction of the Directors, or party of the first part, said party of the second part to receive for making said road, and doing all the labor thereon, and Finding all the Materials except the Plank and the Boards to lay the Plank upon, (which Plank and Boards the Directors are to furnish, when, and where wanted,) at the rate of One Dollars, and Six Cents for Constructing said road, Payable in the following manner: one half in the Stock of said Company. & one half in Cash. as follows on the 15th of July & the remainder at the time the Job is Completed & Accepted by said Directors. It is also understood and agreed that the grade shall in no place be more than one foot in 20 feet on said Section.

In Witness Whereof, the Parties hereto have Subscribed their Hands and Seals this Eighteenth day of April 1851, in presence of

E. W. Cook
Amos Stanbro
A. Robey
} Directors of the Springville and Boston Plank Road Company, of the First Part.

Johnson E. Tyrer

Mud was a deep, sticky impediment to travel. The creation of mud-spanning planks made from local trees made travel easier. This article of agreement from the Springville and Boston Plank Road Company illustrates the beginning of a new industry.

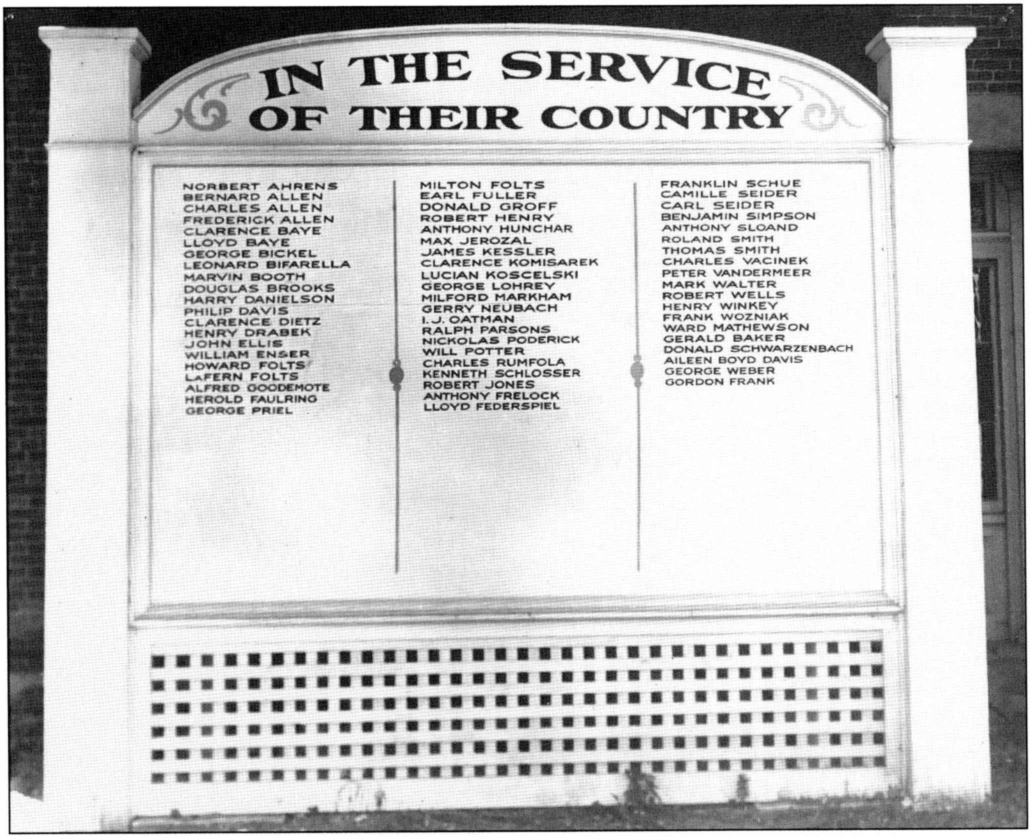

Prominently displayed above are the names of Springville and Concord residents who served in World War II. A World War I plaque that resided at "Old G.I." until 1970 was rededicated at Shuttleworth Veteran's Park in 1985, alongside the Civil War Grand Army of the Republic Log Cabin, as well as more recent memorials for soldiers in Korea, Vietnam, and Operation Enduring Freedom, all sitting on what was once Shuttleworth Pond.

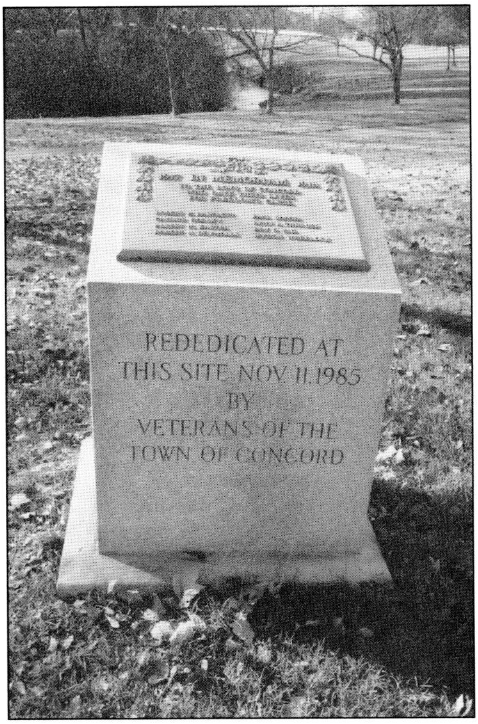

Springville Civilian Defense Committee

Committee on Fire Defense

Gordon K. Rouse, Chief

Instructions To Citizens In

Incendiary Bomb Control and Extinguishment

Be Sure You

1. Be sure you can get to your attic by stairway or ladder.
2. Be sure you always have bath tubs, wash tubs and pails filled with water, and a hose tap connection in the house. Make it possible to reach your attic with your available hose.
3. Be sure you have a garden hose with the regular adjustable nozzle. A stirrup pump or pack pump outfit may be purchased if desired.
4. Be sure you definitely locate the bomb's position.
5. Be sure you use only water SPRAY on the bomb. Careful application of spray will reduce burning time of bomb from fifteen to three minutes.
6. Be sure you search for remaining fires in the area where the bomb has rested and on the floors below.
7. Be sure you open windows to allow smoke to escape after bomb is out.
8. Be sure you make a determined effort to control the bomb before calling the fire department which may be needed for large fires.
9. Be sure you clear unused garrets and unused top floors of all stored burnable material — the best fire prevention at all times.
10. Be sure you realize that a few bombs may contain a SMALL explosive charge. Incendiary bombs are generally safe to approach two minutes after impact.
11. Be sure you have several pails of sand in the house, on the upper floors. Put dry sand on the bomb to cut down heat, then scoop bomb up with shovel and put in pail partly full of sand where it will burn out. Take pail from house immediately.

Do Not

1. Do not lock inside doors.
2. Do not depend solely upon public water supply, if any other means can be used in an emergency. Water mains might become broken.
3. Do not keep your fire fighting equipment in a place where it cannot be reached easily.
4. In attics keep close to the floor where the best air will be found, making it easier for you to breathe.
5. Do not hit the bomb with a SOLID stream of water and do not use commercial extinguishers unless approved by your Fire Department. Soda and acid, the most common, is approved. Hold the thumb over the nozzle to make a spray.
6. Do not be satisfied when the bomb is burned out. Search carefully for hidden fire.
7. Do not be without light and air, if they can be had safely.
8. Do not become frightened and leave the building. FIGHT THE FIRE.
9. Do not neglect good fire prevention housekeeping — good in peace or war.
10. Do not fear incendiary bombs. Respect them. Keep cool. Where possible advance upon an incendiary bomb behind a shield. Anything you can keep in front of you is suitable — chair, small table, wet blanket, etc.
11. Do not shovel up bomb until sand is placed over it.

Anyone Can Control An Incendiary Bomb

Don't Fear Them - Respect Them - Keep Cool

Please Post In Home

These instructions were given to residents to protect themselves and their property in the uncertain times of World War II. Air-raid sirens wailed, and frightened children waited in their darkened homes for the all-clear siren. Vehicles that were allowed to operate did so with sock-like covers over headlights with just a slit for minimal light to escape, lighting the way. Guards were posted at Cascade Railroad viaduct to prevent enemy sabotage, and prisoners of war worked in farm fields. And when it was all over, a celebration sent toilet paper, a scarce commodity, trailing from overhead wires and traffic signals all over the business district.

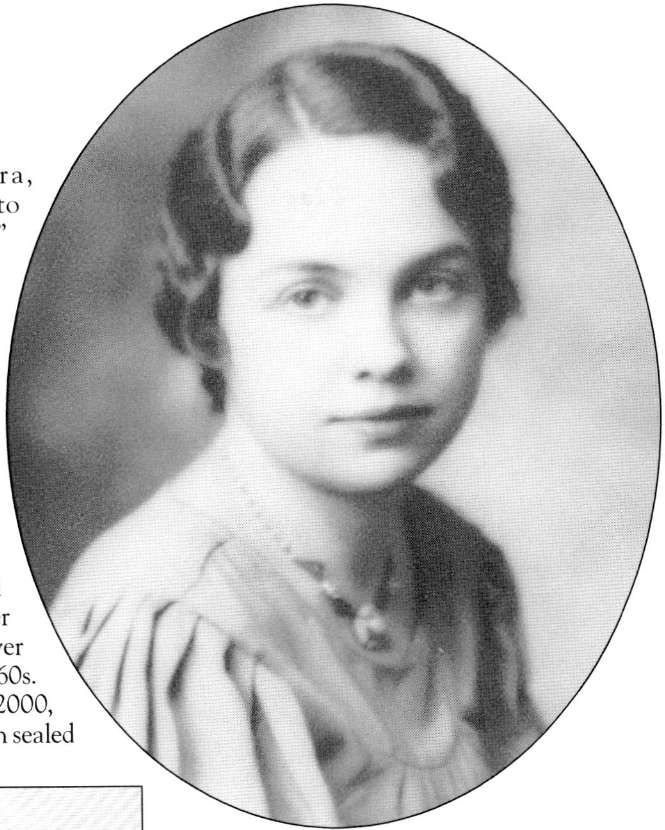

During the Cold War era, schoolchildren were required to participate in "duck and cover" drills, ducking under desks or in windowless hallways to avoid flying glass. Public buildings had food, water, and bedding for large numbers. Some landowners, like John P. and Lorraine Joslin Ellis, even built shelters near their homes. Lorraine Ellis, Griffith Institute, 1930, who turned 100 in 2011, shares her home with her son David and his wife, Jeanne, who operate Oasis Bed and Breakfast. David helped his father build the shelter on weekends over a three-year period in the early 1960s. When the shelter was opened in 2000, no contents were found. It had been sealed since 1971, when John Ellis died.

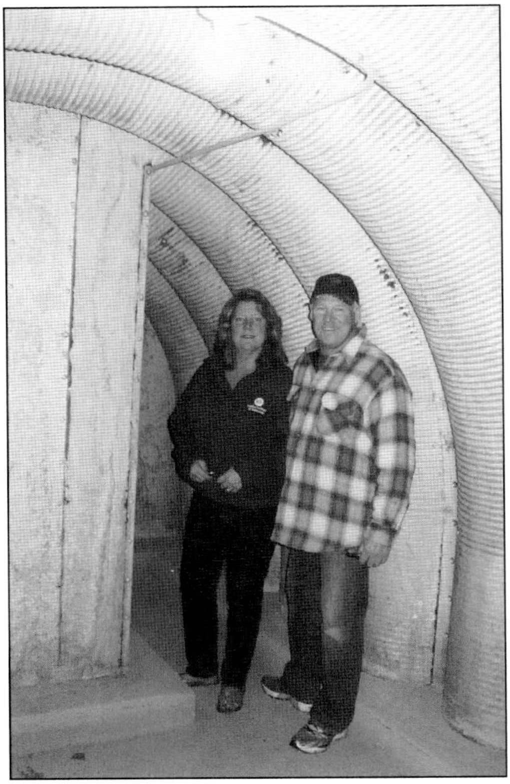

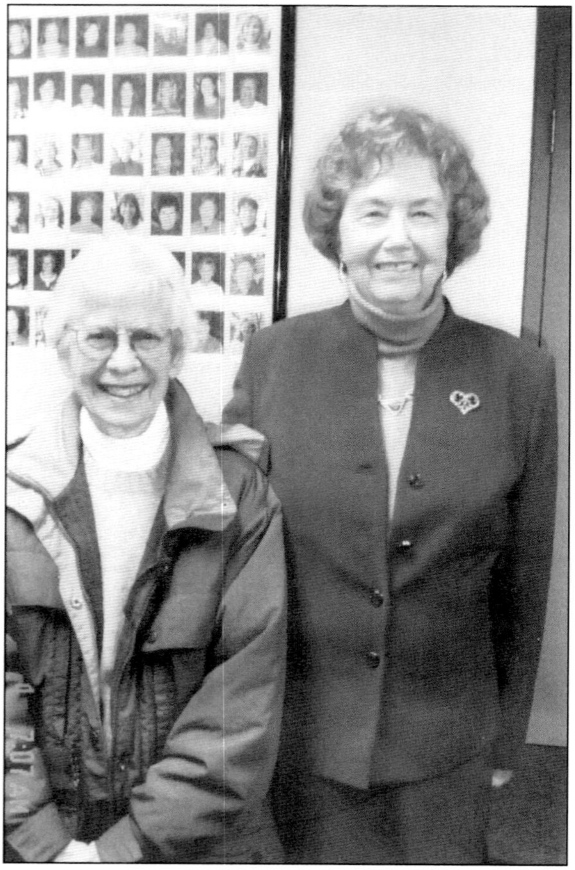

In 1960, Betty Cooke and Edie Palmer, each of whom had a child with severe hearing loss, refused to accept the conventional practice of institutionalizing their children. A committee of parents met at the home of George Schuster Jr. and his wife, Mary, and the League for the Handicapped Preschool Learning Center began. Through their 11 years at the Presbyterian church and 12 years at the Methodist church, hundreds of volunteers held dozens of fundraisers to obtain new programs and equipment. And on land on North Street donated by the Springville Lions Club, they finally built a $1-million-plus facility. Palmer said, "I can remember when we got our first $5, and now the facility has a $4-million annual budget, a staff of 110, serving 130 children at the center, and home visitation for an additional 145 children over a wide area."

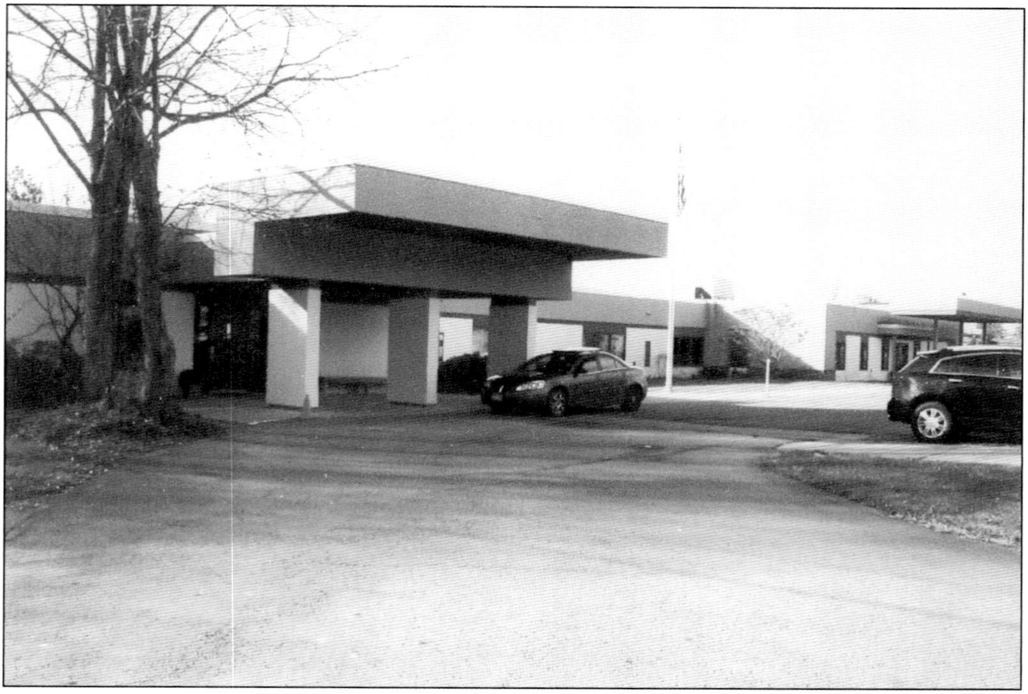

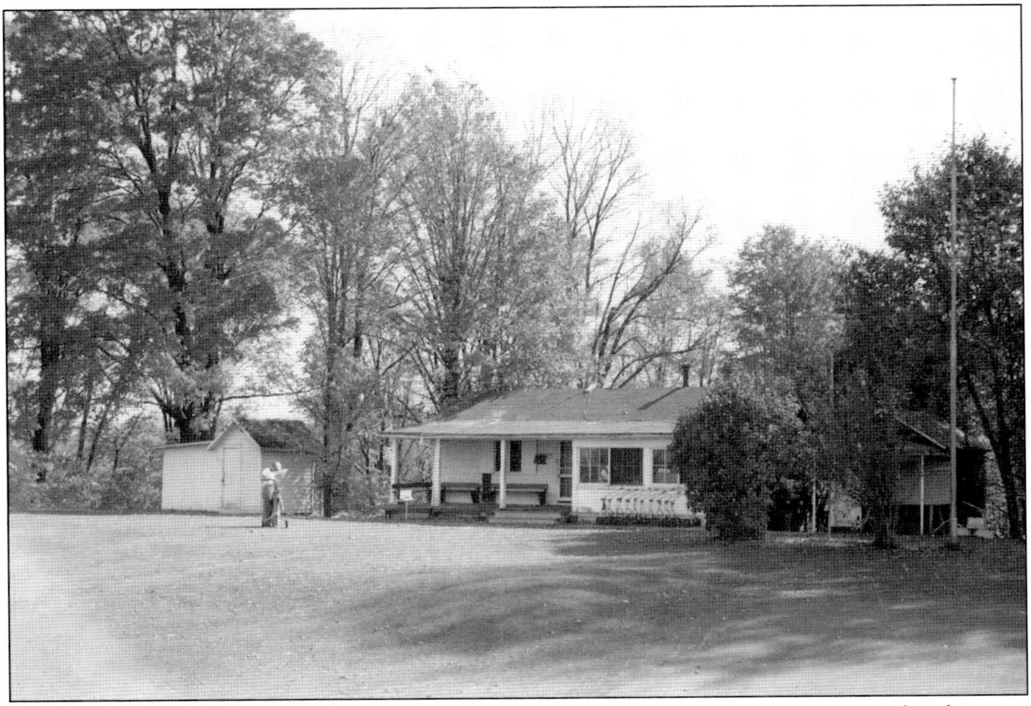

Golfing has a long-standing tradition in the Springville area, going back to a group of enthusiasts who rented land from "Pop" Warner's father, William H. Warner. At Route 391 and Genesee Road, they laid out a course that remained until 1921 near the famous "Maples on Nunweiler Hill." That group, then organized as Springville Country Club with "Pop" Warner as president, purchased the former Buffalo, Rochester & Pittsburgh Railway's Cascade Park. Warner and Dr. R.B. Waite laid out the initial nine-hole course with sand greens; grass greens were not developed until 1929. The June 17, 1926, issue of the *Springville Journal* reported, "There were over 1,200 people at the Springville Country Club Sunday." (Many of Cascade Park's attractions were still in place.) Tree plantings, water source development for irrigation, land acquisitions, additional holes, a club professional, and construction of exceptional facilities have all resulted in one of the finest courses in Western New York.

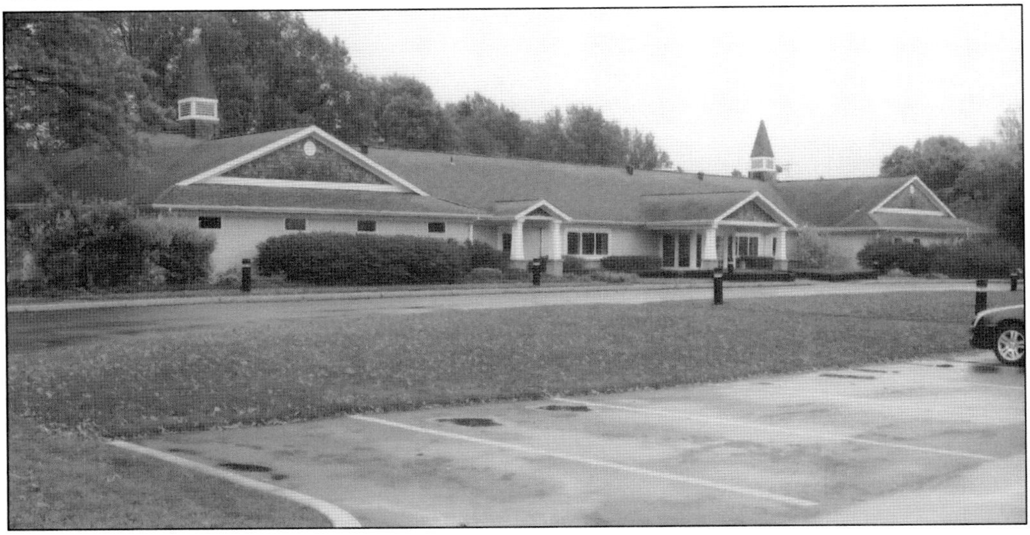

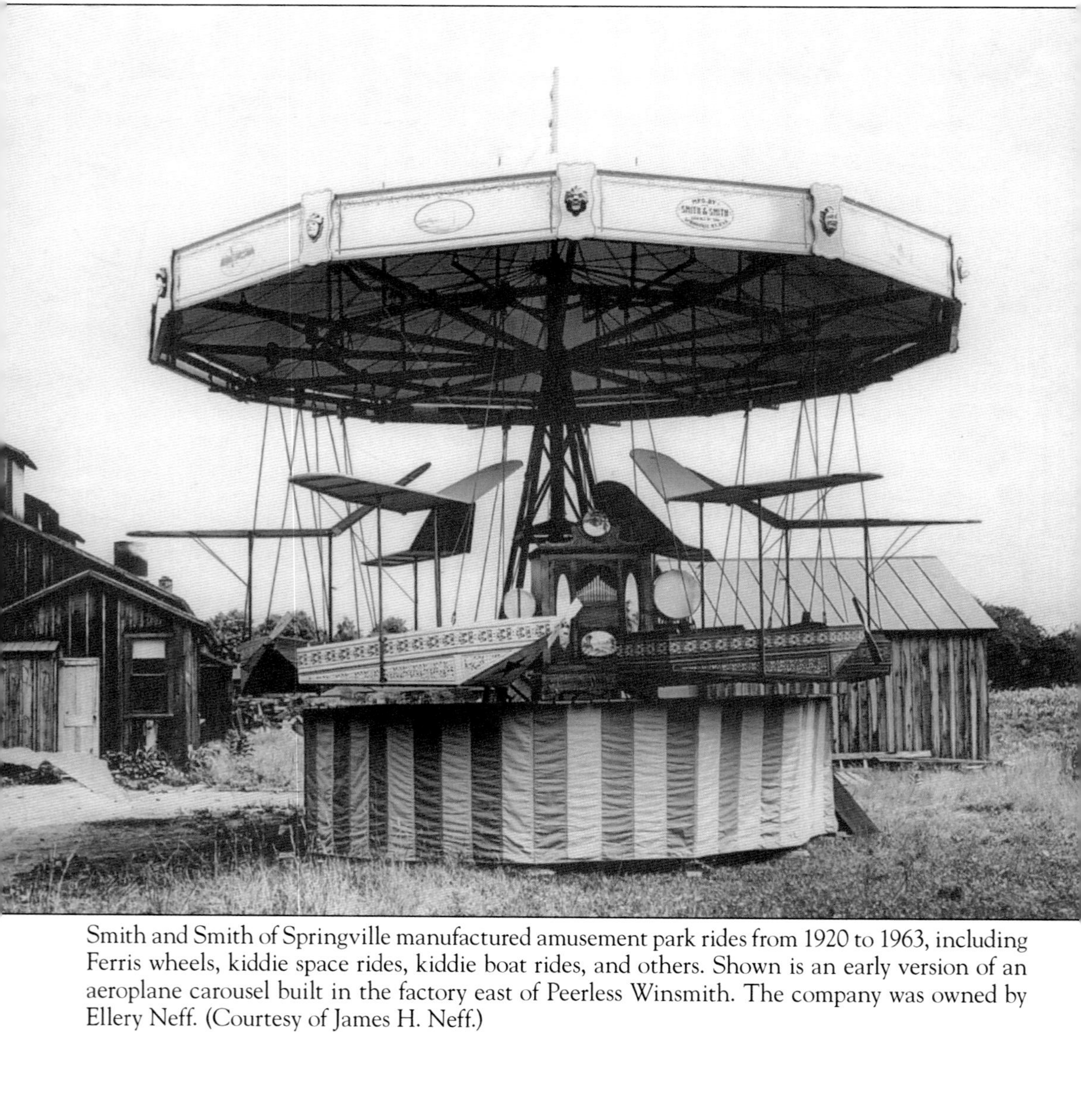

Smith and Smith of Springville manufactured amusement park rides from 1920 to 1963, including Ferris wheels, kiddie space rides, kiddie boat rides, and others. Shown is an early version of an aeroplane carousel built in the factory east of Peerless Winsmith. The company was owned by Ellery Neff. (Courtesy of James H. Neff.)

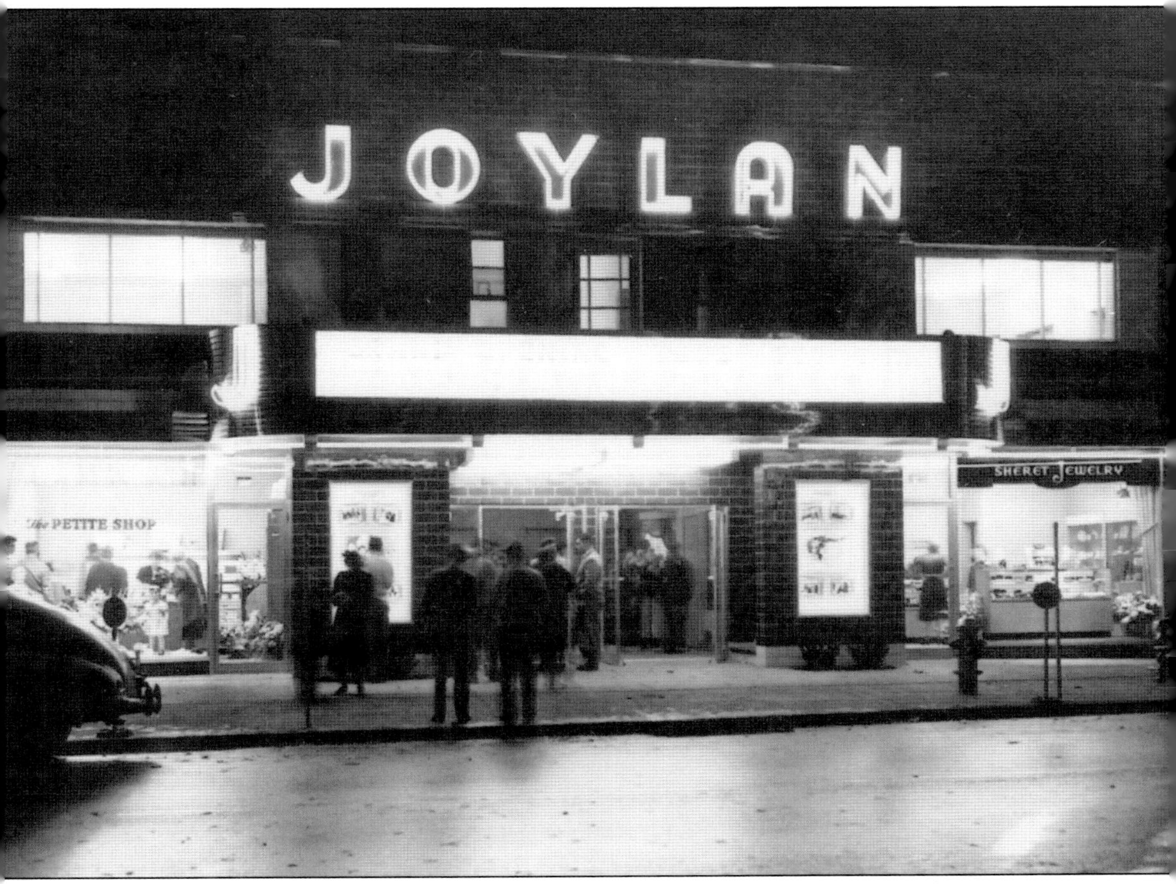

In 1946, Peter and Lena Bifarella purchased the Utrich Hotel. Following its demolition in 1948, they began construction on the Joylan Theater. Opened on October 4, 1949, it was one of the most beautiful and modern theaters in Western New York, and the realization of the Bifarellas' life dream. Ownership of the 671-seat theater remained in the Bifarella-Burns family until 1982. (Courtesy of Ted and Debby Adams.)

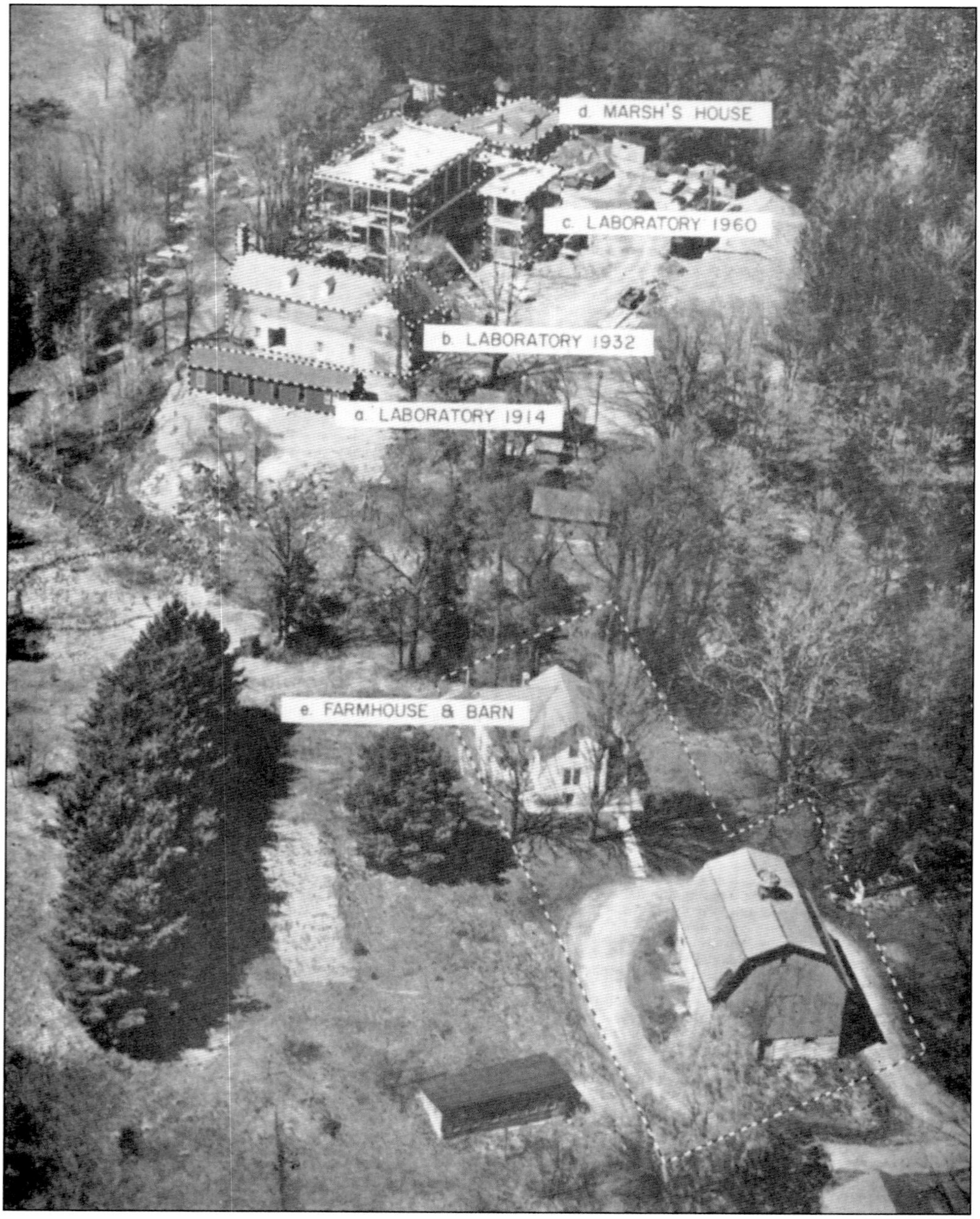

In 1913, Dr. M.N. Brooks of Springville and nine others presented a 31-acre farm on East Main Street to the New York State Institute for the Study of Malignant Diseases (now Roswell Park Memorial Institute). A budget of $15,000 was set for development of the farm, and an additional $20,000 was budgeted in 1915. Following World War I, the institute studied the incidence of cancer in inbred laboratory mice. In 1932, additional expansion took place when an administration and library building was added. In 1959, New York State added a $1-million research building, the only remaining structure of the complex. During the 1960s and 1970s, 60,000 research mice were housed there. Various experiments also included dog and monkey colonies. At various other times, deer, horses, armadillos, fish, and poultry were utilized.

Nicholas Wendel brought his family to Vaughn Street in 1945. At the time, numerous families had backyard chicken enterprises, from which only a couple of empty chicken houses remain. Park and Pollard Company, known for its famous "Lay or Bust" poultry feeds, had a multiacre feeding and care research facility at 432 Franklin Street, and chicks could be purchased at Springville Hatchery. At 54 Franklin Street (now Leisure Laundry), Concord Frozen Foods operated a basement chicken kill-and-dress facility. The only remaining chicken enterprise is Wendel Farm, now managed by the third generation of Wendels: Martin and David. The fourth generation waits in the wings as the Wendels operate a fleet of trucks and trailer-mounted barbecue units, as well as retail poultry, pumpkin, and maple syrup sales. David and Ron Wendel are seen here observing a feeding station in 1990.

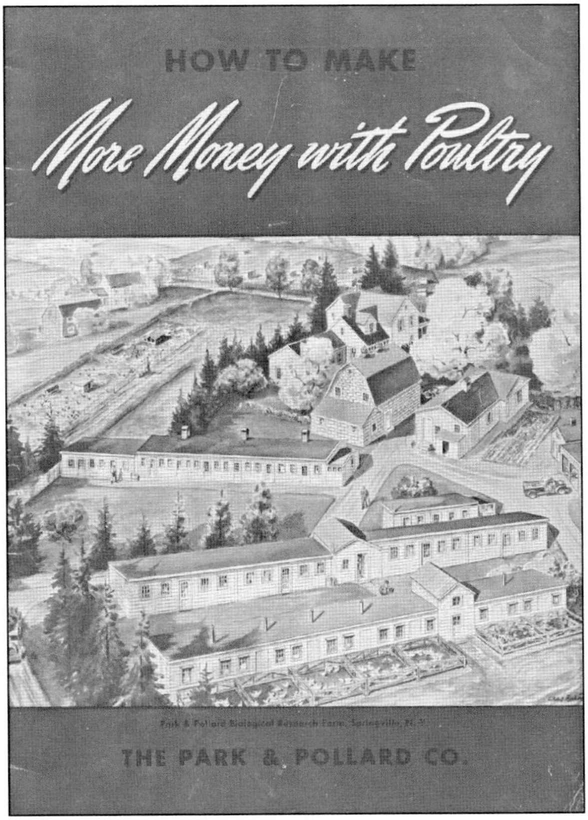

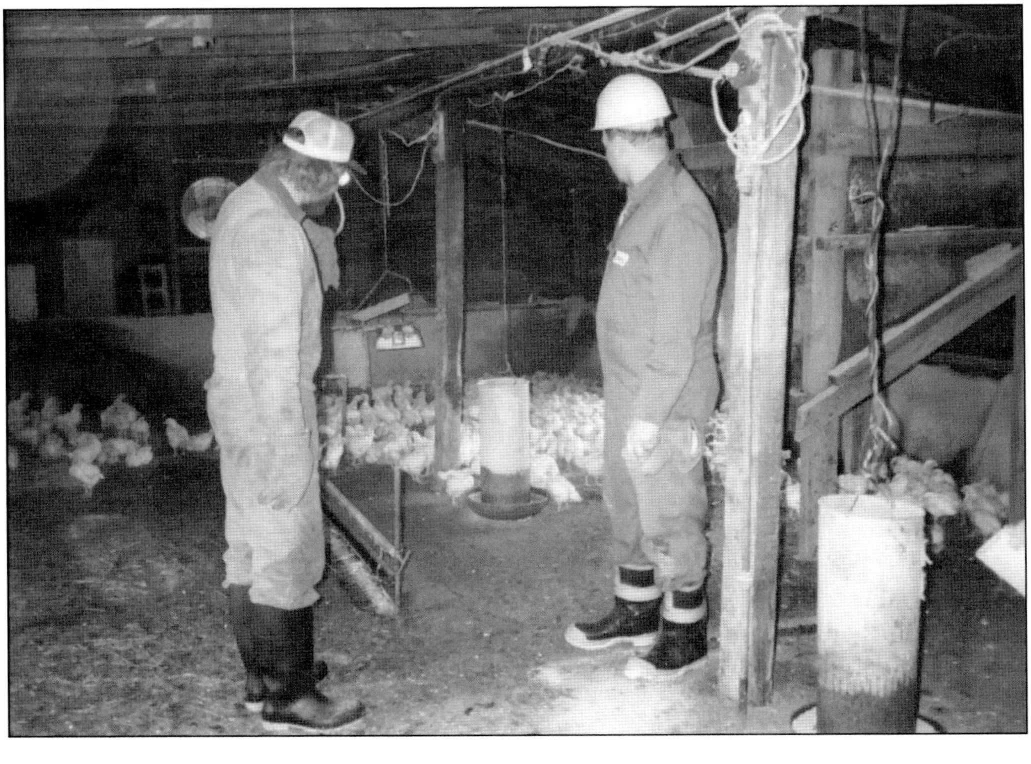

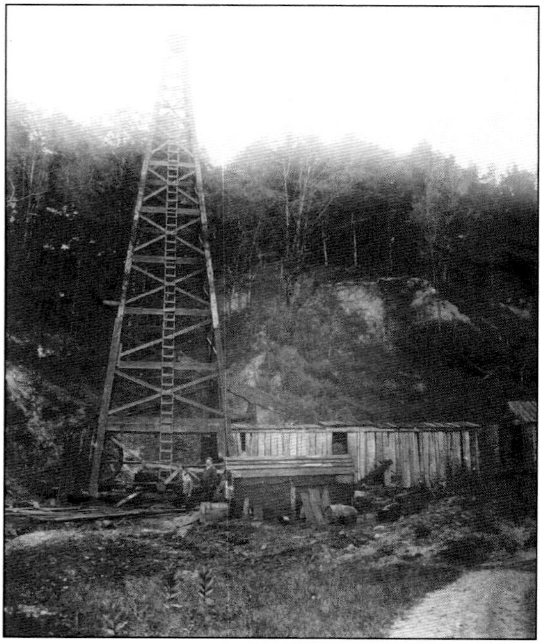

A Zoar Valley well supplied the Springville Natural Gas Company with natural gas. The region has long utilized this resource, and most landowners have leased their mineral rights to energy developers. One particularly productive area is near the intersection of Genesee and Pratham Roads.

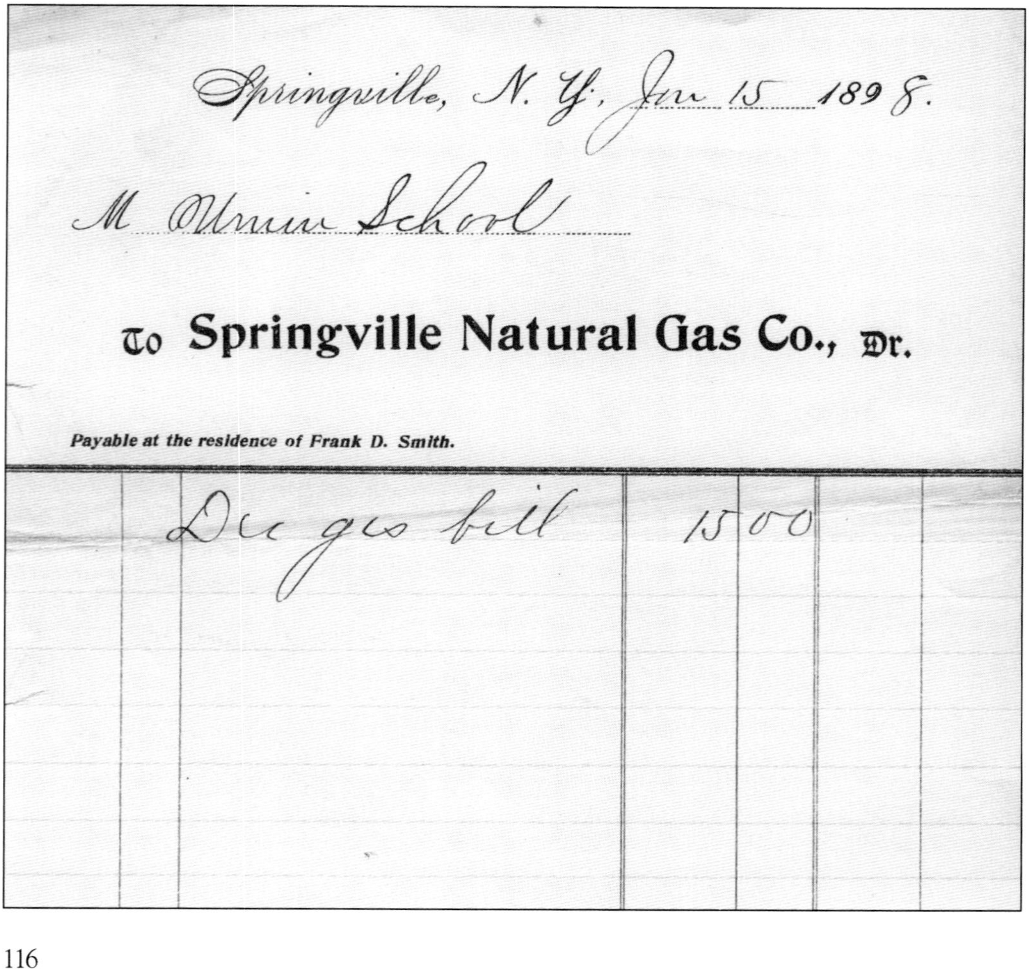

Springville, N. Y., Jun 15 1898.

M Union School

To **Springville Natural Gas Co., Dr.**

Payable at the residence of Frank D. Smith.

Due gas bill	15	00		

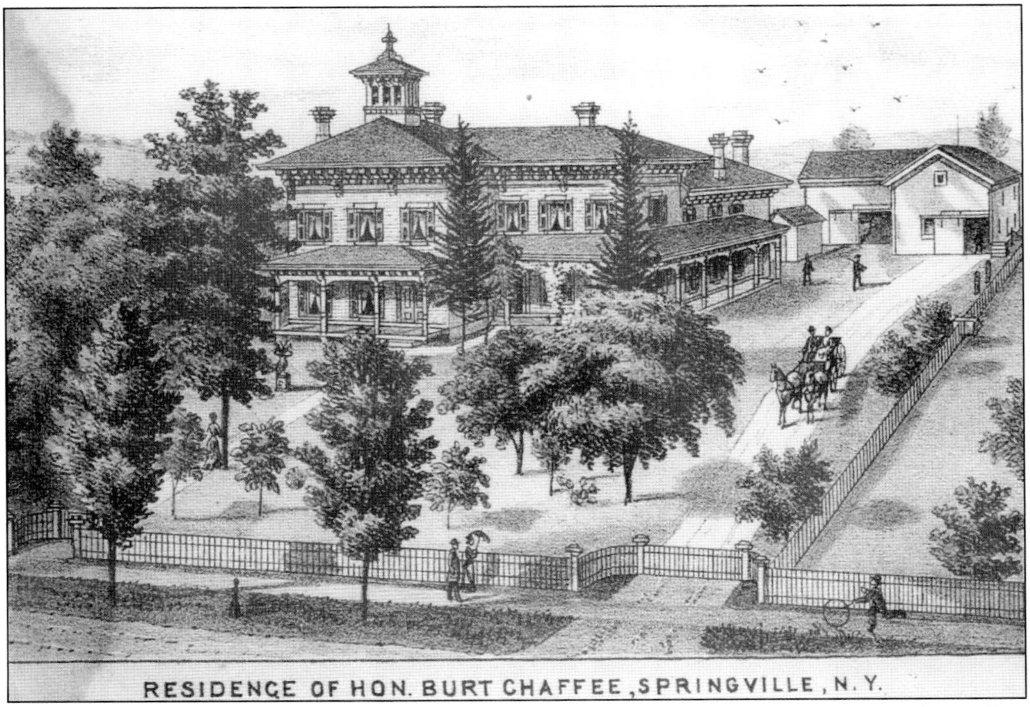

Burt Chaffee (1837–1916) attended Springville Academy and married Jennie B. Richmond in 1871. Jennie managed their home at 224 East Main Street after his death, until 1934. In 1937, elderly care was initiated following the directive of Burt's will: "give her the right as executrix to sell or convey all assets except the Springville homestead with sufficient grounds for a hospital." The care emphasis changed in the 1940s to patients of all ages. A series of volunteer services and fundraisers has assured the growth of Chaffee Hospital and the Jennie B. Richmond Nursing Home. A succession of dedicated members of the board of directors has steered its fortunes through the many challenges of building and staffing. The board has not been without celebrity: Arcade's Fran Stryker, creator of the Lone Ranger, the Green Hornet, and Sergeant Preston of the Yukon, once served. (Above, courtesy of 1880 F.W. Beers Atlas.)

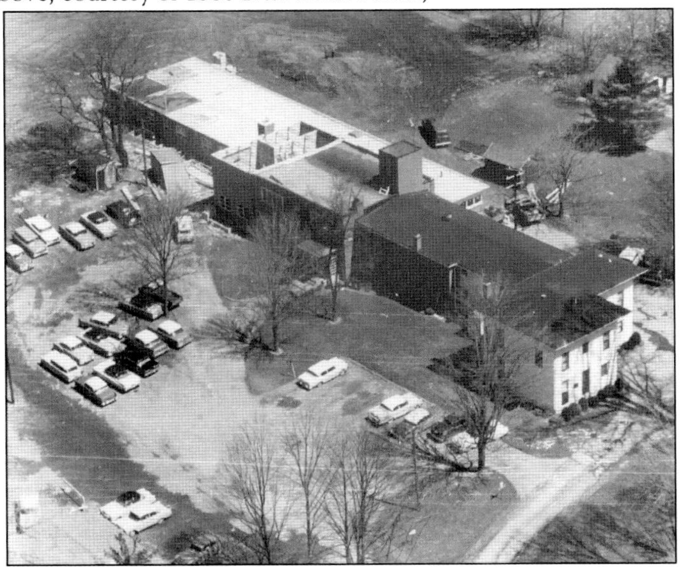

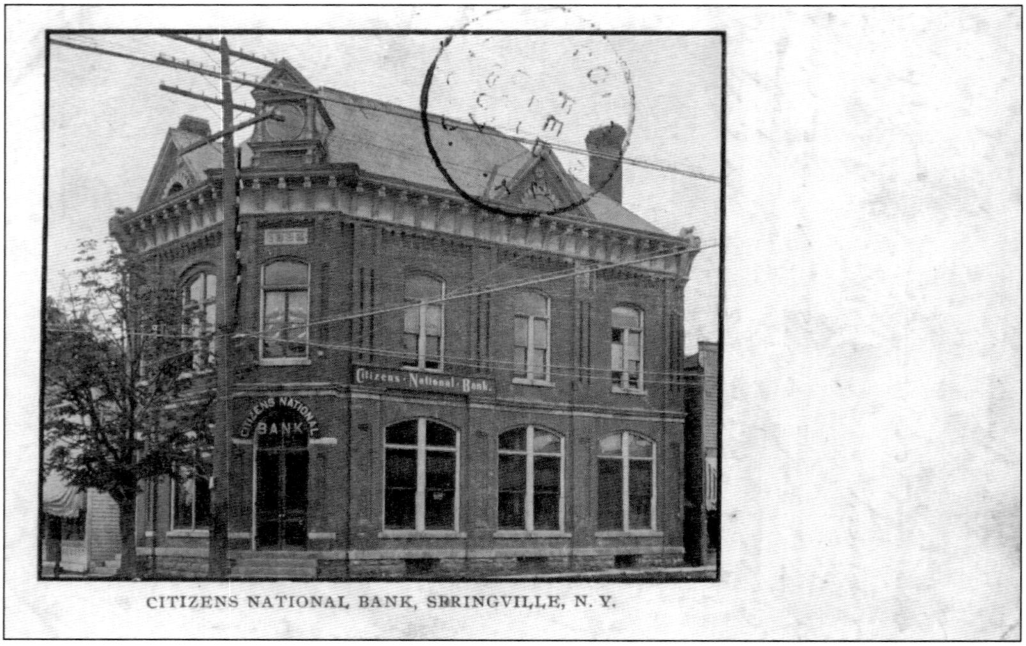

The Citizens National Bank of Springville, at the northwest corner of Main and Buffalo Streets, is seen here around 1902. The second building to the left of the bank is the Utrich Hotel, which was razed to make room for the Joylan Theater. The 1929-series National Bank note bore the engraved signatures of Orin H. Stearns, cashier, and Arnold L. Neubach, president. The now rare and collectible 1902 series bore the actual individually signed bank officers' names. A. Ronald Cady, in his later years, recalled how as a teenager he had carried a briefcase full of currency to the officers for signature for his father, bank officer P.J. Cady. (Below, courtesy of Brian K. Scharf.)

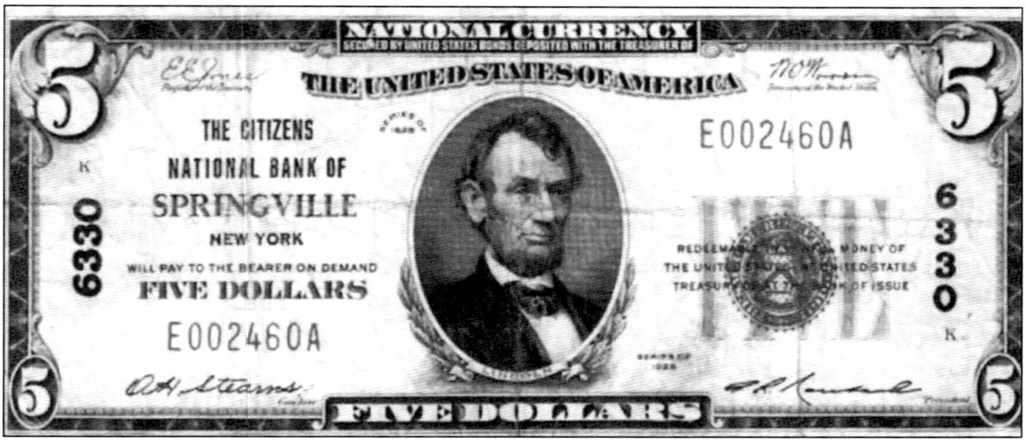

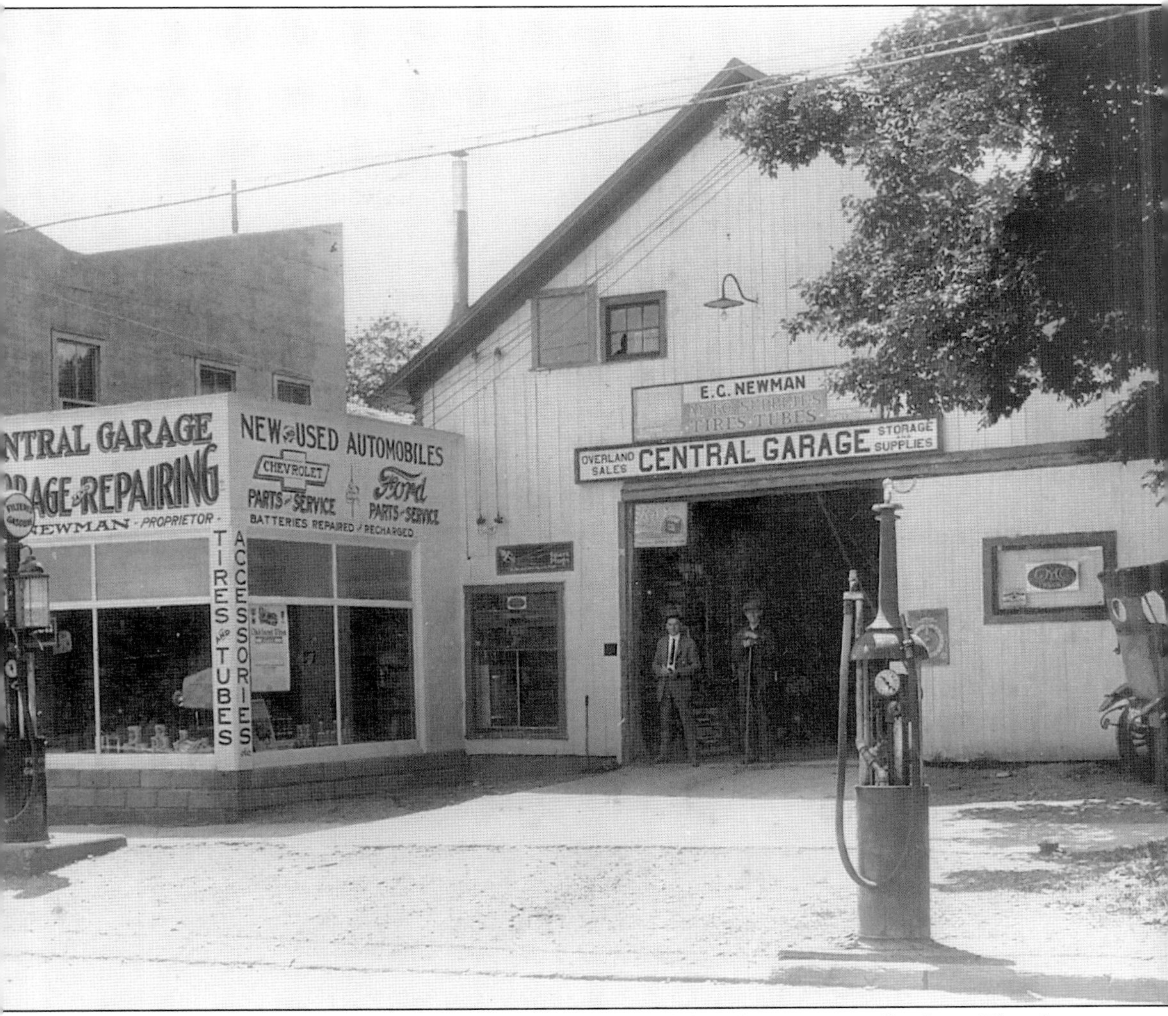

The vintage and location of photographs is often debated, but there are usually clues. The clues here are the curbside gas pumps and the back one-third of the soft-top automobile, likely from the late 1910s or early 1920s. The distinctive roofline to the left is that of the Winkey Building.

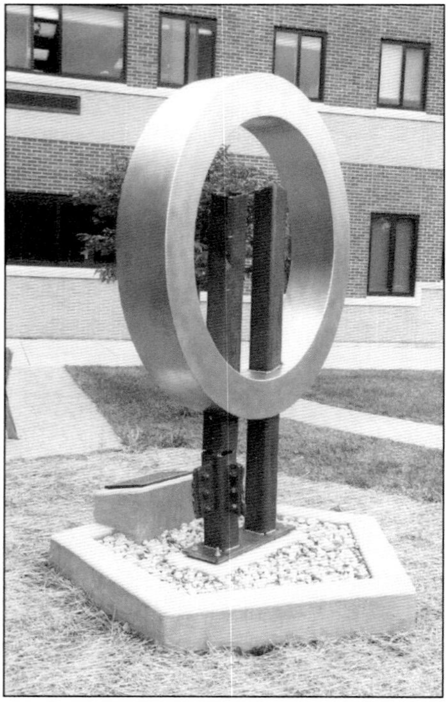

There was a call for entries to students in grades 6–12 to design a 9/11 memorial sculpture utilizing steel obtained from the site of the World Trade Center attacks. A total of 67 concepts were reviewed, and the one submitted by Dakota Ball was deemed the winner. The symbolism was explained as follows: the pieces of salvaged beam represent the twin towers, the circle represents American unity following the attacks, and the five-sided base represents the Pentagon and Shanksville, Pennsylvania, where planes also hit. (Courtesy of Angela Ginnitti.)

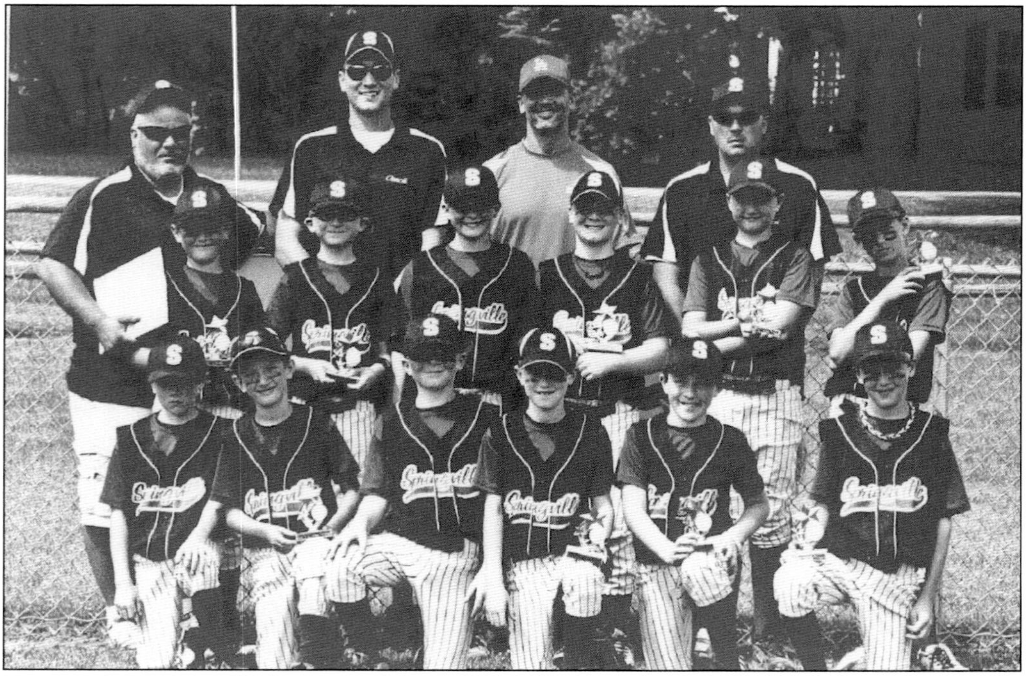

These young Springville history-makers are the 10-and-under Springville team, 2011 Southtowns and Western New York Travel Team champions. They are also ranked in the top 10 of New York State. From left to right are (first row) Jarret Wolf, Andrew Delasondro, Justin Slippy, Justin Paler, Jordan Salzler, and Mason Goodridge; (second row) Joey Lupica, Mike Soboto, Evan Elkins, Sean Berry, Emmitt Collins, and Nick Abdo; (third row) coaches Dan Lupica, Vince Roberts, Jeff Goodridge, and Jeff Wolf. (Courtesy of Joseph Paler.)

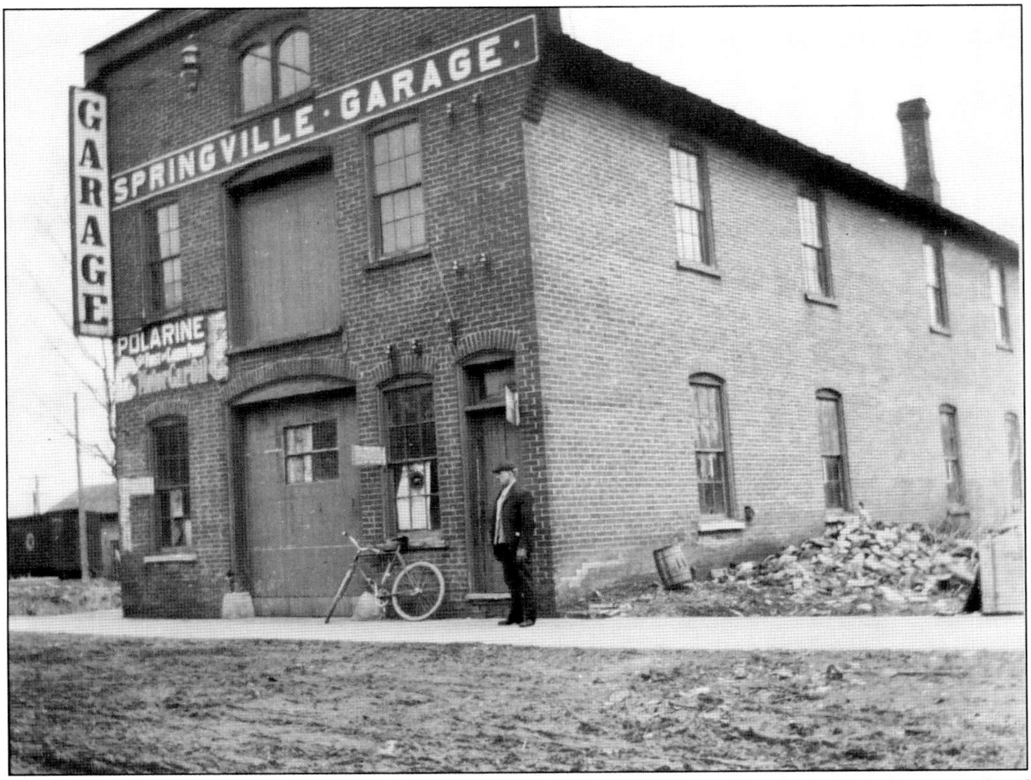

The Polarine Motor Car Oil sign, garage designation, and dirt streets date this photograph of Springville Garage to around 1912. The c. 1920 postcard below reveals a building between the Civil War monument and Godard Hall on Mechanic Street without signage. It does, however, have door and window configurations matching Springville Garage.

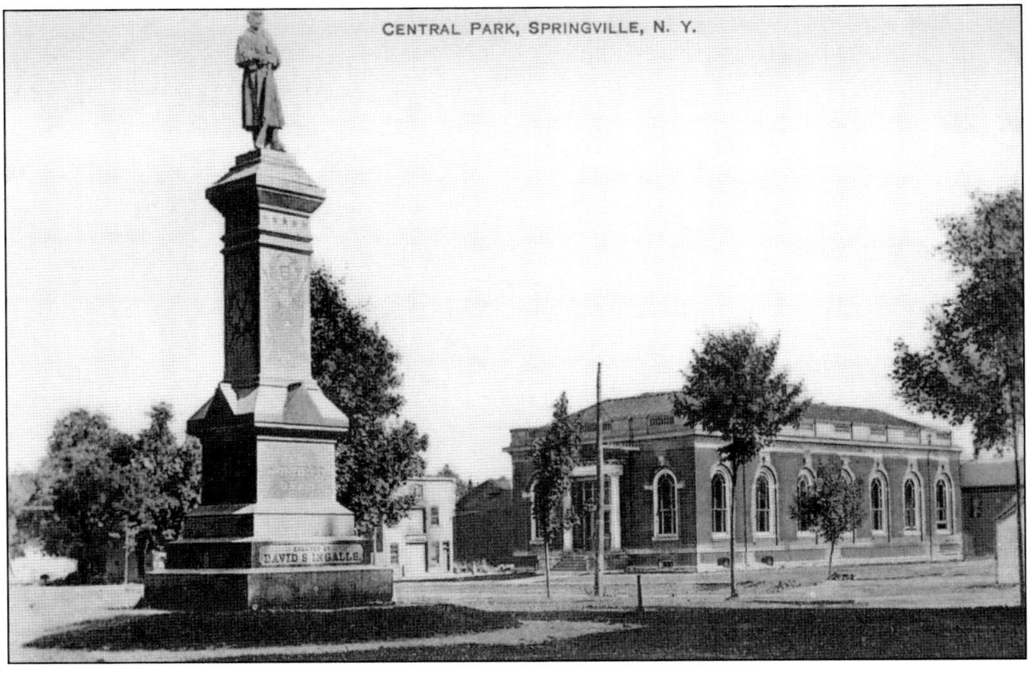

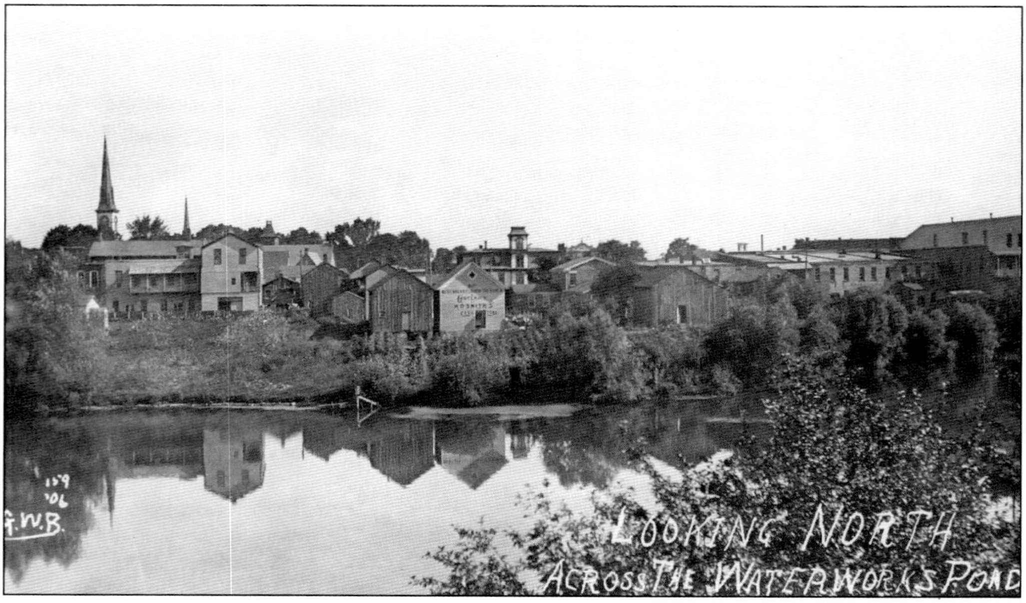

Shuttleworth Pond's useful life ended not far into the 20th century. Early postcards show boaters and waterfowl, but one story still stands out. Mrs. Brooks, wife of Dr. M.N. Brooks, once drove her new electric-powered automobile across South Buffalo Street and into Shuttleworth Pond before climbing to its top and calling for rescue. In the above view, a variety of barns occupies what is now the municipal parking lot. The Leland House and the Presbyterian steeple are easily distinguished. The photograph below is of a c. 1880 South Buffalo Street serving as a pond dam.

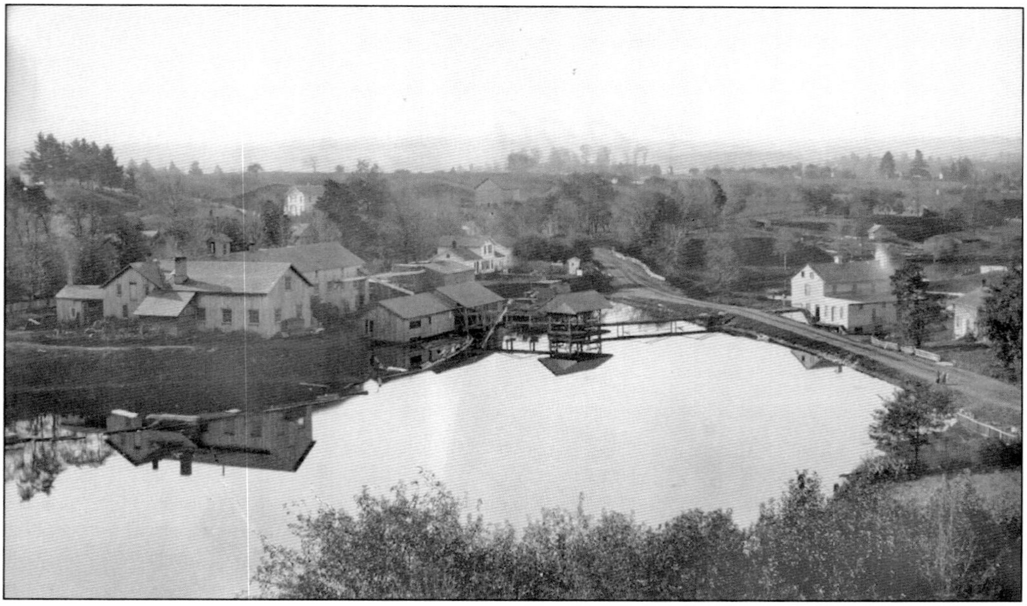

CAYUGA CHIEF, NO. 2.

FOR THE YEAR 1865.

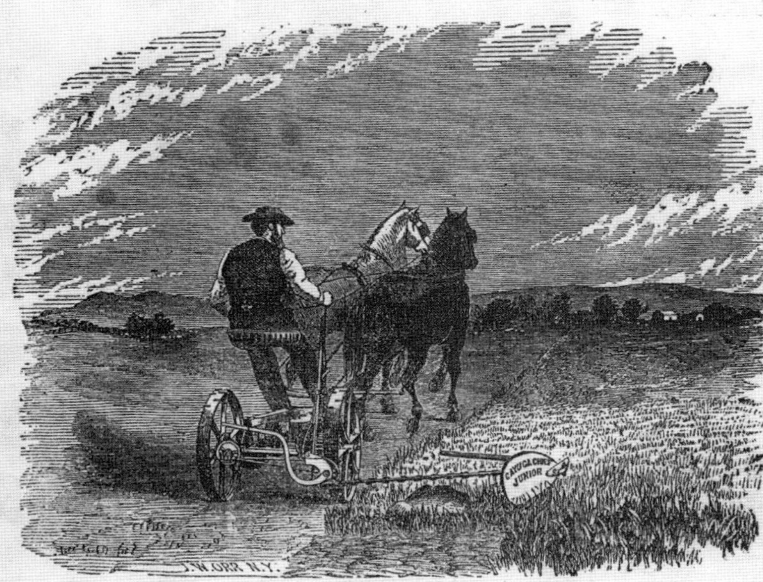

Manufactured at Springville, Erie County, New York, By C. J. SHUTTLEWORTH.

IT HAS NO EQUAL AS A MOWER.

HAVIEG, since the harvest of 1864, enlarged my facilities for the manufacture of Machines, I am now prepared to offer the new improved "CHIEF" to the farming community, as the best and lightest draft Machine in use. Those wishing to purchase Machines will o well to consider the great advantages derived by the use of Machines manufactured at or near the vicinity where used, as they can at all imes on the shortest notice obtain any piece that may be broken or worn out, and save time and cost of sending to foreign places, often undreds of miles from the same.

The CHIEF will be presented to the Farming Community for the coming harvest, warranted perfect in all its parts, and will be sold as low s any other first class Machine, cutting the same width of swath. Every Machine is built with perfect arrangements for the Reaper atachment, complete for $35.00, the attachment can be connected with the Machine when delivered, or any future time when desired.

REFERENCES.

C. J. SHUTTLEWORTH.—*Dear Sir*:—We, the undersigned, have used the "Cayuga Chief, No. 2," purchased of you in July last, to our erfect satisfaction. We have used it in heavy and light grass—standing and lodged—wet and dry—smooth and uneven surface, and in very instance to our *entire satisfaction*. It is simple in arrangements, easily operated, and kept in order without difficulty—strong where trength is required; without great bulk or weight. It will do its work with high or low motion, and excels all other machines that we ave ever seen operate, in *lightness of draft*, it being easy work for a common span of horses, and they do not require to be urged to a high peed to do the work satisfactorily. We believe that its peculiar adaptation to the uneven surface of the ground, its ease of draft and its reat strength and durability give the "Cayuga Chief" superior advantages over any other machine in use.

Philip Ferrin,	Concord.	Isaac C Newton,	"	J W VanValkenburg,	"	F H Clark,	"	H H Phelps,	Aurora.	R Meatyord,	E Hamburgh.
W. H Stanbro	"	James Ryder,	Sardinia.	Thomas Hopkins,	"	Jas Goodemote,	"	Chas Madison,	Sardinia.	H Meatyard,	"
Byron Wells,	"	Lyman Parker,	"	Chas Spencer,	Concord.	Lucius Lincoln.	Otto.	D H Odell,	Brant.	J Darbee, 2d,	"
Wm. P. Mills,	"	R Tillingnast.	"	Jas A Cranston,	"	Samuel Tefft,	"	Nomo Garty,	Hamburgh.	E Conolly,	Holland.
H M Blackmer,	"	Wm Tillinghast,	"	Marvin W Fields,	"	Dewey Tefft,	"	A Shappater,	Evans.	J Kinder, Sen.,	"
Stephen R. Smith,	"	Luther Briggs,	"	Samuel Burley,	"	W Z Lincoln,	"	Louis Miller,	"	J Kinder, Jr.,	"
B W Norton,	"	William Hyde,	"	Hiram Rowland,	Ashford.	Frederick Lahuney,	Boston	Edward Iversoll,	"	Henry Myers,	Eden.
Epaphras Steele,	"	Stephen Savage,	"	J Quackenbush,	"	Wm B Rice,	"	James J Sweet,	Colden.	Benj Webster,	"
N. G. Churchill,	"	Dexter Savage,	"	C A McIntosh,	"	Jos R Alguer,	"	David D Barrett,	"	Wm White,	Collins.
Wm Blackmer,	"	Frederick West,	"	John P Bond,	"	John A Bury,	"	Bichard Wiley,	"	Charles Eels,	Alden.
Wm H Freeman	"	Jerome Rydder,	"	Chas Stowell,	"	A C Shelden,	"	Hymen Lewis,	"	S Hodges,	Glenwood,
Wm Shultus,	"	Daniel Hopkins,	"	Almon Fuller,	"	Lyman Rockwood,	"	O P Buffum,	"	O P Vedder,	Ellicottville.
Wm F Emerson,	"	Charles Long,	"	John G Morrow,	"	Geo Brindley,	"	N Ames,	"	E. Young Arnold,	"
C C Sibly,	"	James Hopkins	"	Daniel W Tickner,	"	Isaac Ormsbee,	"	A W Patridge,	"	S. P. Arnold,	"
Luther Killom,	"	Geo Richmond,	"	A Hufstaler,	"	Frederick Lahrny,	"	Wm Brink;	"		

In 1865, C.J. Shuttleworth used endorsement advertising to sell his Cayuga Chief hay-mowing machine.

A WORD OF EXPLANATION

Names in our History

At a time when the community is taking a look back at its beginnings, it seems appropriate to recognize those families who have been part of our area's long-term history.

It is impossible to compile a complete and accurate listing of family names, due to the incomplete nature of the references available, the lack of precise knowledge on the part of our present day residents, and the limited time I had to accomplish this large task. Some modern residents' surnames are only coincidentally like those of earlier times. I leave it to you to do the necessary genealogy to establish those root connections with the past. And don't miss that opportunity, there is so much to learn about our area and its people.

In my search I found useful THE HISTORY OF THE ORIGINAL TOWN OF CONCORD, BRIGGS, 1883; SPRINGVILLE DIRECTORY, 1912; FIREMAN'S SOUVENIR SPRINGVILLE HISTORY, 1939; and a 1939-40 Telephone Directory. I referred to our present day directory and spoke with many individuals. It was great fun for me and I hope you enjoy the information. Not being professional in this area, any omissions of families were not intentional.

Rosey Sutherland

As a contribution to the town of Concord's 175th anniversary in 1987, Rosey Sutherland researched the community arrival dates of a number of well-known area families and included them in a collectable cookbook.

Names in Springville History

Below is a random list of the families who were the backbone of our community. The date is either a family quotation or from Erasmus Briggs's *History of the Original Town of Concord*. The following is a key to various dates:

(vb date) Village Board records, when they served.

(12) 1912 Springville directory. No definite dates available.

(39) 1939–1940 telephone company directory. No definite dates available at time of printing.

Ackley	(1816)
Adams	(1820)
Ahles	(1890)
Ahrens	(12)
Alford	(39)
Altman	(12)
Anderson	(12)
Andrea	(39)
Andrews	(1943)
Ballard	(1923)
Ballentyne	(1949)
Baker	(12)
Barie	(39)
Barrett	(1810)
Barthel	(vb 1923)
Bartlette	(12)
Bates	(12)
Bauer	(39)
Beach	(1934)
Becker	(39)
Beckerich	(1894)
Belscher	(1880)
Bement	(12)
Benkelman	(39)
Benz	(——)
Benzing	(12)
Bifarella	(1930)
Bigelow	(12)
Blakely	(1838)
Blemel	(1870)
Blasdell	(1864)
Block	(12)
Blohm	(12)
Bly	(pre-1939)
Boberg	(1947)
Bobseine	(39)
Bolton	(39)
Bond	(12)
Booth	(1817)
Botsford	(1847)
Briggs	(1815)
Brooks	(1841)
Brown	(1906)
Burgard	(39)
Burns	(1876)
Capanyola	(1928)
Cary	(12)
Cieszynski	(39)
Ciszak	(1897)
Chandler	(1847)
Childs	(1820)
Clark	(1902)
Clarke	(39)
Clay	(39)
Cobo	(1910)
Cole	(1817)
Cook	(1830)
Coons	(39)
Cooper	(12)
Corsette	(39)
Cotter	(12)
Crandall	(1821)
Cranston	(1834)
Crist	(39)
Crosby	(1874)
Crump	(1838)
Darzewski	(39)
Dash	(1946)
Davis	(1838)
Dewey	(12)
Domes	(1880)
Drabek	(39)
Dunn	(12)
Dye	(12)
Dygert	(1812)
Earl	(39)
Eaton	(1810)
Edwards	(39)
Ellis	(1836)
Emerling	(1858)
Emerson	(1842)
Engle	(——)
Enser	(——)
Erdman	(12)
Errington	(1945)
Evans	(12)
Fagnan	(12)
Farner	(1905)

Fattey	(1868)
Feldman	(1937)
Felton	(39)
Ferrin	(1902)
Ferry	(1912)
Feuz	(1905)
Fisher	(1829)
Follman	(1870)
Folts	(1912)
Foster	(1812)
Fowler	(12)
Fox	(1860)
Frank	(12)
Fuller	(1825)
Gamel	(12)
Ganschow	(1874)
Garlock	(——)
Geiger	(1880)
Gentner	(1873)
Glass	(12)
Glazier	(12)
Goodemote	(1816)
Goodrich	(39)
Gray	(12)
Griffith	(1830)
Hadley	(39)
Hagerer	(12)
Hawkins	(12)
Hampton	(12)
Hansen	(39)
Hanson	(12)
Harvey	(12)
Hauth	(12)
Hayden	(——)
Heary	(12)
Hebdon	(1924)
Heinz	(1926)
Hemmerling	(——)
Hess	(1900)
Hoffman	(12)
Hofmann	(39)
Hughey	(12)
Hunter	(1942)
Hurlburt	(39)
Irish	(1833)
Jackson	(12)
Jermain	(39)
Johnson	(12)
Jones	(12)
Joslin	(12)
Jureller	(12)
Kaufman	(1873)
Kessler	(1897)
Kester	(39)
Kern	(12)
King	(1845)
Kingston	(39)
Klahn	(39)
Klein	(1951)
Knopf	(39)
Krezmien	(1912)
Kruse	(1912)
Kuhn	(12)
LaCosse	(39)
Lambert	(39)
Land	(39)
Langreck	(pre-1920)
Lazell	(12)
Lenz	(39)
Lerminaux	(——)
Lightcap	(——)
Lohrey	(1896)
Loomis	(39)
Lounsbury	(12)
Lowe	(12)
Luce	(39)
Luss	(39)
Luther	(39)
Lux	(1887)
Mahl	(1873)
Manchester	(1838)
Manning	(12)
Martin	(——)
Maul	(1951)
Mayo	(12)
McCarthy	(1912)
McCoy	(12)
Mercer	(39)
Meyer	(1858)
Miller	(12)
Morton	(12)
Mooney	(——)
Mrugala	(1920)
Murphy	(——)
Murray	(12)
Nagel	(12)
Nason	(1895)
Neff	(39)
Nelligan	(12)
Newman	(1912)
Nunweiler	(1918)
O'Connor	(39)
Ott	(1938)
Oyer	(12)

Pearson	(1921)
Perkins	(——)
Peters	(12)
Pfarner	(1800)
Phillips	(1925)
Pierce	(12)
Pitillo	(1938)
Plenz	(——)
Ploetz (Plotz)	(12)
Potter	(1816)
Priel	(39)
Pritchard	(12)
Quackenbush	(1939)
Randall	(1933)
Ratajczak	(39)
Reynolds	(1813)
Rogers	(1901)
Rumfola	(1921)
Russell	(1808)
Safford	(12)
Salzler	(1873)
Scharf	(12)
Schichtel	(1924)
Schneider	(12)
Schroeder	(12)
Schue	(12)
Schweickert	(1889)
Scott	(12)
Seider	(1873)
Sheret	(1930?)
Sherman	(12) .
Shimburski	(——)
Shultes	(1812)
Simon	(1904)
Sixt	(1879)
Smith	(1810)
Snyder	(39)
Spaulding	(1826)
Spencer	(1840)
Stock	(12)
Taylor	(1948)
Thurber	(1843)
Townsend	(1810)
Travis	(12)
Treat	(12)
Trevett	(1817)
Underberg	(1920)
Vacinek	(1915)
Van Dermeer	(pre-1939)
Vaughn	(1832)
Vedder	(——)
Walker	(12)
Wallace	(1928)
Wamer	(1847)
Watkins	(12)
Watson	(1867)
Weir	(1914)
Weismantel	(1865)
Wells	(1816)
Wendle	(1945)
Wheeler	(12)
Widrig	(1885)
Wiedemann	(mid-1800)
Wiley	(1813)
Willett	(12)
Williams	(1947)
Wilson	(1849)
Winkey	(1917)
Winship	(1825)
Wolniewicz	(1890)
Wright	(1844)
Wyatt	(vb 1925)
Zielinski	(1862)
Zimmer	(1876)
Zimmerman	(——)
Zittle	(——)